Revelation

REVELATION

Final Exodus

Mwaniki Karura

Foreword by Mumo wa Kisau

WIPF & STOCK · Eugene, Oregon

REVELATION
Final Exodus

Copyright © 2024 Mwaniki Karura. All rights reserved. Except for brief quotations in critical publications or reviews, no part of this book may be reproduced in any manner without prior written permission from the publisher. Write: Permissions, Wipf and Stock Publishers, 199 W. 8th Ave., Suite 3, Eugene, OR 97401.

Wipf & Stock
An Imprint of Wipf and Stock Publishers
199 W. 8th Ave., Suite 3
Eugene, OR 97401

www.wipfandstock.com

PAPERBACK ISBN: 979-8-3852-2926-0
HARDCOVER ISBN: 979-8-3852-2927-7
EBOOK ISBN: 979-8-3852-2928-4

VERSION NUMBER 012225

Unless marked otherwise Scripture citations are taken from the Holy Bible, New International Version®, NIV®. Copyright © 1973, 1978, 1984, 2011 by Biblica, Inc.™ Used by permission of Zondervan. All rights reserved worldwide. www.zondervan.com The "NIV" and "New International Version" are trademarks registered in the United States Patent and Trademark Office by Biblica, Inc.™

This commentary is dedicated to the late Bishop Evans Mrima, the founder of Gospel Outreach Church—Kenya. He revitalized worship and evangelism. He mentored many young men and women who are now ministering the gospel all over the world. His prologue to every citation of a Bible verse, "The Bible says," pointed and rooted us in the Bible.

Contents

Foreword by Mumo Kisau | xi
Author's Preface | xiii
Acknowledgments | xv

Introduction | 1

Commentary on the Visionary Revelation

Chapter 1
Prologue and Covering Letters to the Seven Churche | 39

Chapter 2
Setting of the Handover of the Visionary Revelation (4:1—5:14) | 68

Chapter 3
Outworking of God's Indiscriminate Decrees (6:1—8:1) | 81

Chapter 4
Divine Rapprochements to the Dwellers of the Earth (8:2—11:19) | 103

Chapter 5
Tribulation of the Church by the Evil Trinity (12:1—14:20) | 130

Chapter 6
Defeat of the Evil Trinity and the Final Judgment (15:1—20:15) | 150

Chapter 7
Eternal Dwelling of The Saints (21:1—22:21) | 200

Summary | 219

Bibliography | 223

RETROSPECTIVE GRAPHIC OVERVIEW OF THE VISIONARY SIMULATIONS

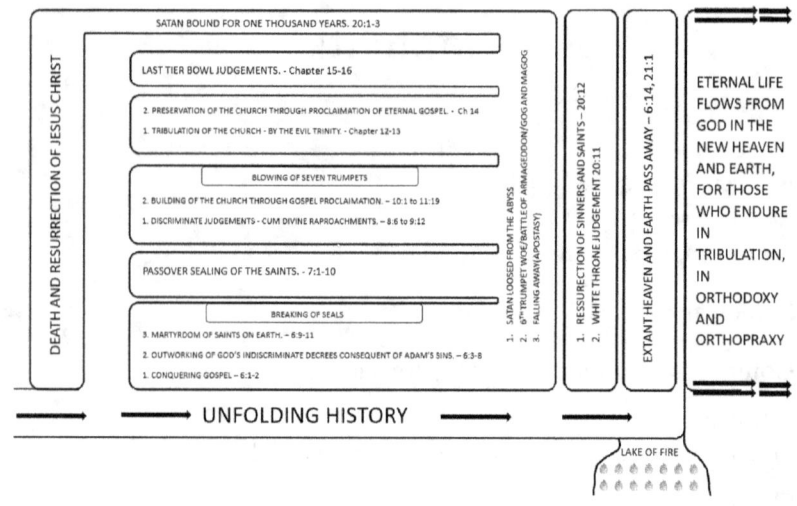

GRAPHIC STRUCTURE OF THE TEXT

Visionary Situation of the Seven Churches (1:1–3:22)	Strategic Acts Embedded in Simulations of Events That Would Happen in the Unfolding History (4:1–20:15)			Visionary New Heaven and Earth as a Strategic Act (21:1–22:5)
	One thousand years, 3½ yrs., 1260 days, 42 months.	A little while Apostasy 3½ days.	End of the current heaven and earth.	
1. Gaps in Orthodoxy 2. Gaps in Orthopraxy 3. Theodicy (Tribulations)	1. 1–4 Seal: (God's decreed rapprochement and judgments consequent of Adam's sins. 2. 1–7 Trumpet: Divine rapprochements in disciplinary judgments, building the church & gospel proclamation. 3. Rev. 12–13 Tribulations by the Evil Trinity. 4. 15–16: Last-tier of God's judgments; the wrath of God is completed in them. 5. Satan is depicted as bound and incarcerated in the bottomless pit.	1. Apostasy depicted as lasting for 3½ days when churches' witness appears dimmed. Also depicted as Satan loosed for a little while, battle of Armageddon, battle between the Lamb and alliance of Gog and Magog. 2. Judgment of beast from the sea and false prophet. 3. Judgment of sinners and Satan/Dragon. 4, Reaping of the righteous and gathering of the sinners into the winepress of the wrath of God.	The end of the former heaven and former earth is simulated as the destruction of the present earth after opening the sixth seal, blowing the seventh trumpet, and passing away of the former heaven and earth.	Eternal life with God and the Lamb in the new heaven and new earth

Foreword

THE AUTHOR DR. MWANIKI Karura has attempted and succeeded in explaining a rather complex apocalyptic narrative for the church of Christ today, thanks to the lockdown that happened due to the COVID-19 pandemic. Karura's choice of the hermeneutical interpretative method is the key that has unlocked the text to a world of unimaginable exploits as the reader is taken through the final exodus that culminates with the two realms: the blissful eternal rest for the saints in a city where the streets are paved with pure gold and the lake of fire for those who are damned for slighting God's grace in the work of the now resurrected son of God.

Even as the reader is taken through the simulation of the epochal events of revelation, one's mouth is left open not only by the amazement and wonder of the happenings but also by the style that the author uses. It is so easy to follow, starting with a schematic diagram and ending with the same as a means of summation of the entire message of the book of Revelation.

Here is a commentary like no other, one that is welcoming and inspiring, more like an interesting oration. Cast in seven chapters, just like the numerical numbers used in the apocalyptic scenes—seven bowls, seven angels, seven seals, etc.—Dr. Karura has used these seven themes perfectly to illustrate the church's final exodus. These seven chapters are memorable and progressively guide the reader, lighting up every chapter of the book.

As mentioned earlier, Dr. Karura has produced an interesting commentary and one that all of us interested in getting the message of the book of Revelation are invited to enjoy its teachings. Here is a work that uses communicative and strategic acts to stimulate faith in our God and encourage us in our sufferings knowing there is light at the end of the tunnel. Karura's intention is to bring the reader to hear what the Spirit is saying to the churches.

In the generous words of Swahili, *karibuni sana*.
—Prof. Mumo Kisau, PhD

Author's Preface

I HAD ARRIVED IN church early for personal devotion before the programmed Sunday service began. The usual din that characterizes collective charismatic worship slowly gave in to a worried quiet as we wondered what had befallen our pastor and his assistant. They had not arrived, way past the time the Sunday service usually began. As one, the church members turned their gaze to the middle of the congregation where I was seated. Though they knew that I had not led a worship service before, their imploring eyes suggested that I do so. I obeyed the unspoken but apparent call. I stood up and led them in the opening prayer, word of exhortation, and songs of praise and worship. I was still on my bed, on an early Sunday morning, where, in the Spirit, I had seen a vision as in a 3-D movie. Little did I know that I was being called and inducted into church ministry.

Having been woken up by the unfamiliar experience, I prayed, prepared, and went to church. Amazingly, all that I had seen in the vision-church that morning played out in the real church. Way after the devotion hour, the pastor and his assistant had not arrived. The congregants looked at me imploringly, just as had happened in the vision-church. It dawned on me that the early morning experience was a divinely led vision to prepare me for my first ministry assignment and induct me into church ministry. Amazed but encouraged, I stood up and, for the first time, led our church congregation in worship. From that day, the pastor took me in as one of the church ministers. A recollection of that Holy Spirit-led vision generates evocations of an assuring calm when I pass through stormy seasons in ministry.

The above experience informs the presupposition I bring to the interpretation of the book of Revelation. It constrains me to interpret the visionary revelation from the supposition that the Holy Spirit superintended all the three stages of its transmission, namely the visionary revelation, narration, and performance reading. Performance reading is aural and demonstrative.

It seeks to draw the reader and hearer into the vision experience. Thus, John narrated only what he saw, heard, and experienced. Contrariwise, some interpreters view the book of Revelation as John's well-thought-out literary work. Such a view supposes that it was John's prerogative to choose the media, genre, and symbolism with which he expressed his theological position regarding God's response to the needs in his audience's historical situation. Richard Bauckham, a proponent of this view, opines, "The Apocalypse of John is a work of immense learning, astonishingly meticulous literary artistry, remarkable creative imagination, radical political critique, and profound theology."[1] Thus, he sees John as a very innovative author.

However, this commentary observes that Revelation narrates a divinely directed visionary revelation of past, present, and unfolding events. These events are simulated using a cast of visionary symbols of worldly and otherworldly personalities, animals, numerical numbers, and time, complemented with explanatory auditions. John describes the visionary characters and simulated events using language conventions, imageries, and symbols of his time. Amazingly, no one has yet developed a suitable biblical criticism method for interpreting visions and dreams in the Bible. This commentary interprets the visionary revelation by analyzing the simulations, the simulated events, the cast of characters, symbols, and auditions. It uses insights from semiosis, cinematography, intertextuality, and analysis of the strategic and communicative acts embedded in the visionary simulations, the evocations they generate, and the intended audience response.

---

1. Bauckham. *Climax of Prophecy,* ix.

Acknowledgments

WRITING THIS COMMENTARY WAS inspired and made possible by two unplanned events. First, like many other countries, my country, Kenya, was on lockdown, courtesy of the deadly COVID-19 pandemic. The government ordered all churches and schools to be closed. This forced sabbatical afforded me time to read and write. Second, some conspiracy theories suggested that the COVID-19 virus was developed by agents of the antichrist to create an opportunity to insert a microchip with the mark of the beast ("666") into people's bloodstreams during vaccination. To enlighten our local church, I decided to do an online series on the book of Revelation.

A daily reading of the book of Revelation for over four years birthed this commentary. I am sincerely indebted to Gospel Outreach Church, Thika, for their love and encouragement. Their hunger and thirst for the word have inspired me to spend lots of time studying the Bible. Reading a Bible text that has been interpreted so divergently and writing a commentary takes a toll on family time. I sacrificed time I would have otherwise spent with my wife, Nyambura. For her patient endurance and encouragement, I am truly grateful.

The concept of strategic acts, which is the bedrock of my methodology, is not my original idea. I stumbled upon it while reading *First Theology: God, Scripture & Hermeneutics* by Kevin J. Vanhoozer. I owe lots of gratitude to him. His bibliography led me to Jürgen Habermas, the originator of the concept in his book *The Theory of Communicative Action and Rationalization of Society*. I used the concept to explain the nature and function of the visionary revelation.

Special thanks are due to the following people for reading the manuscript and giving valuable suggestions: Samuel Ngewa, Professor of New Testament Studies at Africa International University; Kabiro wa Gatumu, Associate Professor of New Testament Studies at St. Paul's University; John Frederick Evans, Professor of Hebrew and Old Testament at Union School of Theology, and Elizabeth Mburu, Associate Professor of Greek and New Testament at Africa International University. Special thanks also to Mark Shaw, Professor of World Christianity and History at Africa International University for introducing me to Wipf & Stock publishers. Finally, special thanks to Mumo wa Kisau, Professor of New Testament Studies at Africa International University, for writing a befitting foreword to the commentary.

Introduction

HERMENEUTICAL CHALLENGE

The book of Revelation narrates a vision in which God revealed the events that would be happening in the unfolding history. Before then, these events were only known to God. They were revealed through visionary simulations. As such, the noun "revelation" (Greek: αποκάλυψις, *apocalypsis*), as used in the text, refers to the visionary simulations as well as the simulated events. Later, the word was used as the title of the narrated version of the visionary revelation. The adjective *apocalyptic* was later adopted to describe the genre of the text and other texts of its kind.

John's revelation is unique in several ways that pose a challenge to its interpretation. First, it was transmitted through three different media. Primarily, it was divinely revealed through visionary simulations. Secondly, John narrated it to the lead pastors of the seven churches in literary prose. Finally, the pastors performance-read the narration to their individual congregations. Over the centuries, the text has been copied and recopied to meet the needs of the expanding church. Thus, the present readers interact with the visionary revelation through reading copies of the original text that was written by John.

Reconstructing the visionary revelation through reading copies of the text at a time when the original language and symbols with which the divine revealer described and portrayed different personalities, objects, actions, and ideas are obsolete is a very challenging task. Moreover, some of the symbolisms used in the visionary revelation were informed by the myths, immediate history, and religious experiences of the primary discourse partners that are not adequately accessible to the present-day readers.

Second, Scripture texts normally narrate God's dealings with his people in the past. Since the events narrated in these texts happened within experienced human history, it is easy for narrators to describe them. It is equally easy, using the available historical and archaeological data, for interpreters to scan the contexts in which these events occurred. However, most of the events simulated in John's visionary revelation were to happen as history unfolds. These events are outside the realm of the lived experiences of the seer, the primary, and even the secondary readers. As such, describing the nature and form of these events is a very challenging endeavor. It is equally challenging to scan the near and distant future contexts in which these events will take place.

Furthermore, in the scriptures that narrate God's dealings with his people in the past, the narrators depict ideal and imperfect mirror-worlds with which they urge readers to conform their real worlds to the ideal mirror-world and to be vigilant against conforming to the imperfect mirror-world. However, the book of Revelation narrates a divinely directed visionary revelation that simulated the outworking of God's decreed judgments and redemptive acts in the unfolding history. The decrees of God can be understood as "the eternal plans of God whereby, before the creation of the world, he determined to bring about everything that happens."[1] This definition can be expanded to include God's decrees consequent of Adam's fall. The visionary revelation also simulated God's acts of preserving and avenging the saints throughout the unfolding history. It finally simulated the saints' ultimate reward of eternal life with God in the new heaven and earth. These visionary simulations engender audience response through evocations generated by seeing the visionary simulations through a performance reading of the book of Revelation.

Third, the mode in which the visionary revelation was transmitted differs from the rest of the New Testament texts. For example, the conception and mode of transmission of the message in the Gospels and Epistles were informed by the need to bridge gaps in the primary readers' historical situations. Therefore, they were shaped by the writers' knowledge of the primary readers' historical situations, the identified needs, the authors' literary skills, and the existing communication styles. However, except in a few instances where he expressed his emotional reaction to what he saw and heard, John was wholly pliable to the dictates of the divine revealer of the visionary revelation. Divine prerogative dictated the genre, simulated events, choice of the visionary cast, symbols, and oral clarifications.

Fourth, normally, Scripture texts seek to bridge gaps in their primary addressee's historical situations using communicative acts, that is, speech acts whose meaning is accessed through understanding. On the other hand,

---

1. Grudem, *Systematic Theology*, 332.

the visionary revelation seeks to bridge gaps in its audience's historical situations using, majorly, strategic acts[2] that are inhered in its visionary simulations. Strategic acts are not intended to convey meaning and be understood. They are intended to generate evocations which compel the audiences to act in ways that can bridge gaps in their historical situations.

In his ably articulated theory of communicative action, Jürgen Habermas avers:

> I count as communicative action those linguistically mediated interactions in which all participants pursue illocutionary aims, and only illocutionary aims, with their mediating acts of communication. On the other hand, I regard as linguistically mediated strategic action those interactions in which at least one of the participants wants, with his speech acts, to produce perlocutionary effects on his opposite number.[3]

Habermas further adds, "Strategic actors are goal-oriented subjects who achieve their ends by way of an orientation to and influence on the decision of other actors."[4] Thus, the revealer of the visionary revelation sought to orient and influence readers to decide to act in ways that would bridge the gaps identified in their historical situations.

In his discussion on Habermas's theory, David Ingram says, "In acting strategically, then, we behave rationally to the degree that we calculate how others will act or can be made to act in ways that either facilitate strategic rationality or hinder the successful pursuit of personal aims."[5] Ingram's explanation suggests that the visionary revelation was intended to facilitate audience allegiance to God's will, patient endurance in tribulation, and to hinder compromises with the sinful world.

Expanding on Habermas's theory, Kevin J. Vanhoozer rightly views "actions that aim to produce an effect on the audience other than by means of understanding as strategic, not communicative acts."[6] Thus, the creator of a strategic action does not intend, with the help of either visionary simulations or speech acts, to achieve agreement but to constrain the visionary or narratee to accomplish a specific purpose.[7] John's visionary simulations of the things that would be outworked in the unfolding history are embedded with strategic acts with which they evoke hate, fear, trauma, admiration, love,

---

2. Habermas, *Communicative Action*, 295.
3. Habermas, *Communicative Action*, 295.
4. Habermas, *Communicative Action*, 87–88.
5. Ingram, *Strategic Rationality*, 432.
6. Vanhoozer, *First Theology*, 185.
7. Magdalena, *Strategic Action*, 39–52.

shame, honor, pride, gratitude, indignation, and amazement, to name just a few evocations. These evocations engender audience actions that can bridge gaps in the audiences' historical situations. Citing Quintilian and Longinus, Craig R. Koester rightly notes that "Creating pictures in the minds of an audience is a powerful means of evoking emotion (Quintilian, *Inst.* 6.2.29–31; Longinus, *Subl.* 15.1–2)."[8] Indeed, creating mental impressions through visionary simulations can be a very effective behavior-change therapy. For example, the fear evoked in seeing God's severe judgments simulated in the visionary revelation can engender repentance.

The following anecdote aptly illuminates the efficacy and impact of strategic acts: I was born and raised in the *Gikuyu* community that lives on the slopes of Mount Kenya at a time when indoor washrooms were unknown. Instead, the bushes served the purpose by day and night. Because of the mortal danger posed by hyenas and leopards after dusk, we were discouraged from leaving the safety of our huts. However, the call of nature would force children, who had not mastered the art of holding on to the reflexes of nature, to demand to be taken out at night for much-needed relief. The concerned mothers would scare the children off the unforgiving night by telling a horrifying story about an imaginary, nocturnal, man-eating animal called *Ndiba Maĩ* (water spitter).

Notwithstanding, when the reflexes of nature pushed, the children would still insist on being taken out. To effectively deal with this problem, mothers would enforce the much-needed discipline by simulating the acts of the water spitter. On a moonless night, the mother would take the child behind the round grass-thatched hut, and while the child was busy relieving itself, she would tiptoe back to the house, get a calabash full of water, walk unnoticed, and splash the water on the child. The child would rush towards the door, shouting, "*Mami! Mami! Ndiba maĩ! Ooi! Ooi!*" (Mummy! Mummy! The water spitter! Ooi! Ooi!). Trembling with fear, the child would cast itself into the safe hands of the mother, who would issue a final reprimand: "I warned you about the marauding water spitter, and you would not heed. See now how you and I would have been devoured tonight!" That strategic act evoked fear and induced discipline to hold on to the call of nature until day break. Such is the power of strategic acts. They work where logical reasoning would fail.

An episode narrated by my friend illustrates the enduring efficacy of evocations generated by strategic acts: One day, during his boyish escapades, he saw a lorry winding through a steep road. Without the knowledge of the lorry driver, he jumped onto the back of the lorry to hike a lift to his village.

---

8. Koester, *Revelation*, 27–150.

As the lorry neared his destination, my friend jumped off the moving truck. Unfortunately, he fell on his hands and knees, sustaining severe injuries. As my friend narrated the story, I experienced an empathetic sensation in my hands and knees, as if I were actually falling on the hard road. That feeling created a lasting fear of ever trying such feats. That sensation is replayed every time I recall the story.

By its nature and function, a single strategic act can generate multiple evocations which can constrain the audiences to act towards solving multiple needs. For example, the evocations generated by the strategic act embedded in the visionary scene simulating the wholesome life in the new heaven and earth (21:1—22:5), complemented by the knowledge that lack of love can debar one from attaining such a glorious eternal abode could rekindle the love of the church in Ephesus. Similarly, it could spur hope and patient endurance in the persecuted saints of Smyrna and engender abhorrence of the heretical teachings of the Nicolaitans in Pergamum. It could also evoke abhorrence of sexual immorality and idolatry in Thyatira as well as resurrect the dead church in Sardis. Again, it could encourage the faithful saints in Philadelphia to persevere in tribulation. It could also revive lukewarm Laodicea. This multifunctional aspect makes strategic acts very effective in evoking faith, patient endurance, and performance of spiritual disciplines.

Finally, over the years, interpretation of the book of Revelation has produced divergent conclusions which are held as irrefutable truths by different Christian groups and scholars. These conclusions have become impenetrable pre-understandings that limit the introduction of new methods of interpretation. Moreover, the challenge of interpreting the visionary revelation is compounded by the fact that a biblical criticism method of interpreting dreams and visions has not yet been developed. Most interpreters of visions and dreams in the Bible interpret their narrated versions as opposed to the actual visions and dreams.

This commentary seeks to help readers overcome the challenges identified in these introductory remarks. Its unique contribution is in identifying that the efficacy of the visionary revelation, to a very large extent, inheres in the evocations that are generated by the strategic acts embedded in the visionary symbols, simulations, and explanatory auditions. Since evocations are generated more by strategic acts than communicative acts, this commentary will comment on the visionary scenes other than the textual verses.

AUTHORSHIP

Ramsey Michaels notes that one of the major issues in the studies of Revelation is the question of whether the emphasis should be placed on Jesus as the divine source of the work or on John as the human author.[9] This commentary supports both positions. It recognizes that God was the divine source of the revelation, Jesus the director of the visionary simulations, and John the seer and narrator of the visionary revelation to the addressees (1:1).

Internal evidence names the visionary as a man named John (1:1; 4; 9) who boldly authenticates the vision with the signature of his name (1:1–2; 22:8). Such boldness suggests that his credentials and persona were highly trusted by his contemporaries to a level whereby his claims to having received divine revelation could be undoubtedly accepted. Such level of trust was vested on the apostles. Thus, this John can be identified as the son of Zebedee. Both Justin Martyr[10] [circa 135 CE] and Irenaeus[11] [circa 180 CE] also identified the writer as John the son of Zebedee. Irenaeus was a protégé of Polycarp (CE 60–155), the bishop of Smyrna who was under the overseership of apostle John.

However, some scholars have analyzed the syntax of the undisputed Johannine texts and Revelation and concluded that their differences warrant a different view.[12] The difference in the syntax can be mitigated by the difference in the genres. Furthermore, the events narrated in the Gospel of John had already happened by the time of writing. They were within experienced human history. As such, the language with which objects and events were described was within the known language conventions. However, Revelation narrates visionary simulations of events that were to happen in the unfolding history, which was not within experienced human history. As such, the syntax of the two narratives is bound to differ. Thus, the difference in syntax does not necessarily suggest difference in authorship. Suffice to say that, the evidence for John's authorship by persons so near to his time convinces us to accept their judgment as the most probable.

AUDIENCE

The visionary revelation was narrated to seven churches in Asia Minor. These are the churches in Ephesus, Smyrna, Pergamum, Thyatira, Sardis,

---

9. Michaels, *Interpreting Revelation*, 21.
10. Eusebius, *Ecclesiastical History*, 4.18.
11. Eusebius, *adv. Haer.* 4.14.1:5.26.1.
12. Ladd, *Revelation*, 171–77.

Philadelphia, and Laodicea. These churches were situated along the road that connected the seven cities. Thus, one postal carrier could pass on the narrated version of the visionary revelation to each of the seven churches.[13] It appears that though these churches had received the same gospel, their responses were impacted by their different historical situations. Judging their responses to the gospel using Jesus' gospel response matrix in the parable of the sower (Matt 13:1–9; Mark 4:1–20), it can be deduced that the gospel seeds in the majority of the members of the church in Sardis had fallen on walking paths and the birds of the air—Satan—had eaten them up. Similarly, in some of the members of the church in Thyatira, the gospel seeds had fallen on rocky soils, and because the soil was shallow, the gospel seedlings were scorched by the sun—sexual immorality and idolatry. In most of the members in the church in Laodicea, the gospel seeds had fallen on fertile soils but under thorns—worries of this life and deceitfulness of wealth and the desires for other things. They had germinated but the budding seedlings were choked by the thorns of double-mindedness. In the churches in Ephesus and Pergamum, the gospel seeds had fallen on fertile soils but were not optimally fruitful. Some were yielding a paltry thirty-fold, while others had a slightly improved yield of sixty-fold. To the sower's delight, the gospel seeds in the churches of Smyrna and Philadelphia had fallen on fertile soils and were yielding optimally at one-hundred-fold. The purpose of the visionary revelation was to evoke response to the gospel for optimal fruitfulness.

OCCASION

Indeed, the meaning of a visionary revelation can be illuminated by a knowledge of the reason that prompted God to show it. The visionary revelation addressed three issues which are explicitly described in the letters to the seven churches (2:1—3:21). One, it addresses concerns arising from theodicy, that is, the church's view and response to persecution by the synagogue Jews (2:9) and tribulations instigated by Satan (chapter 12), the emperor, and overzealous emperor-cult leaders (chapter 13). Indeed, from its inception on the day of Pentecost to the writing of the text, presumably during the reign of Emperor Domitian (81–96 CE), the church faced various forms of persecution by the synagogue Jews and the political powers. N. T. Wright convincingly argues that the persecution of Christians arose as a result of deep divisions between those who claimed to be the heirs of the scriptural promises on the basis of the temple, land, Torah, the race, and those who

---

13. Beitzel, *Moody Atlas*, 267.

claimed the same things on the basis of Jesus and his Spirit.[14] The persecution intensified after CE 90, when the Jewish council cursed the Christians for not supporting their CE 66–73 revolt that led to the destruction of the temple in CE 70.[15]

During his reign, Emperor Domitian demanded worship from his subjects. He demanded to be addressed and recognized as "Our Lord and God (*Dominus et Deus*)."[16] A few decades after Revelation was written, Pliny, the governor of Bithynia, notes that Christians were forced to invoke the pagan gods, curse Christ, and offer sacrifices of wine to the emperor's image.[17] The imprisonment of John (1:9) and martyrdom of Antipas (2:13) show that, as had happened to the three Jewish young men, Shadrach, Meshack, and Abednego, during the Babylonian exile (Dan 3:1–30), staunch Christians chose martyrdom rather than recognize the imposed lordship of the emperor and offer libations to his image.

Some in the church may have felt forsaken by God, while others were likely to renounce their faith to save their lives. G. K. Beale quotes a letter by Pliny the Younger to Trajan referring to people who had apostatized many years earlier and a few as twenty-five years earlier, that is, during Domitian's reign.[18] Thus, Pliny's letter supports the supposition that persecution indeed led to people renouncing the faith. The saints were also subjected to social and economic discrimination in the marketplace (13:16–17). This particular historical situation presented a need to simulate decreed judgments against the persecutors of the saints to assure the persecuted saints of their vindication, thereby engendering patient endurance (16:1–11; 18:1–19:3).

Two, the visionary revelation addressed the risk posed by false prophets and teachers to orthodoxy (2:2, 14–15, 20). Some of the churches were tolerating the heresies referred to as the teachings of the Nicolaitans. Fiorenza opines that the Nicolaitans expressed their freedom in libertine behavior, allowing them to become part of their syncretistic pagan society and participate in the Roman civil religion."[19] Such a situation presented a need to simulate the judgment of the false prophet (19:20) to evocatively engender abhorrence of unwholesome teachings and deeds.

Finally, the visionary revelation addressed gaps presented by nonadherence to orthopraxis—the right practice of the Christian faith. The

---

14. Wright, *New Testament*, 452.
15. Kistemaker, "Revelation," 2001.
16. Beasley-Murray, "Revelation," 1028.
17. Pliny the Younger, 10.97.
18. Beale, *Revelation*, 5.
19. Fiorenza, *Revelation*, 117.

general temptations, trials, and persecutions by the Judaizers and emperor-cult leaders negatively impacted the practice of faith. Furthermore, sections of the church were slack in performing spiritual disciplines. Lovelessness, sexual immorality, and idolatry had infiltrated some churches (2:4, 20). One church was almost spiritually dead, while another was lukewarm in faith (3:1; 3:15). This sad situation presented a need to prompt the audience to practice spiritual disciplines and shun idolatry and immorality.

In summary, a contextual analysis of the personalized covering letters (chapters 2–3) appended to the narrated version of the visionary revelation in chapters 4–22 shows that the overriding occasions in the seven churches were gaps in orthodoxy and orthopraxis. These two gaps threatened to disinherit the saints from the promised temporal and eternal rewards. On the other hand, the effects of tribulation were physically painful. However, those who patiently endured, even to the point of martyrdom, were assured of eternal life. Thus, gaps in orthodoxy and orthopraxis were more spiritually lethal than tribulations.

PURPOSE

Henry Barclay Swete sums up the book's purpose as *sursum corda*, inviting the churches to seek strength in the faith of a triumphant and returning Christ.[20] This commentary builds on Swete's supposition and shows how the book achieves this purpose. It identifies three needs that are addressed by the visionary revelation. One, there was a need to bridge gaps in orthodoxy. Two, the need to bridge gaps in orthopraxy. Three, the need to encourage the saints to endure the sufferings resulting from tribulations.

The visionary revelation is a three-pronged encouragement. First, it simulates God's preservation of the saints as they contend with the evil trinity[21] to evoke hope that inspires patient endurance. Second, it simulates God's rapprochements to humanity in the preaching of the gospel and the outworking of his decrees in retributive and disciplinary judgments on the world and erring saints. These simulations are strategic acts that are intended to generate evocations to jolt the wayward to repent, assure the saints of God's continuous salvific work in the church, and urge the saints to preach the gospel. Third, it reveals the final reward of eternal life in the new heaven and earth to evoke hope and zeal to pursue this eternal bequest.

Notably, John did not interpret, redact, or edit the visionary revelation; he narrated it raw. Similarly, Jesus and the mediating angels were also very

---

20. Swete, *Revelation*, xcvi.
21. The evil trinity is the alliance of Satan, beast, and false prophet.

economical with their explanations (1:29; 7:13–17; 12:9; 14:4–6; 16:13–14; 17:9–15; 20:2). This observation suggests that Jesus and John intended the audience to imaginatively and dramatically see, and be evocatively impacted by, the visionary simulations. An imaginative transfer of the audience to the visionary stages is achieved by a performance reading of the text. Performance readers imaginatively act out the text as they read. These observations suggest that, other than the general introduction (1:1–8) and the seven covering letters and their authenticating prologue (1:9–3:22), the rest of the visionary revelation was not meant to be strictly understood. Rather, it was majorly meant to generate evocations that would engender urgent actions that would eliminate the gaps identified in the historical situations of the seven churches.

The above observation challenges readers to imaginatively reconstruct John's prose narration into its visionary version, see, and respond to the evocations generated by the strategic acts embedded in its symbolisms, simulations, and auditions.[22] Auditions are John's explanations and clarifications of unclear aspects of the visionary revelation. In his article, "Is Revelation a Vision—or an Audition?" Ian Paul notes that Revelation is 55 percent visual, 43 percent auditory, and 2 percent introduction and conclusion. As such, auditions are an important element in interpretation of the visionary revelation. Christopher C. Rowland rightly observes that "Revelation requires the recovery of the ability to hear or read and to be stirred or shocked and scandalized into repentance and action."[23]

STRUCTURE

Two kinds of structures are identifiable: First, the structure of the visionary revelation narrated in 6:1—22:21. Second, the structure of the entire book. An understanding of the two structures can illumine interpretation of the book's message. The structure of the visionary revelation illumines its theme while the structure of the book illumines the relationship between the covering letters (1:9—3:22) and the visionary revelation (4:1—22:21).

Structure of the Visionary Revelation.

Two streams of events that would happen throughout the unfolding history are simulated in the visionary revelation:

---

22. Paul, "Is Revelation a Vision."
23. Rowland, "Book of Revelation," 556.

1. The church's sojourn and pilgrimage in the present heaven and earth throughout the unfolding history: This is represented as a final exodus from the present heaven and earth through the unfolding history into the new heaven and earth. Just as the Israelites were saved through judgments upon Egypt (Exod 7–12), so are the saints avenged by judgments against the evil trinity (9:1–21; 12:7–11; 16:2–7; 18:8–24). Again, just as the deliverance of Israel was achieved by her sealing with the blood of the Passover lambs (Exod 12:1–13), so was the deliverance of the church outworked through a passover sealing of the saints (7:1–10; 11:1; 20:1–3). Just as Israel faced tribulations in the wilderness wonderings, the church also faces tribulation in form of temptations, trials, and persecutions by Satan, the sinful worldly political and economic systems, and compromised cultic systems as she sojourns through the unfolding history (12–13).

2. Imageries from the Egyptian pilgrimage and Babylonian exile and the respective deliverances are used to simulate the church's redemption, earthly sojourn, and pilgrimage as she awaits to enter her Canaan-new heaven and earth. Rahab's and her family's deliverance through the seal of the scarlet cord could also be in view (Josh 2:18–21). This view of the life of the church's sojourn and pilgrimage was common in the apostolic times. Evangelist Mark interpreted Isa 40:3 and Mal 3:1 as pointing to the church's final exodus which was to be led by Jesus Christ (Mark 1:2).[24]

3. The second stream of simulated events consists of the outworking of God's eternal and consequential decrees throughout the unfolding history. Outworking of eternal decrees are identified in simulation of the work of the lamb of God who was slain from the foundation of the world (13:8). Outworking of God's consequential decrees is mainly in rapprochements to the world and erring saints in the gospel of Jesus Christ. It is complemented by retributive and disciplinary judgments on the world and the wayward saints to avenge the persecuted saints and to paradoxically engender repentance. Meanwhile, the saints are sealed as God's possession as they await the establishment of the kingdom of God in the new heaven and new earth where God's presence will eternally abide with them (21: 3–4).

---

24. Karura, *Catalyzing Reader Response*, 178.

Structure of the Book

The book is structured into three main sections: one, a general introduction to the narration of the whole visionary revelation (1:1–8). This general introduction contains the prologue (1:1–3) and the salutations (1:4–8). Two, the general introduction is followed by a narration of a vision of a personality who identifies himself as Jesus Christ. A comparison of the setting and purpose of this vision with Moses' ascent to Mount Sinai (Exod 19:3–9), Isaiah's visions of God (Isa 6:1–8), Ezekiel's vision (Ezek 1:1–28), and Daniel's vision (Dan 7:9–14) show that this vision is an introduction to the letters to the seven churches. It is intended to authenticate the contents of the seven letters by highlighting the divine source of the description of the historical situation of the seven churches (chapters 2–3).

Towards the end of each letter is a transition clause—"Whoever has ears, let them hear what the Spirit says to the churches"—which connects each of the letters to the final section of the book, the narrated version of the common visionary revelation (chapters 4–22). Similar to the letters to the seven churches, this visionary revelation is also introduced by an initial visionary simulation (chapters 4–5) which is also intended to authenticate the visionary revelation narrated in chapters 6–22. This final visionary revelation is the major generator of evocations that would engender actions to solve the needs exposed in the seven covering letters. As such, the seven letters can be described as covering letters to a common visionary revelation. This structure suggests that the seven letters are not stand-alone pieces. They are appendages to the common visionary revelation. As such, they should be interpreted together with the visionary revelation.

VISIONS AND DREAMS IN THE BIBLE

Scripture shows that when God intends people to know him, keep his word, and build their faith, he inspires the writing of Scripture (Exod 31:18; 2 Tim 3:16–17). When he intends them to recall, relive, and be impacted by a past redemptive deed or experience, he institutes memorial ordinances like circumcision (Gen 17:10–13), Passover feast (Exod 12:14–20), baptism (Matt 28:1–20), and the Lord's Supper (Matt 26:26–30; 1 Cor 11:23–26). When he intends them to foretaste and be impacted by his eschatological promises and decreed consequential and disciplinary judgments, he simulates them in dreams and visions (1:19). Memorial ordinances and visionary revelation in dreams and visions constitute sacred texts through different media other than the literary text. Wolterstorff agreeably observes that "the media of divine discourse is even more divers . . . dreams, visions, apparitions, burning bushes, illnesses, national calamities, national deliverances, droughts—on and on."[25]

Leland Ryken aptly notes that dreams consist of "momentary pictures, fleeting impressions, characters and scenes that play their brief part and then drop out of sight, abrupt jumps from one action to another."[26] They are images of occurrences usually played out in the mind when one is asleep. They are mediums through which people relive their conscious and unconscious experiences. The spirit world uses them to communicate with people in the natural world.[27] An example is Nebuchadnezzar's dreams in the book of Daniel chapters 2 and 4.

On the other hand, visions are experienced either in sleep or in a trance. Keener calls the state in which visions are envisioned "an altered state of consciousness." He further notes that "Brain research suggests that the human brain is open to such experiences."[28] Majorly, visions simulate actual events that have occurred, are occurring, or are yet to occur. The efficacy of the visionary revelation is in the joy, desire, fear, trauma, etc., evoked by the audience's foretaste of the simulated events that will undoubtedly happen in the unfolding history. God has used man's ability to dream and to see visions to reveal his plans, will, judgments, and eternal reward to his saints.

Visions Narrated in the Book of Revelation

In agreement with all other New Testament texts, the visionary revelation narrated in the book of Revelation does not constitute a new revelation of God. Instead, it amplifies the teachings of the Old Testament Scripture and the revelation of God in the person and teachings of Jesus Christ. As such, its interpretation can be illuminated by insights from the Old Testament Scripture, the redemptive work of Jesus, and the teachings of Jesus and his apostles.

The visionary revelation sought to solve very grave and urgent issues that were threatening to hinder the progress of the church in Asia Minor (1:3). Trials, temptations, and persecutions by the evil trinity of Satan, the beast from the sea (Rome and its Emperors), and the beast from the land (Rome's provincial governors who also doubled as imperial cult leaders) were strategic acts that were intended to seduce and force the saints to comply

25. Wolterstorff, *Divine Discourse*, 38.
26. Ryken, *How to Read the Bible*, 170.
27. Mbiti, *Concepts of God*, 443.
28. Keener, *Miracles*, 871.

with Satan-induced Romish ideals. Similarly, heresies from false teachers and lukewarm spirituality had infiltrated the church ranks. To counter these grave issues, God showed John visions to evoke repentance, revival from dead works, patient endurance, and practice of spiritual disciplines.

SYMBOLISM IN THE OLD TESTAMENT

Often, the writers of Old Testament texts employed symbolism to communicate their messages. The first covenant between God and Adam was expressed in symbolism. Adam and his wife were given dominion over the cosmos on the condition that they would not breach God's word (Gen 1:28–30, 2:15–17). Breach of the covenant was symbolized as eating the fruit of the tree of knowledge of good and evil.

God's covenant with Abraham was entered through a symbolic act whereby the two parties to the covenant passed between the carcass of a slaughtered animal (Gen 15:9–21). This symbolic ritual signifies a sealing of the covenant. The ordinance of circumcision was instituted as a perpetual reminder of the covenant. Thus, a strict adherence to the covenant was referred to as circumcision of the heart (Deut 30:6; *Greek:* περιτομή *peritomē* [Phil 3:3]), while non-adherence was likened to a mere mutilation of the foreskin (*Greek:* κατατομή, *katatomē*, Phil 3:2).

The blood of the Passover lamb in Egypt was used as a symbol of the death of the firstborns of the Israelites. When the angel of destruction visited their houses to kill the firstborns and saw the symbol of death, he passed over them (Exod 12:12–13). Prophets Isaiah (Isa 14:12–14; 40:6–7), Ezekiel (Ezek 37), Daniel (Dan 2, 7), and Zechariah (Zech 4:1–14; 9–11) employed symbolism to portray their contemporary and future realities.

Normally, the conception of a symbol is informed by the worldview of the audience. A single reality could be represented in different symbolisms to different audiences depending on the worldview of the audience and the intended evocations. For example, in Nebuchadnezzar's dream, the empires of Babylon, Medo-Persia, Greece, and Rome were represented in the symbol of an image made of gemstones, metals, and clay. The divine overthrow of these empires was simulated by showing a small stone that was not hewn by human hands knocking down the huge image to nothingness. However, when the same empires were shown Daniel, an exile in Babylon, they were depicted in symbols of a lion, bear, leopard, and a fourth dreadful beast. These beastly kingdoms were divinely overthrown by one like the Son of Man who came into the scene riding on the clouds of heaven. Notably, Nebuchadnezzar viewed other kingdoms as desirable trophies to be won, hence the choice of representing these kingdoms in form of admirable gemstones and metals. On the other hand, Daniel viewed the same kingdoms as dreadful persecutors of the Jews, hence the choice of representing them in symbols of dreaded beasts. These different symbolisms of the same reality aimed at generating different evocations. The symbolism in Nebuchadnezzar's dream evoked faith and fear of YHWH, whereas it evoked patient endurance and hope of eventual emancipation in Daniel and his audience.

SYMBOLISM AND PORTENTS IN THE BOOK OF REVELATION

Symbolism and portents are the bulwarks of the visionary revelation. The divine author of the visionary revelation used redemptive and judgment episodes in the past to mirror, reveal, and explain the outworking of God's decrees and judgments consequent of humanity's response to God's rapprochements in Jesus and his word. By revealing God's decreed rewards to those who keep his word and his judgments against their persecutors and those who act contrary to his word, God sought to persuade the seven churches to bridge spiritual and ethical gaps in their historical situations. This supposition agrees with Koester's position that "the images through which Revelation 'signifies' its meaning are an element of persuasion. The book is not so much designed to dispense information as it is designed to strengthen its reader's commitments."[29]

Imagery that is informed by events in the people's mythological past, immediate history, and eschatological expectations, as had been illuminated by their inspired teachers and prophets, was a very effective tool to mirror and inspire actions in their time. Caird notes that "a myth is a story told about the remote past but told to explain the present. It must be capable of being re-enacted by those who have found in it a stimulus to the imagination and a spur to action."[30] He further argues that "all genuine convictions require a mythology for their adequate expression and cannot influence the conduct of men until they have bodied forth in powerful imaginative symbols."[31] In agreement with Caird's supposition, this study avers that simulating the visionary revelation using symbols constituted strategic actions that can stimulate the imagination and spur the audience to action.

The revealer used symbols that were familiar to John's audience to enable them assign the intended referents and meaning. Most of the symbols

---

29. Koester, *Revelation*, 44.
30. Caird, *Revelation*, 148.
31. Caird, *Revelation*, 148.

had been used in the existing Scripture in the narration of occurrences similar to those shown in the present visionary revelation. For example, the symbolism of a locust invasion prophesied in Joel 1:4; 2:4 as a judgment against Judah is reused in the visionary revelation simulating the judgment that would be handed down to those who slight God's rapprochements. Similarly, the imagery of the judgment in Exod 7:14–25, in which the waters in Egypt were turned into blood, is reused to simulate similar occurrences narrated in 8:8 and 16:3–4. Again, the beast from the sea, which in the visions of Dan 7:7 represented a future Roman Empire, is reused to represent the Roman Empire in John's days and similar empires that would arise in the unfolding history.

Similarly, the 1,260-days abomination by Antiochus Epiphanes IV between 167 and 164 BCE that caused the desolation of the second temple is used as a symbol to represent the period between the destruction of the Herodian temple and the second coming of Jesus Christ. In fact, to date, the Herodian temple stands desecrated and desolate. The Dome of the Rock, a Muslim temple, stands where the Jewish temple once stood. Some newer symbolisms are also used if an equivalent is not found in Israel's mythological, historical, and religious heritage. For example, the victory of the cross through which Jesus bound the strong man—the Devil (Mark 3:27; Matt 12:29)—until he vandalizes his kingdom by redeeming his captives through the gospel is depicted as the imprisonment of Satan in the bottomless pit for a thousand years.

Unlike symbolisms in the elements and mode of administering the ordinances of the Lord's supper and baptism, which relive and commemorate past redemptive events to revive the partakers' faith and reciprocal obligations,[32] apocalyptic visionary symbolisms represent events in the past, present, and unfolding history in a way that evokes responses that are intended to bridge gaps in the audiences' historical situations. In agreement with this supposition, Keener says, "John's symbolic language is meant as evocative imagery, to elicit particular responses, rather than a detailed literal picture of events."[33] Functionally, showing these symbols constitute strategic actions. On this premise, strategic actions in the visionary revelation are meant to generate evocations of awe, fear, trauma, admiration, esteem, etc., to urge the faithful churches to hold on to faith, awaken the ones in spiritual slumber, resuscitate the dying and breathe life to the spiritually dead.

Moreover, unlike metaphorical symbols that sometimes use euphemisms to soften gory events, apocalyptic visions use the goriest, scariest,

---

32. Karura, *Baptism Lord's Supper*, 24
33. Keener, *Bible Background*, 761.

most explicit, and very captivating symbolic depictions. For example, judgments are depicted as an attack by an army of locusts with scorpion tails that sting to inflict maximum pain. The sins of Rome are represented in the symbol of a prostitute holding a cup full of abominations and filth of her sexual immorality. The pain of eternal separation from God is expressed as a lake of fire kindled by sulfur and brimstone. On the other hand, the eternal abode of the saints with God and eternal life are depicted in the most admirable symbolism: a bride, a city decorated with jewels, a street of gold, a river of life, and a tree of life with leaves that are for the healing of nations.

Similarly, the life span in the new heaven and earth is expressed as forever and ever to evoke contempt for the present transient life on earth and a longing for eternal life. The duration of the church's suffering throughout the unfolding history is described litotically as three and a half years to minimize hopelessness and despondency that is likely to be caused by long periods of tribulations. On the other hand, the period of Satan's defeat by the work of the cross is expressed hyperbolically as one thousand years to elicit great assurance of a severe judgment of Satan.

Functionally, visionary portents are different from visionary symbols. They are signs in whose form and description are embedded messages, doctrines, theological perspectives, or realities that the sign's creator intends to communicate. Their embedded message is noticeable in its whole and constituent parts.

Symbolisms of the Unfolding History

The entire visionary revelation portrays the duration of the unfolding history in both litotic and hyperbolic time symbols depending on the intended evocation in a particular simulated event. When demonstrating that the church will triumph throughout the unfolding history despite great tribulations, the unfolding history is litotically depicted as forty-two months. The saints' resistance and sure triumph in this period is compared to the historical situation in the time of the Maccabean revolt between 167 and 164 BCE. This comparison encourages the saints by demonstrating that their painful resistance to forced emperor worship by the evil trinity will similarly come to an end sooner than later.

To assure the church that the time of her suffering will be short-lived and that God will protect her and supply her needs throughout the unfolding history amid tribulation by the devil and his cahoots, the unfolding history is litotically portrayed as lasting for a time, times, and half a time (12:14). This period compares with the time Elijah was sustained by the ravens and the widow of Zarephath (1 Kgs 17:1–24) during a ravaging dearth and persecution by Ahab and Jezebel.

When the unfolding history is portrayed as the period when the church, represented by the two witnesses preach the gospel amid great opposition, it is depicted as 1,260 days (11:3). This period is again litotically compared to the Jewish endurance and resistance against Antiochus Epiphanes IV. The comparison assures the church that she too will triumph and emerge out of her struggles sooner than later.

When expressed as a time when Jesus' death destroys the work of the devil, the unfolding history is hyperbolically depicted as a thousand years of Satan's detention. Consequently, the kingdom of God on earth, when the work of Jesus gives the saints unassailable victory, is established and lasts for a corresponding period of a thousand years. This hyperbolic depiction assured the saints that the work of Jesus has achieved a sustained and overwhelming victory over the devil.

AUDITIONS IN THE VISIONARY REVELATION

The visionary revelation consists of simulations of present, unfolding, and eschatological events by a symbolic cast complemented by auditions. Auditions are oral clarifications that explain obscure visionary symbolisms and simulations. They are communicative acts which complement the strategic acts in the symbols and simulations. Functionally, they are interpretive cues that are intended to minimize the vision's ambiguity.

The symbolic cast can be identified with the saying "I saw." Simulations are identifiable by the deeds ascribed to each character. On the other hand, oral clarifications can be identified with the phrase "I heard." The cast simulating the outworking of God's redemptive and judgment decrees, acts of the Roman Empire, emperor, and provincial kings, and theological themes are represented in symbols of earthly beings, inanimate objects, terrestrial objects, celestial beings, and mythological beasts. The choice of the symbol was dictated by the symbol's effectiveness to generate the intended evocations.

At times, John is enjoined as one of the visionary characters (10:8). In his description of symbols, simulations, and oral clarifications, he used language conceptions that were common and available in his time. Of course, the human conceptual limitation does not allow very exact descriptions of the symbols that represented aspects and events that were yet to be fulfilled in the unfolding history. Some were not comparable to anything that John had ever seen or heard. However, the descriptions and expressions were sufficient to generate the intended evocations.

COMMUNICATIVE ACTS IN REVELATION

The personalized covering letters to the seven churches (2:1–3:21) are mainly communicative acts. They prompt responses more by convincing and convicting the audience than by generating evocations. Primarily, they highlight the audiences' historical situations, the religious gaps therein, and the needed remedial actions. Positive values are highlighted, and the churches are encouraged to uphold them. Vices are also exposed, and the culprit churches are urged to forsake them. Finally, to enthuse compliance with the exhortations and warnings, the churches are promised various rewards, which include divine recognition and eternal life with God in the new heaven and earth.

STRATEGIC ACTS IN THE CHRISTIAN SCRIPTURE

Functionally, the Christian Scripture is to a lesser extent aimed at imparting knowledge. It is largely skewed towards calling people to faith and transforming character. In other words, it is less of a doctrinal but more of a relationship-building text. Being a text that aims at building the covenant relationships between man and God, the Bible uses various strategic acts to evoke positive attitudes, desires, and aspirations to uphold the covenantal stipulations. Vanhoozer rightly notes that "the criterion for success in 'strategic' action is simply bringing about an intended result, some change in the world, other than understanding. The intended result may produce an effect on a hearer or reader."[34]

In both the Old and New Testaments, strategic acts have been used to evoke positive responses to God's various rapprochements. For example, the ten judgments against Egypt were intended to compel Pharaoh to free Israel. Likewise, God's miraculous food and water provisions to the Israelites in the wilderness were primarily meant to supply their needs. Secondarily, but significantly, they acted as strategic acts to induce faith in God. This aspect is shown in the statement "I have heard the grumbling of the people of Israel. Say to them, 'At twilight, you shall eat meat, and in the morning,

---

34. Vanhoozer, *First Theology*, 185.

you shall be filled with bread. Then you shall know that I am the LORD your God'" (Exod 16:12).

When Naaman went to Israel's king to be introduced to a healer, Prophet Elisha said, "Let him come to me, that he may know that there is a prophet in Israel" (2 Kgs 5:8). Indeed, the miracle of Naaman's healing was a strategic act that evoked faith in the God of Israel. After being healed, Naaman said, "Behold I know that there is no God in all the earth but Israel . . . From now on, your servant will not offer burnt offerings or sacrifice to any god but Yahweh" (2 Kgs 5:17). The effects of evocations generated by strategic acts are quick and effective.

Sometimes, God uses strategic acts to call people to ministry. An example is God's act of calling Moses in the burning bush (Exod 3:2). Another was the supernatural consumption of Gideon's sacrifice by fire (Judg 6:19–21). The heavenly throne vision of Isa 6:1–13 was a strategic act through which God confirmed his call to ministry. It was narrated to authenticate Isaiah's prophecy. So was the vision of Ezekiel in which he was told to eat a scroll (Ezek 1–3). The miracle of the mighty catch of fish that prompted Peter, James, and John to forsake all and follow Jesus (Luke 5:1–11) was a strategic act. Finally, Paul's conversion and call were to a large extent prompted by a strategic act on his way to Damascus (Acts 9:4–5).

Performing miracles to elicit faith is a strategic act. It engenders change through means other than by understanding a message. However, later narrations of the miracles are not necessarily strategic acts. Mostly, they are rhetorical devices that are used to convict and convince the readers about the authenticity of the word of God, who alone has supernatural power to work out the narrated miracle. Jesus' miracles amazed both the recipients and eyewitnesses. He would also use verbal strategic acts to magnify the evocative efficacy of his miracles. Mark records instances where Jesus performed miracles both in the open and in secret but would tell the recipients not to broadcast them, knowing too well that they would not keep quiet (Mark 8:36). The amazingness of the miracles compelled the recipients to, all the more, publicize them. Jesus' purpose in telling the beneficiaries not to broadcast the miracles was also a strategic act that elicited wonder and faith when hearers and later readers noted that though the recipients were told not to broadcast the miracle, they nevertheless could not keep quiet. Karura rightly says, "It is arguable that Jesus' injunction was loosely given to be disobeyed . . . This can be identified as one of Jesus' methods of increasing the reach and impact of his ministry."[35]

---

35. Karura, *Catalyzing Reader Response*, 223.

Strategic Acts in the Visionary Revelation

Observably, the evocative nature of the visionary revelation's setting, stage arrangement, the cast of characters, symbols, and simulated events suggest that the visionary simulations are intentional strategic acts.

Steps in Identifying Revelation's Strategic Acts and their Intended Evocations

1. A performance reading of the text that makes the reader dramatically see every visionary episode, hear every audition, and be impacted by everything that John saw and heard.

2. Identification of the original audience's visionary situations.[36] Borrowing from Bitzer, a visionary situation can be defined as a complex of persons, events, objects, lifestyle, and relations presenting an actual or potential need which can be completely or partially removed if a vision or narration of it, introduced into the situation, can so constrain human decision or action as to bring about a significant modification of the need.

3. The personalized covering letters to the seven churches uncover the gaps in their historical situations that prompted God to show this evocative visionary revelation (2:1—3:22). This information should be complemented by scanning the seven churches' religious, social, cultural, economic, and political contexts that are availed by historians, geographers, and archaeologists.

4. Identification of the evocative cues in the simulation of the outworking of God's decrees throughout the unfolding history and symbolic portrayal of the events, personalities, expression of time periods, and celestial and hellish places shown in the visionary revelation (i.e., hyperbole, litotes, foils, wonder, goriness, explicitness, New Jerusalem, lake of fire, etc). Visionary hyperbole exaggerates while litotes diminish issues to increase their evocative efficacy.

5. Establishing the nature and functions of the simulated acts, symbols, and portents by illuminating them with echoes from their apparent allusions in the Hebrew text, the sayings of Jesus, and the teachings of the apostles in the New Testament texts.

---

36. Bitzer, *Rhetorical Situation*, 1–14.

Efficacy of Strategic Acts in the Visionary Revelation

In her analysis of how Apocalypse creates its effect, Adela Yarbro Collins rightly notes:

> The apocalypse is as evocative as it is expressive. Not only does it display attitudes and feelings; it also elicits them ... The Apocalypse handles skilfully the hearers' thoughts, attitudes, and feelings by using symbols and a narrative plot that invites imaginative participation. This combination of effective symbols and an artful plot is the key to the power of apocalyptic rhetoric.[37]

Yarbro identifies rhetoric as the linguistic vehicle that was used to communicate Revelation's evocations. However, rhetorical structuring and cues are noticeable only in the first three chapters. First, John starts the narration with a common introduction that evokes keen listening, hearkening, and faith (1:1–3). By noting that the revelation was from God via Jesus and mediating angels, John absolved himself from its conception. He placed it squarely on the omniscience of God, thereby enhancing the revelation's efficacy. Second, as a good amanuensis, he wrote Jesus' personalized letters to each church. Each letter highlighted the church's historical situation and shortcoming which the visionary revelation sought to solve. Finally, he ended each covering letter with the catchphrase "He who has an ear, let him hear what the Spirit says to the churches." In ordinary rhetorical language usage, this catchphrase is used at the beginning or end of an address to underscore the importance of the content and to urge audience response. It also acts as a warning of dire consequences for not responding. "What the Spirit says to the churches" are the exhortations in the personalized covering letters to each of the churches and the evocations generated by the strategic acts embedded in the visionary simulations.

Argumentation, which is a major feature of rhetoric, is not a feature of the visionary revelation or its narrative version. Since narrative prose is the second-tier medium in the three media through which the message of revelation is transmitted, it should be used as fodder for reconstructing the visionary revelation wherein strategic acts are the primary generators of evocations. An imaginative "seeing" of the visionary revelation in the reading or hearing of the text is an essential step in the process of its interpretation.

The visionary revelation narrated in 6:1—22:21 simulates "what must take place after this." Apparently, some of the things that "must take place after this" were already happening by the time John saw the vision. The

---
37. Collins, *Crisis and Catharsis*, 144–145.

structure of the visionary revelation builds climactically, from the introduction of the author and director (chapters 4–5) to God's rapprochements in redemptive acts and judgments (chapters 6–9), rapprochements in the church's preaching of the gospel (chapters 10–11), church's tribulation by the evil trinity (chapters 12–13), Jesus' preservation of the saints till he calls them home (chapter 14), God's acts of vengeance against the persecutors of the saints (chapters 15–20), and finally, the establishment of the kingdom of God in the new heaven and earth (chapters 21–22). This structure is itself strategic. It builds and heightens suspense, thereby arousing the reader's interest and enthusiasm to respond. The exhortation, "Blessed is the person who reads aloud the words of this prophecy, and blessed are those who hear and keep what is written in it, for the time is near" (1:3), further urges the audience-response.

The events described as "what must take place after this" are symbolized and simulated hyperbolically, litotically, and explicitly. They are also symbolized and simulated in the goriest form on one hand and most excellent on the other hand. For example, the final judgments of Satan, the beast from the sea, the beast from the land, and sinners are simulated by throwing their role players into a lake of fire kindled by sulfur and brimstone (19:20; 20:10). This simulation arouses deep fear, in the audience, of ever facing such judgment, thereby prompting repentance.[38] Disciplinary and retributive judgments are also portrayed in the most gruesome manner to intensify their evocative power. For example, death is represented in the symbol of the blood of a corpse (16:3); pain is compared to the pain of being stung by scorpions for five months, whereby victims seek to die but death eludes them (9:5–6). On a positive note, the unfolding history was expressed in litotes (an understatement) of short periods like 3½ days, 1,260 days, time times and a half, and 42 months to minimize hopelessness and despondency as a result of envisaging long periods of tribulation.

On the other hand, those who would overcome the devil's wiles and the allure of worldly pleasures are rewarded with eternal life with God in the new heaven and new earth. God's presence in the new heaven and new earth is represented by a humongous ark of his presence, depicted as a holy jewel-bedecked city—the New Jerusalem (21:11–14). Here, eternity is portrayed as a street of gold (21:21), while eternal life is symbolized as a river of life flowing down its middle. The tree of life which bears fruits every month, which represents unceasing satisfaction, is shown growing beside the river. Its leaves are said to be for the healing of nations (22:2). It represents complete wellness in the new heaven and earth. Such a presentation is a strategic

---

38. Taylor, *Ezekiel*, 248.

act that evokes a deep desire to live in the new heaven and earth, thereby engendering a lifestyle that would guarantee an afterlife in such a glorious abode.

Symbolic contrasts and foils are also part of the devices used to magnify desirable things and diminish the undesirable ones. For example, a symbolic vision stage in the heavens (4–16) is contrasted with a symbolic vision stage in the wilderness (17–20). This contrast highlights the righteous outworking of God's decrees from his heavenly throne and the judgments against the great harlot that are outworked on earth. It urges and nudges the reader to shun the undesirable and choose the desirable and pursue it. Explaining that there was no one in heaven, on earth, or under the earth who was worthy to open the scroll was a rhetorical foil to magnify the person of Jesus and his redeeming work once he is revealed as the one who was worthy. It was also meant to catalyze belief in the gospel about him.

Yarbro rightly observes that the purpose of Apocalypse is to overcome the intolerable tension between reality and hopeful faith—cognitive dissonance, that is, a state of mind that arises when there is a great disparity between expectations and reality.[39] Such cognitive dissonance prompts the reader to respond by working out to change the present reality to conform to the expected reality.

To enhance the efficacy of its strategic acts, the visionary revelation employed explicit symbolism. For example, the idolatry of Rome and her subjects is symbolically simulated by "an immoral woman holding a golden cup full of the abominations and the impurities of her sexual immorality" (17:4). This dramatized simulation of Rome's idolatry would make the audience puke at imaginatively "seeing" the cup's contents. Such a simulation is meant to make the reader cringe in abhorrence of her sins. It is also meant to stigmatize the tempter, the sinner, and sin, thereby engendering resistance to sin.

Application of Strategic Acts in the Visionary Revelation

Since most of the simulated events happen throughout the unfolding history, the readers are impacted by the evocations from strategic acts generated by the visionary simulations and also by the strategic acts generated by the simulated events as and when they are outworked in their lifetime.

The text of Revelation was written to a faith community. It is not a political, economic, or social satire, as has been suggested in some circles. However, its polemics against an ungodly and unjust system can be a

---

39. Collins, *Crisis and Catharsis*, 141.

deterrent to wantonness. It can speak sense to people who behave as if they will live in this world forever. It can also tame societies and call individuals to their spiritual, moral, and ethical senses. However, outside the Christian hope of living eternally in the new heavens and new earth, its promises and prescriptions are hollow, a mere psychological and sociological catharsis.

Revelation can breathe sense to a world that, in one way or another, is being used by Satan to vex and persecute Christians. The historical situations of Christians in many parts of the world today are similar to the situations in the ancient Roman Empire. In the Western world, Christians are contending with systems that are constitutionally stifling the witness of the gospel. Reproving sin is considered to be offensive to some groups. In some countries, preaching Jesus as the only way in their pluralistic worldview may land one in prison. Others have legislated against preaching the gospel in schools supposedly, to give children the right to choose how to live their lives. Church groups in some countries support the sin of Jezebel by advocating for gay and lesbian rights. The visionary revelation should jolt these churches to repent from their compromise.

Middle Eastern countries and Africa have witnessed a proliferation of Islamic fundamentalists such as Al-Qaida, ISIS, Muslim Brotherhood, Hezbollah, Al-Shabaab in Somalia, and Mboko–Haram in Nigeria. Some states like Iran, Iraq, Saudi Arabia, Pakistan, and Afghanistan have institutionalized Islamic fundamentalism as part of their national ethos. In these countries, Christians are marginalized and stigmatized and, worse still, hunted to be killed. Christians in these countries need the evocations generated by the strategic acts in the visionary revelations to elicit endurance in persecutions as they witness Christ.

Some communist countries have also continued to block entry of the Christian faith. For example, in North Korea, reading Christian Scripture is considered a capital offense. Leaders of these countries should hear the narrative of the visionary revelation to evoke repentance, faith, and hope.

The Global South is currently generally poor. Lack of resources is the biggest hindrance to the preaching of the gospel. Though Christianity has flourished, it is in danger of being syncretized to another gospel for lack of sound biblical training. The message of the visionary revelation should urge leaders who ascribe to the Christian faith to curb wanton corruption and lift their populace from poverty.

Of all the sixty-six books of the Christian Bible, Revelation is touted as the most difficult to interpret. Nonetheless, its evocative nature makes it the easiest to apply. Though the events simulated in the visionary revelation are described through concepts and language conventions of the first century, the embedded strategic acts generated evocations and reader responses similar to the evocations it would generate in all Christian generations. Again, it addressed gaps in historical situations that are similar to historical situations of Christians throughout the unfolding history. Similarly, the need to repent, patiently endure, love, urge holy living, and practice Christian disciplines in the first century is generic to Christians throughout the unfolding history. The challenge lies in learning to read the text in a way that imaginatively transports the reader to the vision stage just as the Holy Spirit transported John, see every symbol, cast of characters, simulation, hear every explanation, and then respond to the evocations generated by the strategic acts in the visionary simulations.

Applying evocations generated by the strategic acts embedded in the visionary revelation to the secondary readers requires a thorough scanning of their historical situations in order to establish the specific issues that may be a threat to orthodoxy, an impediment to orthopraxy and, an exposure to issues of theodicy. These three are the major issues addressed by the visionary revelation. Questions to ask: 1) What are the peculiar trials, temptation, and persecutions in the specific audience's historical situation? Once established, they should be countered by the visionary scenes that evoke responses that would fortify the saints against these aspects of the great tribulation. 2) Are there any heretical teachings derailing or likely to derail their faith? These should be matched with the visionary simulations that evoke abhorrence of sin, heresy, and pursuit of righteousness. 3) Are there shortfalls in the audience's performance of Christian disciplines? Any shortfall in this area can be overcome by highlighting visionary simulations that urge repentance and performance of these spiritual disciplines.

METHODOLOGY OF INTERPRETATION

Interpretation methods of the book of Revelation are many and varied. R. H. Charles has done a good study of the history of interpretation of the text from antiquity to his time.[40] Similarly, Craig, D. Koester has done a good literature review on the interpretation of Revelation.[41] Since then, more studies have been done, but the hermeneutical terrain has not changed much. Recent trends tend to compare it to extra-biblical Jewish apocalyptic writings. Seemingly, these Jewish writings sought to give meaning to the religious, social, and political contradictions resulting from the community's shattered hopes due to the traumatic overthrow of the temple and their continued rule by foreign powers. The Jews were first conquered

---

40. Charles, *Studies in Apocalypse*, 1–50
41. Koester, *Revelation*, 151–206.

by Nebuchadnezzar, and a sizeable population of their nobility was exiled in Babylon between BCE 604 and BCE 586. Afterward, they were colonized by the Persians (BCE 536–333), Greeks (BCE 333–164), and Romans (BCE 69–CE 476). A few years before John narrated his visionary revelation, the Herodian temple was destroyed during the CE 66–73 Jewish revolt. Later on, Jerusalem was overrun after the CE 132–136 Bar Kokhba revolt. George W. E. Nickelsburg aptly notes:

> "Why?" and "wither?" are the questions raised by these writers (4 Ezra, 2 Baruch, and the Apocalypse of Abraham) as they ponder the events of 70 CE. The first question refers to the problem of theodicy: Why has a just God allowed the sinful Gentiles to defeat the covenant people and devastate their land and God's temple? The second question relates to reconstruction: What will take the place of the temple as the people attempt to pick up the broken pieces of their life and their religion?[42]

Jewish apocalyptic writings also sought to interpret the Jewish hope of the restoration of Israel under the leadership of a divine Messiah.[43] Ryken rightly places this type of literature in the category of fantasy.[44] Its writers interpreted their difficult historical situation using insights from the community's eschatological promises.

On the other hand, the visionaries and narrators of the canonical apocalyptic visionary revelations were directed by the omniscience of God. Thus, the primary distinction between Jewish apocalypticism and God's omniscience-guided apocalypticism is that the former interpreted its audience's historical situation guided by the writers' finite understanding of the community's hopes and promises. Thus, it can be speculative. However, writers of the canonical apocalyptic texts narrated divinely inspired visionary simulations of the outworking of God's eternal and consequential decrees in the unfolding history. These visionary revelations were embedded with strategic acts with efficacy to generate evocations that, if responded to, would bridge the gaps in the audiences' historical situations.

The supposition that the visionary revelation was a divine production does not allow any interpretive suggestion that disregards this notion. For example, an interpretation that recognizes the fact that the omniscience of God wholly directed the visionary revelation would not accept the notion that the infinite knowledge of God would allow a simulation of Nero's presumed resurrection (*Nero redivivus*).

42. Nickelsburg, *Jewish Literature*, 270.
43. Tomasin, *Judaism Before Jesus*, 29.
44. Ryken, *Bible as Literature*, 165.

So far, these five methods of interpreting the text of Revelation have been proffered:

1. The Preterist method which supposes that the book of Revelation was written to meet the church's needs in John's days and should be read in its historical context. Therefore, some preterists see events recorded in Revelation as having been fulfilled in John's time. However, though it is agreeable that some events revealed in the book were happening in John's time, most would occur as history unfolds.

2. The idealist method supposes that the book of Revelation contains principles that can encourage the church of all ages. This position assumes that the book was written to guide the church of all ages. In this understanding, readers are expected to draw principles to guide their Christian lives.

3. The historicist method supposes that the book of Revelation is a record of the things that were to happen from the time of John to the second coming of Jesus. However, it is necessary to note that the visionary revelation is not a detailed chronological road map of historical events. The vision was shown to John who narrated it to specific audiences that lived in a particular time in history to solve particular needs in their historical situations.

4. The futurist method supposes that the book of Revelation is a prophecy that records eschatological events. Whereas some events, such as the last judgment and the establishment of a new heaven and new earth are futurist, positioning all the events recorded in the book as futuristic poses a big hermeneutical challenge. The audience to which it was written, including a large part of the secondary audience, would not benefit much from the text.

5. The eclectic method uses all the above methods to get into the meaning of the book of Revelation. Therefore, it could be more fruitful than the other four methods.

Each of these methods has some merit. However, due to the unique genre and multiple media in which the revelation was transmitted, new approaches are welcome. The hermeneutical method used in this commentary may not be strictly categorized as any of the above. It is based on the suppositions that:

1. The visionary simulations of the events revealed in John's visions were majorly strategic acts. They were not shown to merely explain present or eschatological events. Rather, they were shown for their evocative

efficacy to encourage the saints in the seven churches to endure tribulations and to provoke actions that would bridge the gaps in Christian orthodoxy and orthopraxis. As such, a fruitful interpretation necessitates identification of the strategic acts embedded in the visionary simulations and the evocations they generate. It also calls for identification of the needs that these evocations were intended to resolve. To illuminate the function of the different scenes of the visionary revelation, the adopted hermeneutical method also incorporates insights from cinematography.

2. In addition to the other events that are simulated in the visionary revelation, God's judgments that would be executed on the fallen world in the unfolding history are also simulated. This supposition calls for an interpretation that incorporates insights from judicial processes to shed light on the nature and purpose of these judgments.

3. To illuminate the effectiveness of visionary portents and symbols, the interpretation of the visionary revelation also incorporates insights from semiosis—the study of signs and their significations.

4. Application of the evocations generated by the strategic acts to the secondary audience is premised on the observation that the church in the unfolding history faces historical situations similar to those that were faced by the primary audience. Though they present themselves in different forms, lovelessness, spread of false teachings, trials, persecution, martyrdom, immorality, idolatry, spiritual deadness and lukewarmness that were affecting the primary audience, are the same issues affecting the church of today. As such, the evocations generated by the strategic acts embedded in the visionary revelation can fully solve needs in the secondary audiences' historical situations.

Observably, the scenes are structured in such a way that successive scenes are simulated in a manner that adds more information and clarifies previous scenes. Therefore, interpretation outcomes of its constituent scenes should be provisionally held until the entire visionary revelation has been studied and interpreted.

A Performance Reading of the Book of Revelation

The multiple media in which the revelation was transmitted demands that it be interpreted in a way that appreciates the unique contribution of each medium, that is, the visionary simulations, narrative prose, and performance reading of the text. In performance reading, the reader immerses themselves into every simulation described in the text. Immediately after reading John's short prologue and greetings, just as John was transported in the Spirit to the different vision halls, the readers should allow themselves to be imaginatively transported to these vision halls, that is, Patmos (1:9), the visionary heaven (4:1), wilderness (17:1), and high mountain (21:10) where John saw the different visionary simulations. In such vantage positions they can see and overhear every detail of the visionary simulation.

Performance reading immerses the reader into the visionary simulation. It evokes empathy for the oppressed righteous and love for righteousness. It equally arouses righteous indignation against the sinner and happily welcomes the judgment of the oppressor. These emotions evoke hatred for sin that leads to repentance. It also evokes admiration for holiness leading to holy living.

Insights from the Administration of Law and Justice

Anthony C. Thiselton has noted that "the theme of God's judgments is the vindication of the oppressed."[45] In agreement with Thiselton, this commentary notes that the bulk of God's judgments in the unfolding history serve a disciplinary purpose. They are handed down to deter offenders from relapsing into sin and warn their ilk. The Kenyan judges often pronounce these words as they read the sentence to the convicts: *"Ili hii iwe funzo kwako na kwa wengine, nimekufunga kifungo cha miaka fulani"* (In order for this judgment to serve as a lesson to you and others, I sentence you to serve a jail term of this number of years). In such cases, the judgment is both retributive to vindicate the offended party and disciplinary to correct the offender's behavior and to deter others.

Visionary simulations of disciplinary judgments are strategic acts aimed at jolting sinners to repentance. They are also aimed at deterring the audience from falling into sinful habits. Moreover, narrations of visionary simulations of consequences for either holy living or otherwise can evoke abhorrence of sin, repentance, endurance of tribulation, and maintenance of orthodoxy and orthopraxy. The intended purpose of judgments simulated in the visionary judgments can be identified by identifying the strategic acts inherent in the visionary simulation, the evocations they would generate, and the envisaged response of the audience.

---

45. Thiselton, *Study of Theology*, 190.

Insights from Cinematography

This visionary revelation was shown to John over 1,900 years ago. Interestingly, it is comparable to today's virtual reality 3-D movies. The 3-D movie glasses virtually transport the audience beyond the cinema screen into the arena of the action. Similarly, the Holy Spirit transported John into the arena where the things that were, and the things that would soon take place were being simulated (4:1; 17:3; 21:10). Simply put, John was not airlifted but in the spirit walked into the future, beholding every aspect of the outworking of God's eternal and consequential decrees throughout the unfolding history. He became both an audience and, at times, part of the cast (10:8–11) There, he saw, experienced and at times participated in the simulation of the events that were being revealed in the visionary revelation. Similarly, by a performance (imaginative) reading of the prose version, interpreters should allow themselves to be transported to the vision stages where the visionary simulations are shown. Leland Ryken aptly notes that such an experience "gives us the shock treatment."[46]

SUMMARY

Unlike other biblical texts which use communicative acts as rhetorical devices to convince and convict their audiences, the visionary revelation uses strategic acts to generate evocations that engender actions that bridge gaps in the audience's historical situations. As such, the conventional verse-by-verse commentary, which is suited in investigating the intended meaning of communicative acts in literary prose texts, would not be suitable in investigating the evocations generated by the strategic acts embedded in the visionary simulations and the intended audience responses. A commentary that would adequately illumine these aspects is one that would comment on the visionary scenes, identify the embedded communicative and strategic acts, the evocations they generate, and the intended reader responses.

OUTLINE OF REVELATION

I. General Introduction
    A. Prologue 1:1–3
    B. Salutations 4–8
    C. Authentication of Visionary Revelation 1:9–20

46. Ryken, *Bible as Literature*, 170.

- D. Personalized Covering Letters to the Seven Churches 2:1—3:20
    1. Covering letter to the church in Ephesus 2:1–7
    2. Covering letter to the church in Smyrna 2.8–11
    3. Covering letter to the church in Pergamum 2:12–17
    4. Covering letter to the church in Thyatira 2:18–29
    5. Covering letter to the church in Sardis 3:1–6
    6. Covering letter to the church in Philadelphia 3:7–13
    7. Covering letter to the church in Laodicea 3:14–22
II. Vision Authenticating the Visionary Revelation 4:1—5:14
- A. Calling of John to the vision hall 4:1
- B. The setting of the vision hall and cast of characters 4:2—4:11
    1. God on his throne 4:2–7
    2. Worship by the seraphs 4:8–9
    3. Worship by the twenty-four elders 4:10–11
- C. Sealed scroll handed to Jesus 5:1–14
    1. A sealed scroll in the hands of God 5:1–4
    2. Jesus takes the scroll 5:5–7
    3. Joint worship of God and the Lamb
        a. Worship by the Seraphs & Elders 5:8–10
        b. Worship by Angels 5:11–12
        c. Worship by the redeemed from every people group 5:13–1
III. Unfolding History in Perspective 6–8:1
- A. The outworking of God's decrees on the fallen world in history 6:1—8:1
    1. The first seal opened 6:1–2
    2. The second seal opened 6:3–4
    3. The third seal opened 6:5–6
    4. The fourth seal opened 6:7–8
    5. The fifth seal opened 6:9–11
    6. The sixth seal opened 6:12–17

7. Sealing of the elect 7:1–17
   a. Four harming angels 7:1
   b. Another angel restrains the harming angels 7:2–3
   c. Sealing of the 144,000 7:4–8
   d. The sealed multitudes from all people groups 7:9–10
   e. Angels join in worshiping God 7:11–12
   f. Introduction of the great multitude by one of the elders 7:13–17
8. Seventh seal opened 8:1

IV. Divine Rapprochements in Disciplinary and Retributive Judgments 8:2—11:19
   A. Outworking of Decrees of Disciplinary and Retributive judgments 8:2—11:14
      1. Seven trumpet-blowing angels appear 8:2
      2. Angel with golden censer full of prayer and incense 8:3–5
      3. Seven trumpet-blowing angels prepare to blow 8:6
      4. Blowing the first trumpet 8:7
      5. Blowing the second trumpet 8:8–9
      6. Blowing the third trumpet 8:10–11
      7. Blowing the fourth trumpet 8:12–13
      8. Blowing the fifth trumpet 9:1–12
      9. Blowing the sixth trumpet 9:13—11:14
         a. Disciplinary judgment by four angels 9:13–21
         b. Conquering Gospel by a Holy Spirit filled Church 10:1—11:14
            i. Mighty angel with a small scroll 10:1–3
            ii. Voice of seven thunders 10:4a
            iii. John told to seal message of the seven thunders 10:4b
            iv. Order to seal message of the thunders countermanded 10:5–7
            v. John ordered to take the small scroll 10:8–10

           vi. John commissioned to prophesy 10:11
           vii. Measuring the temple of God 11:1–2
           viii. The two witnesses prophesy 11:3–6
           ix. The two witnesses killed 11:7–10
           x. The two witnesses come to life 11:11
           xi. The two witnesses ascend to heaven 11:12
           xii. Severe earthquake 11:13–14
      10. Blowing the seventh trumpet 11:15–19
           a. Heaven speaks 11:15
           b. Twenty-four elders worship God 11:16–18
           c. God's Temple opened at 11:19
V. Tribulation of the church by the Unholy Trinity 12:1—14:20
   A. Satan against the seed of the woman 12:1—13:1
   B. The beast from the sea 13:2–10
   C. The beast from the earth 13:11–18
   D. The Lamb and 144,000 victorious saints 14:1–5
      1. The Lamb on Mount Zion 14:1–4
      2. New song in heaven which only the 144,000 could sing 14:5
   E. Angel with eternal gospel 14:6–7
   F. Angel announces the fall of Babylon 14:8
   G. Angel warns against the worship of beast 14:9–13
   H. Harvest of the earth 14:14–20
      1. Son of Man comes seated on a cloud 14:14
      2. Son of Man harvests the earth 14:15–16
      3. Angel harvests grapes 14:17–20
VI. Defeat of Evil Trinity, Satan and Final Judgment 15:1—20:15
   A. Seven angels with seven last plagues introduced 15:1
   B. Victorious saints worship God before the throne 15:2–4
   C. Seven angels prepare to pour wrath on earth 15:5—16:1
   D. Seven angels pour out God's wrath on earth 16:2–21
      1. First bowl poured 16:2

      2. Second bowl poured 16:3

      3. Third bowl poured 16:4–7

      4. Fourth bowl poured 16:8–9

      5. Fifth bowl poured 16:10–11

      6. Sixth bowl poured 16:12–16

      7. Seventh bowl poured 16:17–21

E. John in the wilderness vision stage 17:1—21:8

   1. Judgment of Babylon (Harlot City) 17:1—19:5

      a. Woman sitting on east 17:1–15

      b. Overthrow of the harlot city 17:16–17

      c. Identity of the harlot city 17:18

   2. Aftermath of the fall of the harlot city 18:1–24

      a. Announcement of the fall of the great harlot city 18:1–3

      b. Warnings against being unequally yoked with the harlot city 18:4–8

      c. Dirge by kings of the earth 18:9–10

      d. Dirge by merchants of the earth 18:11–17

      e. Dirge by shipmasters and seafaring men 18:18–19

      f. Call to the heavens to rejoice over Babylon's fall 18:20

      g. Mighty angel demonstrates fall of Babylon 18:21–24

      h. Rejoicing in heaven over the fall of Babylon 19:1–5

      i. Inauguration of the reign of God/the marriage of the Lamb 19:6–8

      j. Blessedness of being invited to the marriage supper 19:9–10

   3. Judgment of Beast, False prophet, Kings of the earth and their armies 19:11–21

      a. Introduction of the rider of a white horse and his army 19:11–16

      b. The great supper of God 19:17–21

          i. Birds of prey called to the great supper of God 19:17–18

           ii. Beast and kings of the earth fight against rider of the white horse 19:19
           iii. Beast and the false prophet are thrown into the lake of fire 19:20
           iv. Slaying of the kings of the earth and their armies 19:21
      4. The nature of Satan's judgment 20:1–15
         a. Binding of the devil for a thousand years 20:1–3
         b. Jesus' and the saints' rule for a thousand years 20:4–6
         c. Release of Satan after the thousand years 20:7
         d. Satan, Gog and Magog fight against Jesus and the saints 20:8
         e. Destruction of Gog and Magog 20:9
         f. Satan thrown into the lake of fire 20:10
         g. White throne judgment 20:11–15
            i. The present heaven and earth flee from God 20:11
            ii. Dead judged 29:12–13
            iii. Death and Hades thrown into the lake of fire 20:14
            iv. Final judgment of sinners 20:15
VII. Eternal Dwelling of the Saints 21:1—22:21
   A. New Heaven and New Earth 21:1–8
      1. Inauguration of the new heaven and new earth 21:1
      2. The holy city, the New Jerusalem 21:2–8
   B. John on the mountain stage 21:9—22:21
      1. New Jerusalem: Ark of God's presence 21:9–14
      2. Measuring of the city 21:15–17
      3. The glory of the city 21:18–21
      4. Lightings in the city 21:22–25
      5. Qualifications for admission into the city 21:26–27
   C. Eternity and eternal life 22:1–5
   D. Call to respond to the evocations 22:6–21

GRAPHIC STRUCTURE OF THE TEXT

Visionary Situation of the Seven Churches (1:1–3:22).	Strategic Acts Embedded in Simulations of Events that Would happen in the Unfolding History (4:1–20:15)				Visionary New Heaven and Earth as a Strategic Act (21:1–22:5).
	One thousand years, 3½ yrs., 1260 days, 42 months.	A little while Apostasy 3½ days.	End of the current heaven and earth.		
1. Gaps in Orthodoxy 2. Gaps in Orthopraxy 3. Theodicy (Tribulations)	1. 1–4 Seal: (God's decreed rapprochement and judgments consequent of Adam's sins. 2. 1–7 Trumpet: Divine rapprochements in disciplinary judgments, building the church & gospel proclamation. 3. Rev 12–13 Tribulations by the Evil Trinity. 4. 15–16: Last-tier of God's judgments, the wrath of God is completed in them. 5. Satan is depicted as bound and incarcerated in the bottomless pit.	1. Apostasy depicted as lasting for 3½ days when churches' witness appears dimmed. Also depicted as Satan loosed for a little while, battle of Armageddon, battle between the Lamb and alliance of Gog and Magog. 2. Judgment of beast from the sea and false prophet. 3. Judgment of sinners and Satan/Dragon. 4, Reaping of the righteous and gathering of the sinners into the winepress of the wrath of God.	The end of the former heaven and former earth is simulated as the destruction of the present earth after opening the 6th seal, blowing the 7th trumpet, and passing away of the former heaven and earth.		Eternal life with God and the Lamb in the new heaven and new earth

Observation From the Graphic Structure

The graphic structure of Revelation shows that, as a first step, Jesus revealed the visionary situations of the seven churches. He then showed visionary simulations of God's redemptive deeds in the work of the Lamb and the gospel, present occurrences that were impacting church life, disciplinary and retributive judgments on persecutors of the church, sinners and the Devil, the victory of Christ, and finally, the reward of the righteous in the new heaven and earth. Simulations of these events were embedded with strategic acts that were intended to generate evocations to urge and nudge responses that would eliminate gaps in the historical situations of the seven churches. They can also be applied to eliminate similar and diverse faith gaps in the historical situations of the secondary readers.

Commentary on the Visionary Revelation

Chapter 1

Prologue and Covering Letters to the Seven Churches

PRELIMINARY OBSERVATIONS

THE PROLOGUE (vv. 1–3), salutations (vv. 4-8), and the initial visionary scene authenticating the entire visionary revelation (vv. 9–20) constitute the general introduction of the entire visionary revelation. It is followed by seven personalized covering letters (2:1—3:22) for the single narrated version of the visionary revelation (4:1—22:21). These covering letters are aesthetically structured and rhetorically nuanced to expose the gaps in the audience's historical situations and to draw them to read, hear, imaginatively see, believe, and respond to the evocations generated by the strategic and communicative acts embedded in the visionary simulations narrated in chapters 6:1—22:21.

REV 1

Prologue 1:1-3

[1] *The revelation of Jesus Christ, which God gave him to show his servants what must soon take place. He made it known by sending his angel to his servant John,* [2] *who testified to everything he saw, that is, the word of God and the testimony of Jesus Christ.* [3] *Blessed is the one who reads aloud the words of this*

prophecy, and blessed are those that hear it and observe what is written in it for the time is near.

George R. Beasley-Murray rightly notes that "the term revelation is capable of expressing a variety of meanings. It can signify the act of unveiling or the object which is uncovered."[1] John uses the term "revelation" to describe a visionary simulation of "what must soon take place." It also suggests that, before this revelatory moment, the nature and timing of "what must soon take place" were only privy to God.

A reading of this text together with chapter four and five suggests that the genitive "of Jesus Christ" singles him as the one appointed to reveal the outworking of God's decrees and the issues that would befall the church in the unfolding history. Indeed, the revelation is wholly a Jesus project. He appeared to John in a vision at Patmos, caused him to be in the Spirit, commanded him to write what he was to see, dictated the seven covering letters to accompany the visionary revelation narrated in 4:1—22:21, and directed the entire visionary revelation. On his part, John was a pliable amanuensis who was commanded to only write what he saw and heard (vv. 1:11).

The things he saw were described as "what must soon take place." The word "must" shows the certainty and inescapability of the simulated events. As such, it also draws the readers to respond appropriately to the visionary simulations and, eventually, to the actual events as they are outworked as history unfolded and continues to unfold. The full phrase shows that Jesus used a cast of angels to simulate "what must soon take place." John was just a faithful amanuensis who narrated everything he saw and heard to the seven churches in Asia Minor in prose.

By saying that he is the one who bore witness to the word of God and the testimony of Jesus Christ (vv. 2), John invoked his high ethos as a stamp of authenticity of all that Jesus revealed to him. In saying that he testified to everything that he saw, John further shows that he was faithful in relaying everything that he was told to relay. John calls all that he saw "the word of God and the testimony of Jesus Christ." This description shows that the visionary revelation was the word of God to the seven churches. It is the testimony of Jesus Christ to the extent that he is the one who revealed it to John. It also urges the audience to respond to God's rapprochement in the gospel of the salvation that Jesus wrought by his death (5:9–10).

The beatitude in vv. 3 urges those who would read or hear to respond to the prophecy. Here, John refers to the visionary revelation as a prophecy. Indeed, it fulfils all the functions of a prophecy. As in other prophetic oracles which both forthtell and foretell, it addresses the things that are, that

---

1. Beasley-Murray, *Revelation*, 50.

is, the historical situation of the audience, and also reveals the things that are to come, that is, the things that would be outworked in the unfolding history. Thus, it is a prophecy in visionary simulations of things that were and things that would come to pass in the unfolding history.

Salutation 1: 4–8

⁴John, to the seven churches in the province of Asia Minor: Grace and peace to you from him who is, and who was, and who is to come, and from the seven Spirits before his throne, ⁵and from Jesus Christ, who is the faithful witness, the firstborn from the dead, and the ruler of the kings of the earth. To him who loves us and has freed us from our sins by his blood, ⁶and has made us a kingdom and priests to serve his God and Father, to him be glory and power forever and ever! Amen. ⁷Behold, he is coming with the clouds, and every eye will see him, even those who pierced him, and all peoples on earth will mourn because of him. So shall it be! Amen. ⁸"I am the Alpha and the Omega." Says the Lord God, "who is, and who was, and who is to come, the Almighty.

Unlike other non-canonical apocalyptists who do not stamp their works with their signatures, John forthrightly names himself as the seer of the visionary revelation (vv. 4). He must have earned trust as one who could receive and disseminate divine truth. His primary audiences are also specific—the seven churches in Asia Minor. As such, secondary readers ought to approach the message as eavesdroppers to the message between Jesus and the specific churches. Wishing his audience grace and peace from God, the seven Spirits and Jesus Christ is a common cliché in the introductions of letters in John's milieu (Rom 1:7; 1 Cor 1:3; 2 Cor 1:2; Gal 1:3; Eph 1:2).

Describing God as "who is, who was, and who is to come" highlights his eternal nature in comparison to temporal powers that were persecuting the saints. I. Howard Marshal, Stephen Trevis, and Ian Paul rightly point out that the description "develops the understanding of the divine name"[2] (Exod 3:14). Describing the Spirit using a numeral adjective "seven," which shows completeness, underscores the Spirit's thorough work of probing the churches' historical situations, identifying the existing gaps, and prescribing the appropriate visionary revelations that would generate apt evocations to engender actions that would solve them.

Describing Jesus as "the faithful witness" highlights his fidelity in revealing every aspect of the visionary revelation. The title "firstborn from the dead" underscores Jesus as the first person to resurrect from the dead.

---

2. Marshal et al., *Revelation*, 363.

It also suggests that there are other persons who will likewise resurrect at the general resurrection of the dead (20:13). The title "ruler of the kings of the earth" highlights Jesus' sovereign rule over the affairs of the world. It is a synonym of his other title: King of kings and Lord of lords. This exalted description of their true Lord must have been intended to diminish the saints' perception of the power and sway that the kings of the land had assumed over them. John caps the description of the Godhead by glorifying Jesus with a very uplifting and befitting doxology: "To him who loves us and has freed us from our sins by his blood, and has made us a kingdom and priests to serve his God and Father, to him be glory and power forever and ever! Amen" (vv. 5–6). In biblical parlance, the word "blood" is mainly used as a metonymy for life and a euphemism for the death of Jesus Christ. John uses the term "blood" to underscore that Jesus willingly died for the sins of the world. This way, he qualified us to be a kingdom of priests to serve his God and Father in holiness (1 Pet 2:9).

The saying "He is coming with the clouds and every eye will see him" (vv. 7) echoes Acts 1:9–11 and Dan 7:13–14 and highlights the certainty of Jesus' second coming. The saying encourages the saints to patiently endure temptations, trials of their faith, and persecutions as they witness Christ to the world and eagerly wait for the blessed hope—the appearing of the glory of their great God and saviour, Jesus Christ (Titus 2:13). The phrase "even those who pierced him" (vv. 7) further emphasizes the fact that his return will be visible to all and that nobody will be exempted from his righteous judgment. This nuance is meant to evoke a reflective disquiet among those who may have slackened in faith, prompting them to act to bridge any gaps in their faith and praxis.

"'I am the Alpha and the Omega,' says the Lord God, who is and who was and who is to come, the Almighty" (vv. 8) is an assertive clause similar to "I am God Almighty (*Elshadai*)" (Gen 17:1), which highlights God's omnipotence, omniscience, and omnipresence. The title *Elshadai* affirmed God's ability to fulfil his covenant with Abraham. Again, he identified himself as YHWH—the living God (Exod 3:14). This title contrasted him with other non-living, human concepts of God and idols in Egypt and Palestine. "I am Alpha and Omega, the one who is, who was, and who is to come" (vv. 8) combines God's attributes expressed in the titles *Elshaddai* and *YHWH* to express his sovereign and immutable nature. It is intended to engender the saints' trust in God's ability and dependability.

AUTHENTICATION OF THE VISIONARY REVELATION (1:9-20)

⁹I, John, your brother and companion in the suffering and kingdom and patience endurance that are ours in Jesus, was on the island of Patmos because of the word of God and the testimony of Jesus Christ. ¹⁰On the Lord's Day I was in the Spirit, and I heard behind me a loud voice like a trumpet, ¹¹which said: Write on a scroll what you see and send it to the seven churches; Ephesus, Smyrna, Pergamum, Thyatira, Sardis, Philadelphia, and Laodicea.

By describing himself as a brother and companion in suffering (vv. 9), John identifies himself as one with his addressees in suffering, kingdom, and patient endurance. The phrase, "suffering and kingdom and patient endurance that are ours in Jesus" shows that suffering for the sake of the kingdom of God is the lot of believers in Jesus Christ (John 16:33; 2 Tim 3:12). Thus, the statement is an exhortation to enduringly seek the kingdom of God. It is also a rhetorical nuance to solicit the addressees' response to the evocations generated by the visionary simulations. The past tense in the phrase "was on the island called Patmos" suggests that John had already been freed from exile by the time of narrating his visionary experience.

The Lord's day was the first day of the week when believers met for corporate worship and holy communion (1 Cor 16:2). It is the day when Jesus rose from the dead and appeared to his disciples (Luke 24:41-43). To be in the Spirit, in this sense, was to be in a Spirit-induced trance in which one could, in vision, see simulations of the outworking of God's decrees in the unfolding history.

The loud voice like a trumpet displays clarity and dispels any ambiguity in what Jesus was about to tell and show John. Recording Jesus' command to John to write what he hears and sees absolves John from being understood as the conceiver of the visionary revelation. It rightly places its conception on Jesus Christ, thus increasing its evocative efficacy. God's visionary revelation was addressed to specific churches. However, it can be applied to the universal church throughout the unfolding history since she experiences similar challenges in orthodoxy, orthopraxis, and in matters of theodicy (1 Cor 10:13).

¹²I turned around to see the voice that was speaking to me. And when I turned, I saw seven golden lampstands, ¹³and among the lampstands was someone like a son of man, dressed in a robe reaching down to his feet and with a golden sash around his chest. ¹⁴The hair on his head was white as wool, as white as snow, and his eyes were like blazing fire. ¹⁵His feet were like bronze glowing in a furnace, and his voice was like the sound of rushing waters. ¹⁶In his right hand, he held seven stars, and coming out of his mouth was a sharp double-edged sword. His face was like the sun shining in all its brilliance. ⁱ⁷ When I saw him, I fell at his feet as though dead. Then he placed his right hand on me and said, "Do not be afraid. I am the first and the Last." ¹⁸ I am the Living One; I was dead, and now look, I am alive forever and ever! And I hold the keys of death and Hades. ¹⁹ Write, therefore, what you see, what is now, and what will take place later. ²⁰ The mystery of the seven stars that you saw in my right hand and of the seven golden lampstands is this: The seven stars are the angels of the seven churches, and the seven lampstands are the seven churches.

"Voice" in verse 12 stands in synechdoche of voice for the speaker for the person speaking. The symbol of lampstands describes the church in relation to her mission of lighting up the world (Matt 5:14; Rev 11:4). Walking among the churches depicts Jesus as the overseer of the church (1 Pet 2:25). It borrows its imagery from the scene in Gen 3:8 where God was similarly walking in the garden of Eden in the cool of the day. This portrayal forebodes its use to underscore Jesus' care, thorough knowledge of the historical situation, and sovereign power over the church in Ephesus (2:1).

Describing the one walking among the lampstands as looking "like a son of man" (vv. 13) suggests that he was an otherworldly being personified in human form. It identifies him as Jesus who in the Gospels took upon himself the title "the Son of man" of Dan 7:13–14 (Mark 2:10; 8:31). His priestly garments highlight his functional office of mediator between men and God (1 Tim 2:5–6). His white hair (vv. 14) compares him with the ancient of days (Dan 7:9), thereby affirming his deity. His fiery eyes demonstrate his omniscience and hence his ability to discern the seven churches' historical situations. According to Poythress, bronze was used to make weapons of war.[3] As such, his bronze-like feet demonstrated his power to execute judgment against the erring church (2:22–23). This portrait forebodes its use in Jesus' warning to the church in Thyatira (2:18) not to underrate his ability to judge her errant members.

His great voice, like many waters, shows the unmistakably audible and authoritative word of the speaker (Ezek 1:24; 43:2; Rev 14:2). It also impressed upon the audience the gravity of his message. The seven stars in his right hand (vv. 16a) denote the speaker's superintendence over the stars—the under-shepherds of his church. Holding something with the right hand demonstrates the holder's power over the thing so held. It also shows its great value and honor.[4] As such, the symbolic holding of seven stars in

---

3. Poythress, *Returning King*, 79.
4. Ryken, *Biblical Imagery*, 728. Hanson, "Right Hand," 191.

his right hand also symbolizes Jesus' power over the under-shepherds of his flock. This portrayal also forebodes its usage in Jesus' warning to the churches in Ephesus (2:1) and Sardis (3:1).

A sharp double-edged sword is identified as the word of God (Eph 6:17 and Heb 4:12). As used here, it refers to an instrument of judgment. It also portends its use in Jesus' encouragement and warning to the church in Pergamum (2:12; 16). It assured her of severe judgment against her persecutors. It also served as a warning to the unrepentant among her members. His brightly shining face (vv. 16c) draws its imagery from Moses' experience on Mount Horeb as he received the Torah. It compares his role of receiving and relaying the vision to the church to Moses' role of receiving and relaying the law to the Israelites (Exod 34:29–30). This portrait served to enhance the evocative efficacy of the visionary revelation.

When John saw the speaker, he fell at his feet as though dead. This incident demonstrates the reverence due to the speaker. The statement "Fear not, I am the Alpha, the Omega, and the living one. I died, and behold I am alive forevermore, and I have the keys of death and Hades (vv. 17–18) identifies the speaker as the glorified Christ. Saying that he has the keys of death and Hades points to his power over death and Hades. Having the key of death and Hades also denotes that by his death, he rendered death, that reigned by the power of sin, powerless over the believer. As such, the shade of the symbol "key" here is different from its shade in the phrase "key of the bottomless pit" in 9:1 which refers to allowing Satan and his demonic host to engender obduracy among persecutors of the saints and unbelievers. It is also different from the nuance in 20:1–3 where the symbol "key" refers to the power inherent in the death of Jesus to overcome the devil's nefarious schemes against believers. These three different shades of the symbol "key" need to be rightly delineated in the interpretation of the three different scenes where the symbol "key" occurs.[5] The saying was also meant to inspire hope in the resurrection, more so to those who were undergoing persecution to the point of martyrdom.

As John concludes his prologue, he notes Jesus telling him, "Write the things that you have seen, the things that are and those that are to take place after this" (vv. 19). The "things that you have seen" were the contents of the vision he was seeing on the Patmos vision stage (vv. 12–20). Some of the "things that are" are described in the personalized covering letters (2:1—3:22). The rest of the "things that are" are simulated in the main visionary revelation (6:1—22:21). These are the things that were happening at the time of writing the text, like the preaching of the gospel, wars, famines and

---

5. Beale and Campbell, *Revelation*, 182.

plagues resulting to deaths (6:1-8). Other examples of "things that are" are the tribulations instigated by the evil trinity (chapters 12-13). The "things that are to take place after this," are simulated in the visionary revelation narrated in 6:1—22:21.

In summary, this scene introduces the entire visionary revelation. It summons the reader to hear and respond to the evocations generated by the communicative and strategic acts embedded in the visionary simulations. It also catalyzes audience belief and response by noting that the source of the revelation was God and that its mediators were Jesus, various angels, and John. These persons are of undoubtable ethos, thus enhancing the believe value and trustworthiness of the visionary revelation. The scene presents Jesus in his post-resurrection glory (vv. 13-14, 16b) and portrays his functional role as a preserver of his saints (vv.13, 16a), judge of the wayward and rewarder of the overcomer (vv. 15).

PERSONALIZED COVERING LETTERS FOR THE NARRATED VERSION OF THE VISIONARY REVELATION (REV 2:1—3:22)

Preliminary Observations

Chapters 2:1—3:22 contain seven personalized covering letters that were collectively appended to the narrated version of the visionary revelation (4:1—22:21). They describe the gaps in each church's historical situation to highlight the needs that were intended to be solved by the churches' response to the evocations generated by the strategic and communicative acts embedded in the visionary revelation. Thus, these descriptions are expressed in plain speech with minimal symbolism and metaphors to minimize ambiguity.

Structure of the Seven Covering Letters

The structures of the seven personalized covering letters are similar and adopt the following format:

1. Jesus names the addressee church.
2. Jesus introduces himself to the addressee church using aspects of his symbolic portrait (1:12-20). These aspects are chosen depending on the intended evocation. The symbolic portraits show the attributes

that Jesus uses to shepherd and judge the particular church. They are highlighted to either warn, comfort, or exhort the church.

3. Jesus commends the church for her good deeds.
4. Jesus highlights the church's shortcomings.
5. Jesus exhorts the church to correct her shortcomings.
6. Jesus further commends the church for her good virtues.
7. Jesus promises rewards to those who would overcome.
8. Transition to the main visionary revelation using the phrase "He who has an ear, let him hear what the Spirit says to the churches." This phraseology is a double-entendre idiomatic expression that is embedded with a warning of dire consequences for slight and paradoxically an exhortation to respond to the evocations generated by the strategic acts in the visionary simulations. It carries the same rhetorical force as God's warning and exhortation in Isa 6:9–10, Jesus' warning and exhortation in Mark 4:1–12 and Matt 13:1–17. As such, these seven letters should be read as appendages to the common visionary revelation narrated in 4:1—22:21.

Covering Letter to the Church in Ephesus

[1] *"To the messenger of the church in Ephesus, write: These are the words of him who holds the seven stars in his right hand and walks among the golden lampstands.*

The explicit naming of the addressee shows that the message in this covering letter is specifically addressed to the church in Ephesus. However, the other six churches were free to read and apply the message to their specific visionary situations. An issue that affects believers in one church can quickly creep into another church in the same religious, political, social, and economic contexts. Jesus introduces the contents of the letter to the Ephesians as "the words of him who holds the seven stars in his right hand and walks among the lampstands" (vv. 1). Holding something with the right hand demonstrates that the thing so held is secure, honored, and that the holder has power over it. In the present context, it demonstrates that Jesus has sovereign power over the seven stars—pastors. It also demonstrates that he values and honors them. Showing Jesus walking among the lampstands demonstrates his overseership of the lampstands—churches. This opening statement is aimed at warning the church in Ephesus not to slight Jesus' diagnosis of the gaps in her historical situation and the offered prescription—the evocations that would be generated by the visionary simulations narrated in 6:1—22:21. It shows that if slighted, he can defrock the pastor and disown the particular church congregation.

> ²*I know your deeds, your hard work, and your perseverance. I know that you cannot tolerate wicked people, that you have tested those who claim to be apostles but are not, and have found them false.* ³*You have persevered, endured hardships for my name, and have not grown weary.* ⁴*Yet I hold this against you: You have forsaken the love you had at first.* ⁵*Consider how far you have fallen! Repent and do the things you did at first. If you do not repent, I will come to you and remove your lampstand from its place.*

Jesus knew the state of this church. Her toil and perseverance were indeed commendable. She could not tolerate evil men. She had tested those who claimed to be apostles and found them false. Jesus observes that she was also enduring patiently for his name and was not growing weary (vv. 2–3). However, all that good was being eclipsed by her waning love (vv. 4). Allowed to continue, lack of love for God, one another, and the lost can slowly but surely kill a church. Paul teaches, "If I give away all I have, and if I deliver my body to be burned, but have no love, I gain nothing" (1 Cor 13:3). Jesus calls decline in love a fall, from which he urges this once-loving church to repent by doing the things she did at first (vv.5). The consequence of lovelessness is extinction of the church (vv. 5).

> ⁶*But you have this in your favour: You hate the practices of the Nicolaitans, which I also hate.* ⁷*Whoever has ears, let them hear what the Spirit says to the churches. To the victorious one, I will give the right to eat from the tree of life, which is in the paradise of God.*

To her credit, the church had tested and shunned the works and teachings of the Nicolaitans (vv. 6). Without supporting evidence, some in the second century supposed that Nicolaitans were followers of Nicolas the elder who was chosen to oversee tables in Jerusalem.[6] The personalized covering letter of the visionary revelation (4:1—22:21) to the church in Pergamum shows that this heretical group condoned sexual immorality and eating food sacrificed to idols (vv. 14–15). God's nature abhors idolatry. As his name קנא, *qann'* (jealous), suggests, it arouses his jealousy (Exod 34:14).

This letter closes by urging this church to respond to the evocations generated by the strategic acts in the visionary simulations narrated in 6:1—22:21 with the double entendre idiomatic expression "He who has an ear,

---

6. Gilmour, *Interpreter's Commentary*, 950.

let him hear what the Spirit says to the churches" (vv. 7). This clause serves two purposes. It urges the audience to hearken to the admonition and exhortations in the letter. It is also a very strong warning to those who would not harken and respond to the evocations that would be generated by the strategic acts embedded in the visionary revelations narrated in 6:1—22:21. Structurally, it also serves as a transition clause connecting the letter to the main visionary revelation narrated in 4:1—22:21. This transition clause is placed towards the end of each of the seven covering letters to the churches (2:7; 11; 17; 29, 3:6; 13; 22). Use of the Greek singular interrogative pronoun τί (*what*) in this clause rightly suggests that "what the Spirit says to the churches" is a common single communication attached to the covering letters to all the seven churches. This observation further suggests that "what the Spirit says to the churches" is actually the content of the visionary revelation narrated in 4:1—22:21.

Promise to the Overcomer

To urge the church in Ephesus to hearken to what the Spirit says to the churches, Jesus promised overcomers the right to eat the fruit of the tree of life, which is in the paradise of God (vv. 7). The paradise of God refers to the new heaven and new earth, where God, the Lamb, and the saints will dwell eternally (21:1–3). The imagery of the tree of life is borrowed from Gen 2:9. In this scene, it is reused as a symbol for an eternity free from sin, death, and want. As in all the promises to the seven churches, the victors will be given eternal life. However, it is described differently as, the tree of life (vv. 7), the crown of life (vv. 10), not to be hurt by the second death (vv. 11), hidden manna (vv. 17), being sustained in the book of life (3:5), and being made a pillar in God's temple (3:12).

Visionary Situation of the Church in Ephesus

The church in Ephesus was outwardly vibrant. Her labor and toil in the work of God were commendable (vv. 2). She was also patiently enduring hardships for the sake of the name of Jesus. However, her faith was threatened by the teachings of false apostles. To her credit, she had tested and found them to be false. She also abhorred the deeds and teachings of the Nicolaitans which Jesus also hated. However, she was waning in the most important Christian virtue—love (1 Cor 13:13). In summary, the Ephesus church was right in doctrine, faith, and practice, but was lapsing in love. The judgment noose for lovelessness was slowly tightening.

Gaps in the Visionary Situation of the Church in Ephesus

The church needed an action that would urge her to uphold her good works, toil, patient endurance, and shun false apostles and teachers. There was also a grave need to reverse her decline in love. The communicative acts in this personalized letter, together with the strategic acts embedded in the visionary simulations narrated in 6:1—22:21, were aimed at generating evocations that would urge the church to uphold their good works and rekindle her waning love.

Covering Letter to the Church in Smyrna

[8]To the messenger of the church in Smyrna, write: These are the words of him who is the First and the Last, who died and came back to life.

This covering letter is specifically addressed to the church in Smyrna. Jesus introduced himself to her as the "first and the last" (vv. 8). This introduction carries the notion that beside him, there is no other. The embedded communicative act aimed at countering the church's intimidation by her persecutors. Describing himself as the one who died and rose again assured the saints of their resurrection even if they were martyred for their faith during the envisaged ten-day persecution (vv. 10).

[9]I know your tribulation and your poverty—yet you are rich! I know about the slander of those who say they are Jews but are not but are the synagogue of Satan.

By asserting that he knows this church's tribulation and poverty (vv. 9), Jesus identifies with her situation, thereby comforting her in the knowledge that Jesus knows her afflictions. The reward of their perseverance in tribulations and poverty for the sake of Christ was reckoned as great riches. Similarly, by saying that he knows the slander of those who say they are Jews but are not but a synagogue of Satan, Jesus empathized with their persecution by the Jews. The Judaizers may have been slandering this church for their poverty and form of faith (Acts 15:1). By labelling Judaizers "the Synagogue of Satan," Jesus shows that true worship was not practiced in these buildings. Indeed Christians, who may not have been visiting the synagogue but worshiped God in Spirit and in truth (John 4:23), were the true Jews (Rom 2:28–29). This statement had the rhetorical efficacy to enhance the Smyrnaean's spiritual self-esteem.

¹⁰Do not be afraid of what you are about to suffer. I tell you; the devil will put some of you in prison to test you, and you will suffer persecution for ten days. Be faithful, even to the point of death, and I will give you the crown of life.

Jesus' omniscience foresaw a ten-day persecution orchestrated by Satan in which some church members would be thrown into prison (vv. 10). Satan's purpose would be to force them to renounce their faith. The fact that this persecution was limited in time and space shows that it may have been a limited persecution. Perhaps there would be a ten-day festival celebrating the emperor which would lead to persecution of those who would not participate. Craig Keener notes that "Christians who were not seen as Jewish had no protection against civil requirements for participation in the emperor cult."[7] The encouragement "be faithful even to the point of death and I will give you the crown of life" suggests that the saints were being persecuted to the point of martyrdom. The promise of eternal life is used to motivate the church to maintain her faithfulness in the face of deadly tribulations. Eternal life is presented as a crown that is earned through faithfulness to the course of Christ.

¹¹Whoever has ears, let them hear what the Spirit says to the churches. The victorious one will not be hurt at all by the second death.

Like all the other seven personalized covering letters, this one is also connected to the narrated version of the main visionary revelation (4:1—22:21) by the clause "He who has an ear, let him hear what the Spirit says to the churches" (vv. 11). Jesus promises those who would be victorious that they will not be hurt at all by the second death. Not being hurt by the second death is put in progressive parallelism to further explain "the crown of life" (vv. 10b). Mention of the second death presumes a first death from which they are raised by the death of Jesus (Col 3:1). In the context of the Smyrnaeans, the first death explains their death in sins and trespasses (Eph 2:1-10) from which they were raised upon faith in Jesus. The second death refers to eternal separation from God for those who would be judged unworthy of eternal life.

Promise to Overcomers

The victors are promised the crown of life (vv. 10, 11b). The genitive "of" in this verse is an epexegetic genitive. It shows that eternal life and the crown of life are synonymous. It is thus expressed to concretize an abstract reality.

---

7. Keener, *Background Commentary*, 770.

Thus, there will not be a physical crown called the crown of life. Jesus further emphasized this promise in a parallel statement: "The victorious one will not be hurt at all by the second death" (vv. 11). The gift of eternal life is a very apt promise to engender patient endurance of severe tribulation and to inspire the church to respond to the evocations embedded in the visionary revelation narrated in 6:1—22:21.

Visionary Situation of the Church in Smyrna

The saints in Smyrna were poor. Poverty has a way of attracting the sins of envy and theft (Prov 30:9). They were also being slandered by the synagogue Jews (vv. 9). Sustained slander has the potential to kill the church's self-esteem, leading to compromise with the persecutors' whims. Notwithstanding these problems, the church was faithful to the word of God (vv. 9). Unbeknownst to her, this church was facing a looming ten-day persecution that would result in the death of some of her members.

Gaps in the Visionary Situation of the Church in Smyrna

The self-esteem of this slandered church needed to be raised. The question of theodicy in view of Christian persecution must have been the topmost among the troubling issues. Unless such issues are addressed, they are likely to foment despondency and compromise of the church's zeal, resulting in lukewarmness or apostasy. The church needed to have her hopes raised by an assurance of vengeance against her persecutors. Because of her excellent standing thus far, she needed evocations that would enhance her resolve in patient endurance.

Covering Letter to the Church in Pergamum

12 To the messenger of the church in Pergamum, write: These are the words of him who has the sharp double-edged sword. 13 I know where you live, where Satan has his throne. Yet you remain true to my name. You did not renounce your faith in me, not even in the days of Antipas, my faithful witness, who was put to death in your city—where Satan lives.

This third letter is specifically addressed to the church in Pergamum. Jesus introduced himself as "who has the sharp double-edged sword" (vv. 12). Bruce Malina and John J. Pilch rightly suggest that "the sharp two-edged sword points to the word as discerning, scrutinizing and judging."[8] As used in this context, the sharp double-edged sword represents Jesus' office as a judge of the persecutors of the saints and those who approved the teachings of Balaam and the Nicolaitans (vv. 16). The communicative act in Jesus' words aimed at assuring the church that he will use the double-edged sword to vindicate her against her oppressors.

The word "yet" in the statement "I know where you live—where Satan has his throne. Yet you remain true to my name" (vv. 13b) highlights the church's great faith. The great tribulation of the saints in trials, temptations, and persecutions to the point of martyrdom earned the town the description "where Satan has his throne." Sin enthrones Satan in people and localities. However, some scholars have identified this description as pointing to the pervasive emperor worship which was evidenced by an image of the emperor in the city.[9] Plausibility of this suggestion is diminished by the fact that Ephesus, which had an image of Diana, was not described in the same manner (Acts 19:35).

14Nevertheless, I have a few things against you. There are some among you who hold to the teachings of Balaam, who taught Balak to entice the Israelites to sin so that they ate food sacrificed to idols and committed sexual immorality. 15Likewise, you also have those who hold to the teaching of the Nicolaitans. 16Repent therefore! Otherwise, I will soon come to you and fight against them with the sword of my mouth. 17Whoever has ears, let them hear what the Spirit says to the Churches.

The church's commendable practice of faith was threatened by a subtle encroachment of false teachings and practices, described as the teachings of Balaam (vv. 14). Balaam was a prophet for hire who advised Barak to have Midianite women entice the Israelites to commit sexual immorality (Num 25:15; 31:16). Some in the church of Pergamum had also embraced the teachings of the Nicolaitans (vv. 15), from which they are urged to repent (vv. 16). This admonition underscores the church's responsibility to purge sin in her rank and file. A little leaven can leaven the whole dough (Gal 5:9).

Use of the word "otherwise" in the phrase "repent, therefore! otherwise" shows that the outworking of God's disciplinary judgments depends on whether people realize their fallenness and repent. If they do not, disciplinary judgment is executed in their lifetime to peradventure evoke repentance. If they adamantly fail to repent, the final retributory judgment is executed at the end of time. The letter transitions to the visionary revelation

---

8. Malina and Pilch, *Revelation*, 56.
9. Cory, *Revelation*, 29.

with the phrase "whoever has ears, let them hear what the Spirit says to the churches" (vv.17).

Promise to the Overcomer

¹⁷ᵇ*To the victorious one, I will give some of the hidden manna. I will also give that person a white stone inscribed with a new name, known only to the one who receives it.*

The Israelites were given manna from heaven, food that they had not known to sustain their lives during the exodus, and to show them that man shall not live by bread alone but by the word that comes from the mouth of the Lord (Deut 8:3). The Greek adjective describing the manna is κεκρυμμένου (*kekrummenou*), perfect participle singular genitive of κρύπτω (*kruptō*), which could mean hidden or laid up. In this context, the translation "laid up" is more probable. The symbol of manna, a life-sustaining heavenly food as used in the visionary revelation, may therefore represent eternal life, which is laid up to be granted the victorious saints at the eschaton.

In the Greco-Roman world, stone pebbles were used as admission tokens for public occasions.[10] Using imageries from such a context, the symbol of a white stone may have symbolized admission of the saints into eternal life. No one can truly know the identity of those who have been admitted to eternal life except those who enter. These promises must have evoked the audience's desire to work on any shortcomings that may hinder their entrance to eternal life.

Visionary Situation of the Church in Pergamum

Pergamum is described as a city where Satan's throne is (vv. 13)—a city rampant with Satan-instigated trials, temptations, and persecutions. The death of Antipas shows that some in the church were persecuted to the point of martyrdom (vv. 13). This particular martyrdom was aimed at scaring the rest of the saints out of their faith. Yet, the church did not recant her faith. Notwithstanding, the church risked being overrun by heresies and practices peddled through the doctrine of Balaam and the Nicolaitans.

---

10. Caird, *Revelation*, 42.

Gaps in the Visionary Situation of the Church in Pergamum

The identified visionary situation highlighted the need to: 1) Encourage this brave church to hold on to her faith and work of service. 2) Raise her hope and encourage the persecuted saints to endure to the very end. 3) Repent the sins of idolatry and sexual immorality. The admonition in this personalized covering letter and the evocations generated by the strategic acts in the visionary revelation narrated in 6:1—22:21 aims to solve these needs.

Covering Letter to the Church in Thyatira

[18]To the messenger of the church in Thyatira, write: these are the words of the Son of God, whose eyes are like blazing fire and whose feet are like burnished bronze.

This personalized covering letter of the visionary revelation is specific to the church in Thyatira. By identifying himself as the Son of God, Jesus highlighted his divinity to raise his message's trustworthiness. The portrait of his eyes as a blazing fire communicates to the church that her visionary situation cannot be hidden from his searching eyes. His feet that are like burnished bronze describe the strength with which he would fight and judge Jezebel and her followers.

[19]I know your deeds, love and faith, your service and perseverance, and that you are now doing more than you did at first.

Verse 19 highlights Jesus' approval of this church's orthodoxy, orthopraxis, and their positive response to Christian suffering. In its textual context, it functions as a foil that highlights the great damage being inflicted, by the teachings and behavior of Jezebel, on an otherwise admirable life of faith.

[20]Nevertheless, I have this against you: You tolerate that woman Jezebel, who calls herself a prophet. Her teaching misleads my servants into sexual immorality and the eating of food sacrificed to idols. [21]I have given her time to repent of her immorality, but she is unwilling. [22]So I will cast her on a bed of suffering, and I will make those who commit adultery with her suffer intensely unless they repent of her ways. [23]I will strike her children dead. Then all churches will know that I am he who searches hearts and minds, and I will repay each of you according to your deeds.

This church's good works (vv. 19) could not compensate for her tolerance of immorality and idolatry spurred by the teachings and actions of a self-styled prophetess tellingly referred to as Jezebel. This title compares her deeds to those of the idolatrous wife of King Ahab, who turned the king of Israel and the nation from worshiping the true God to serving her idols (1 Kgs 16:29–33; 21:25–26). The present Jezebel's teachings and behavior could likewise, if not checked, turn this great church to idolatry and immorality. Keener opines that Thyatira had trade guilds with a patron deity to whom the traders celebrated and worshiped. Christians willing to engage in such trades would be forced to compromise with these idolatrous practices.[11]

The judgment upon this self-styled prophetess and those who committed adultery with her was already passed (vv. 22–23). However, its execution was being delayed to give her and her accomplices a chance to repent. Highlighting this delay in execution of the judgment shows that God does not delight in the death of a sinner (Ezek 33:11). It should be interpreted as an act of grace. However, if Jezebel and her followers do not repent, they would be struck with disease (vv. 22). The punishment would be extended to her children, who would be struck dead (vv. 23). These deadly judgments could be identified as either the judgments unleashed on the unbelieving world after the third and fifth angels blew their trumpets or the woe visited on the unbelieving world after the first bowl-wielding angel poured God's wrath on the world. The pronounced judgment is aimed at jolting the church in Thyatira and eavesdropper readers to shun Jezebel's teachings and to repent of their idolatry and immorality.

[24]Now I say to the rest of you in Thyatira, to you who do not hold to her teaching and have not learned Satan's so-called deep secrets, 'I will not impose any other burden on you. [25]Except to hold on to what you have until I come.'

A good number of the saints in Thyatira had not bowed to the teachings and influence of Jezebel. She and her ilk paraded their evil teachings as "deep secrets." However, Jesus exposed these "deep secrets" as satanic (vv. 24). By saying that "I will not impose any other burden on you, except to hold on until I come" (vv. 24–25), Jesus is affirming that salvation and sustenance are free gifts of God. God does not lay burdens on the believers except a call to faithfulness. The phrase "until I come" emphasizes the necessity to sustain the faith to the very end (2 Tim 4:7).

Promise to the Overcomer

[26]To the one who is victorious and does my will to the end, I will give authority over the nations—[27]that one will rule them with an iron sceptre and will

---

11. Keener, *Revelation*, 133.

dash them to pieces like pottery—just as I have received authority from my father. ²⁸I will also give that one the morning star. ²⁹Whoever has ears, let them hear what the Spirit says to the churches.

A believer's victory is achieved by doing the will of Jesus without wavering. To urge believers in Thyatira to constantly be fervent in love, faith, service, and perseverance, Jesus promised the victors authority over the nations. This bequest is expressed with the words of the promise of God to David (Ps 2:8–9) and his divine successor—Jesus (vv. 27). The symbol of an iron scepter in this context does not represent authoritarian rule. Most probably, it stands for effectiveness of the gospel. The Greek verb interpreted as rule, ποιμαίνω (*poimainō*), refers to care/shepherding. This description echoes Jesus' parable in Matt 24:45–47. Like the servant in the parable, Jesus has put the believer in charge of his household to feed his servants at the proper time. Again, in Luke 10:19, Jesus promises the church power to tread on snakes and scorpions and to overcome all the power of the enemy and that nothing will harm them. The gates of hell cannot prevail against the church (Matt 16:18–20).

Jesus promises to give the saints the morning star. The Greek word δίδωμι (*didōmi*), "give," could also stand for the verb "make." Thus, the promise could be to make the believer the morning star. The phraseology could have been borrowed from Dan 12:3. The morning star is a bright shining planet (Venus) that reflects light on the dark world before dawn. It was used in Dan 12:3 as a symbol of the glorious gift of eternal life that will be accorded those who turn many to righteousness. Like the rest of the letters, Jesus transitions to the main visionary revelation with the phrase "whoever has ears, let them hear what the Spirit says to the churches."

Visionary Situation of the Church in Thyatira

The church in Thyatira was a church of extremes. On one extreme were love, faith, service, and perseverance. At the time of this visionary revelation, she was doing more good deeds than she had done at first (vv. 19). Jesus' urge to her to persevere suggests that she may have been undergoing forms of tribulation. On the other extreme, she tolerated the teachings of Jezebel. Some of her members were involved in idolatry. History teaches that in this industrial city, there were trade guilds. Each guild had a patron deity to which members offered sacrifices.[12] Christians willing to join these guilds would

---

12. Mounce, *Revelation*, 87.

knowingly or unknowingly eat food sacrificed to these deities.[13] These are part of the prohibitions to the gentile converts by the first church council in Jerusalem (Acts 15:20).

Gaps in the Visionary Situation of the Church in Thyatira

This church needed to be encouraged to continue in works of love, faith, service, and patient endurance. But more pressing, she needed to be jolted to abhor and resist the teachings and practices of Jezebel, the self-styled prophetess. There was also a dire need to have those who had succumbed to her teachings to repent.

Covering Letter to the Church in Sardis

[1] To the angel of the church in Sardis, write: These are the words of him who holds the seven Spirits of God and the seven stars. I know your deeds; you have a reputation of being alive, but you are dead.

This covering letter of the visionary revelation is specific to the church in Sardis. By saying that the words addressed to the church in Sardis were from the one who has the seven Spirits of God and the seven stars (vv. 1), Jesus was emphasizing that his worrying diagnosis of the church's visionary situation could not be faulted, since he has the Spirit who searches all things. He also controls the shepherds of the church, who are depicted as being held in his hands. This introductory statement is rhetorically nuanced to show that Jesus was the source of the revitalizing Spirit. He was also in charge of the under-shepherds of this church. As such, she needed to come to him for life and revival. The saying "I know your deeds" (vv. 1) calls the church out of her self-deception that she was alive when she was, in fact, spiritually dead.

[2] Wake up! Strengthen what remains and is about to die, for I have found your deeds unfinished in the sight of my God. [3] Remember, therefore, what you have received and heard; hold it fast, and repent. But if you do not wake up, I will come like a thief, and you will not know at what time I will come to you.

Sin was about to engulf the entire church. She needed to wake up, that is, to realize her pitiable state and strengthen what remains and was about to also die. The description of her deeds as "unfinished in the sight of God" suggests that the church was religiously attractive but spiritually repelling.

---

13. Wright, *New Testament and People of God*, 363.

PROLOGUE AND COVERING LETTERS TO THE SEVEN CHURCHES 59

The admonition "hold fast" suggests inconsistency in her deeds. If she does not heed the call to wake up, the coming of the Lord would find her as unprepared as a victim of robbery. There will be no time to prepare but to face the wrath of God in judgment. Jesus' statement that he will come like a thief does not describe his desire to catch her in the wrong. Rather, it is a call to repentance.

Promise to the Overcomer

⁴Yet you have a few people in Sardis who have not soiled their clothes. They will walk with me dressed in white, for they are worthy. ⁵The victorious one will, like them, be dressed in white. I will never blot out that person's name from the book of life but will acknowledge that name before my father and his angels. ⁶Whoever has ears, let them hear what the Spirit says to the churches.

Amid widespread apostasy in Sardis, a small remnant had not succumbed to peer pressure into sin. "Soiling their garments" is a metaphorical expression describing the act of forsaking a godly lifestyle and sliding into sin. The phrase "they will walk with me dressed in white" is Jesus' promise to this faithful remnant of a sinless afterlife in his presence. Saying that "for they are worthy" shows that these faithful remnants will have earned this reward by staying true to the faith amidst widespread apostasy. Jesus' extension of the reward of the faithful to those who would victoriously hearken to his admonition and repent in verse 5 is an indirect but powerful rapprochement to those who had soiled their garments. He is stirring them to covet the reward that had been promised the faithful perchance to stir them to repentance. He transitions to the main visionary revelation with the refrain "whoever has ears, let them hear what the Spirit says to the churches."

Visionary Situation of the Church in Sardis

The church in Sardis was living a lie. She was in sinful, slumber-soiled garments (vv. 4). She appeared lively in her religious rituals, but sin had strangled her spiritual life. Only a paltry few among her rank and file had not soiled their garments. Indeed, almost everything that qualifies a congregation to be called a church—holiness, orthodoxy, and orthopraxis—was about to die.

Gaps in the Visionary Situation of the Church in Sardis

The gaps in this church's historical situation are summed up in the statement "wake up! And strengthen what remains and is about to die." There was a need to jolt the church to repentance and pursuance of orthodoxy and orthopraxis. There was also a need to encourage the few saints in Sardis who had not soiled their garments to continue in faith amid a dead multitude.

Covering Letter to the Church in Philadelphia

⁷"To the messenger of the church in Philadelphia write: These are the words of him who is holy and true, who holds the key of David. What he opens, no one can shut, and what he shuts, no one can open."

Similar to other churches, this message is specifically addressed to the church in Philadelphia (vv. 7). In describing himself as holy and true, Jesus highlights his lofty ethos. Holiness is his character, while the truth is a virtue with which he leads his saints and judges the world. The phrase "who holds the key of David" derives its expression from both the OT and NT, where the metaphor "key" stands for authority (Isa 22:20–22; Matt 16:19; Rev 1:18; 3:7; 9:1; 20:1). Holding the key of David stands for having Messianic authority. The next statement, "what he opens, no one can shut, and what he shuts, no one can open," points to Christ's sovereign power.

⁸I know your deeds. See, I have placed an open door that no one can shut before you. I know that you have a little strength, yet you have kept my word and have not denied my name.

The statement "I know your deeds" does not just refer to a mere awareness of what the church in Philadelphia was doing. It is a commendation for keeping God's word and not denying the name of the Lord notwithstanding opposition and her little strength (vv. 8). "Placing an open door that no one can shut before you" suggests that since Jesus is the one who has the key of David, no one else can thwart the work that he is doing in this church. This is a very strong encouragement to this church to keep trusting in Jesus. The door is opened by the blood of Jesus, their testimony and total surrender to the point of death (12:11).

⁹I will make those of the synagogue of Satan, who claim to be Jews though they are not, but are liars—I will make them come and fall down at your feet and acknowledge that I have loved you. ¹⁰Since you have kept my command to endure patiently, I will also keep you from the hour of affliction that will come on the whole world to discipline the inhabitants of the earth.

The synagogue Jews who boasted of being Jews but were against the Christian faith are described as those of the synagogue of Satan. In cahoots with Satan, they were persecuting the church. They would be made to come, fall at the saints' feet, and acknowledge that Jesus loves his own. This reversal of fortunes is assured in the promise "I will also keep you from the hour of affliction that will come on the whole world to discipline the inhabitants of the earth" (vv. 10). This preservation could be referring to the Passover-sealing of the saints before the judgments simulated when the seven angels blow their trumpets (7:1—9:21).

¹¹I am coming soon. Hold on to what you have so that no one will take your crown.

The second coming of Christ was and is a certainty. The statement in the verse "I am coming soon" is not merely stating a fact. It expresses the unfolding history in a litotes to inspire hope in the assurance that the time for the church to receive her eternal bequest was nearer than when she first believed (Rom 13:11). Jesus drew his idiom from athletics to describe the present state of this church. Like good athletes, they were running a good race of their faith and deeds, and if they persisted, they would be given a crown. However, if they relaxed, someone else would take their crown. Hearing that someone else may take their crown is not a fact of the Christian walk. It is an idiomatic expression that underscores the need to jealously guard their faith notwithstanding their present success. This caution is more preventive than curative. It also shows that the looming danger of falling away from the faith is an ever-present possibility.

Promise to the Overcomer

¹²To the victorious one, I will make a pillar in the temple of my God. Never again will they leave it. I will write on them the name of my God and the name of the city of my God, the New Jerusalem, which is coming down out of heaven from my God; and I will also write on them my new name. ¹³Whoever has ears, let them hear what the Spirit says to the churches.

To motivate them to hold on to their faith, Jesus promised to make the victorious saints pillars in the temple of God in which they would live forever (vv. 12). Furthermore, the permanency of the pillars shows that this figure of speech is a metaphor for eternal life. The temple on earth represents the meeting place between humans and God. In this visionary revelation, it represents the ever-present *shekinah*. Having the name of God, the New Jerusalem, and Jesus written on them affirms that God, Jesus, and the victorious saints will perpetually dwell in the new heaven and earth. Similar to the other letters, this one transits to the visionary revelation narrated in 4:1—22:21 with the double entendre phrase "whoever has ears, let him hear what the Spirit says to the churches" (vv. 13).

Visionary Situation of the Church in Philadelphia

Most likely, this church was being taunted by the Judaizers (vv. 9) who adhered to the religious but empty rite of circumcision (Greek: κατατομή, *katatome*) as a necessity for salvation. However, they were not keen on the circumcision of their hearts (Greek: περιτομή, *peritome*) (Phil 3:2–3).

The world was about to witness affliction, at a time that Jesus called the "hour of affliction," to discipline the earth's inhabitants (vv. 10). However, the saints will be sealed so that the affliction will not come upon them (7:3). As used here, earth's inhabitants stand for unbelieving humanity.

The church had little strength (vv. 8), perhaps in many spheres such as finances, civic power, and learning. Paul had before intimated that "not many of the Christians were wise by human standards; not many were influential; not many were of noble birth" (1 Cor 1:26). However, against expectations, they had endured patiently and kept his word and had not denied the faith (vv. 8).

Gaps in the Visionary Situation of the Church in Philadelphia

Jesus identified three gaps in this church's visionary situation that needed to be addressed: 1) Need to be assured that God would keep them in the hour of affliction. 2) Need to raise her spiritual esteem to counter the taunting of the Judaizers. 3) Need for encouragement to patient endurance in her existing and future tribulations.

Covering Letter to the Church in Laodicea

[14]*"To the church in Laodicea write: These are the words of the Amen, the faithful and true witness, the ruler of God's creation."*

The parallelism in the three titles "the Amen," "the faithful," and "true witness" highlights Jesus' trustworthiness. Together with the emphasis that he is the ruler of God's creation, the statement aims to rebuke the church for her lukewarmness towards the one who would never fail.

15I know your deeds that you are neither cold nor hot. I wish you were either one or the other! 16So, because you are lukewarm–neither hot nor cold–I am about to spit you out of my mouth. 17For you say, 'I am rich; I have acquired wealth and do not need a thing.' But you do not realize that you are wretched, pitiful, poor, blind, and naked. 18I counsel you to buy from me gold refined in the fire so you can become rich, and white clothes to wear to cover your shameful nakedness, and salve to put on your eyes so you can see.

The faith of the Laodicean church was not reflected in their deeds. As James would say, "Faith without works is dead" (Jas 1:17). The idiom "lukewarm" describes confessing Christians who had compromised their faith with the popular culture of their time. Paul describes such Christians as "lovers of money and pleasure rather than lovers of God—having a form of godliness but denying its power" (2 Tim 3:2–5). The Laodicean church understood this idiom because the city inhabitants were familiar with lukewarm water from nearby springs.[14] Saying, "I am about to spit you out of my mouth" is a dramatized metaphor to highlight Jesus' displeasure with the church's compromising lifestyle. For her behavior, Jesus described her as wretched, pitiful, poor, blind and naked. Together, these five adjectives describe the great depth into which this church had backslidden. Jesus is redirecting her to true riches—uncompromising faith in Jesus also referred to as gold refined by fire (1 Pet 1:7). He is also urging them to pursue righteousness—white clothes to cover her shameful nakedness (Gen 3:10–11). Like the Pharisees, she is oblivious of her grave state. She ignorantly thinks that she is standing when she is actually fallen.

19Those whom I love, I rebuke and discipline. So be earnest and repent. 20Here I am! I stand at the door and knock. If anyone hears my voice and opens the door, I will come in and eat with him and he with me.

Jesus' saying "Those whom I love, I rebuke and discipline" is derived from Prov 3:11–12. It refers to the rebuke in vv. 15–16 and the disciplinary judgments simulated after the seven angels blew their trumpets (8:1–13). His desire to have this church change is shown in the plea "So be earnest and repent" (vv. 19). The plea is followed by a reconciliatory rapprochement: "Behold, I stand at the door and knock. If anyone hears my voice and opens the door, I will come in and eat with him and he with me" (vv. 20). The rebuke, rapprochement, and the evocations in the narrated version of the

---

14. Keener, *Bible Background*, 774.

visionary revelation attached to this covering letter were a loud knock on the door that looked forward to a positive response. Eating together signifies reconciliation. Thus, notwithstanding her pitiful state, Jesus is calling for reconciliation.

Promise to the Overcomer

[21] To the victorious one, I will give the right to sit with me on my throne, just as I was victorious and sat down with my father on his throne.

Jesus urged this church to repent by promising the overcomers a right to sit with him on his throne. Jesus is fronting his glorification after overcoming death as an affirmation that they too will be so rewarded if they overcome. This promise refers to the yet-to-be-consummated reign of Jesus and the church.

Visionary Situation of the Church in Laodicea

The city of Laodicea was a center of banking, pharmacies, and cloth manufacturing.[15] The church was equally materially endowed. But unfortunately, her pursuit of riches and the attendant satisfaction had left little room for faith and spiritual disciplines. As a result, she was spiritually comatose and in danger of severing her relationship with Jesus. Beale rightly notes that "Like Israel in Hosea's time, the Laodiceans are probably doing well economically because of some degree of willing cooperation with the idolatrous trade guilds and economic institutions of their culture . . . spiritual compromise because of economic factors has been identified as an unavoidable temptation for Christians living in the major Asia Minor cities (Pergamum and Thyatira)."[16]

Gaps in the Visionary Situation in Laodicea

There was a need to jolt the church to spiritual consciousness. She needed to be as zealous for faith and spiritual disciplines as she was in pursuit of worldly pleasures. A visionary revelation that would simulate the painful consequences of compromise with sin and unbridled pursuit of fleeting

---

15. Keener, *Revelation*, 160.
16. Beale, *New Testament Use of Old Testament*, 70.

worldly pleasures at the expense of eternal pursuits would jolt them to change their ways.

Summary of the Visionary Situations of the Seven Churches

The cumulative visionary situation revealed in the seven covering letters:

1. Christians in this region faced persecution by the competing emperor cult and the Jews. Fiorenza agreeably notes, "After the destruction of Jerusalem and the temple, the self-interest of Jewish communities in Asia Minor demanded that they get rid of any potential political "trouble makers" and "messianic elements" in their midst, and Christians certainly seemed to be among them."[17] Persecution could force believers to compromise with the worldly ideals, thereby killing orthodox Christianity or changing it into a syncretized faith. This situation presented the need to simulate the latent workings of God in a way that would encourage them in times of tribulations.

2. Presence of itinerant false apostles who were teaching false doctrines. This context presented a need to arouse vigilance lest the saints are diverted from orthodoxy.

3. There were heretical groups—Nicolaitans who taught the gospel of grace without denouncement of former sinful ways. Their teachings were comparable to the teachings of Balaam, who taught Balak and the Moabites to entice the Israelites to eat food sacrificed to idols and to commit sexual immorality (Num 25:1–5; 31:16). This situation presented the need to urge the saints to shun and repent all forms of evil.

4. Some of the churches were afflicted with poverty. Such churches could easily be lured to compromise their faith to better their economic fortunes. Thus, they needed to be urged to despise the shame of worldly poverty when compared with the rich reward of their faith and perseverance.

5. There were synagogue Jews who were slandering Christians and their faith. They prided in legalism and would often foment persecution of the nascent church that preached salvation by grace through faith in Jesus Christ. This situation presented a need to affirm the Christians.

6. Lovelessness was stalking the church in Ephesus. There were also dead and lukewarm churches like Sardis and Laodicea; this visionary situation presented a need to urge the saints to fervency in their spiritual

17. Fiorenza, *Revelation*, 194.

walk by simulating the reward of victory in Christian living and the severe judgments on the opposers of God and his saints.

Some interpreters consider Christian persecution to be the overriding occasion of the visionary revelation. However, an analysis of the visionary situation of the seven churches, in the seven personalized covering letters, shows that orthodoxy and orthopraxis were the overriding visionary situations. True, issues of persecution had the potential of harming the Christians socially, economically, and physically to the point of martyrdom. Nevertheless, after perseverance, they stood to earn the worthy prize of eternal life. However, gaps in orthodoxy and orthopraxis were spiritually lethal. They could derail the saints from the new covenant blessing, thereby disinheriting the churches from God's eternal promises.

Application of the Message in the Seven Covering Letters

The seven covering letters primarily exposed the seven churches' visionary situations. The strategic acts embedded in the simulations of the visionary revelation narrated in 6:1—22:21 were intended to generate evocations that could engender actions to bridge the gaps that had been identified in the seven churches' visionary situations. Accordingly, without the contribution of evocations generated by the strategic acts in the annexed written version of the visionary revelation, the exhortations and admonitions in these letters are provisional. Thus, whereas there are several application points in these personalized covering letters, a complete application is only feasible after identification of the evocations generated by the strategic acts embedded in the entire visionary revelation. On the other hand, an interpretation of the attached visionary revelation without an eye on the seven covering letters would not yield the intended response. A synchronic reading of the letters and the narrative version of the visionary revelation is a necessary step in the interpretation process.

The needs that occasioned the visionary revelation are common to the church of all ages. She undergoes the same tribulations in the form of trials, temptations, and persecutions that peccability and a world against everything good and godly bequeath humanity. Every kind of persecution by the state and alternative religions calls for patient endurance. Every temptation and trial that results from humanity's peccability calls for resistance with every iota of will and prayers (Matt 26:41).

The current church exists in similar historical situations to the ones in the seven churches in Asia Minor. For example, like the churches in Smyrna, the church in the Middle East, and the Muslim belt in Africa and

Asia undergo high levels of persecution for their faith. Similarly, like the church in Laodicea, the church in North America and other affluent nations have slid into pursuit for affluence at the expense of orthodoxy and works of faith.[18] Though, as Philip Jenkins rightly suggests, the center of Christianity has shifted to the Global South,[19] unorthodox doctrines like prosperity gospel and other culturally influenced forms of syncretism are threatening to overrun orthodoxy in these areas. On her part, like the church in Thyatira, the church in the Global North risks being overrun by the sin of Jezebel. In this region that was once the bastion of orthodoxy, same-sex marriages are being accepted as a norm even by sections of the church. Today's great prostitute holding the cup of her immorality can be identified in most of the world's cities. Indeed, the visionary situation of the seven churches can be identified all over the world.

Application of the visionary revelation should first consider investigating the historical situation in which the particular church finds herself. The urgency and grave importance of the message of Revelation demands that it be made relevant to the church to urge her to patiently endure the various tribulations and uphold orthodoxy and orthopraxy as she sojourns in her final exodus to her eternal abode.

---

18. Storkey, "Materialism," 575–76.
19. Jenkins, *New Christendom*, 191–92.

Chapter 2

Setting of the Handover of the Visionary Revelation (4:1—5:14)

PRELIMINARY OBSERVATIONS

MOSES' PHYSICAL ASCENT TO the top of Mount Sinai to meet with God and receive the written covenant was narrated to primarily authenticate the covenant and to enforce adherence to its stipulations (Exod 19:3–9). The visionary ascents of prophets Isaiah (Isa 6:1–8), Ezekiel (Ezek 1:1–28), and Daniel (Dan 7:9–14) to the visionary heaven, where they encountered God, were enabled, experienced, and narrated to authenticate their prophecies and to increase their believability. They were a visionary version of the rhetorical authentication formula of divine communication: "Thus says the Lord."

Similarly, John's narration of his visionary encounter with Jesus in Patmos and the display of his unmistakable divine attributes (1:9–20) were intended to authenticate the contents of the seven personalized covering letters and to urge adherence to their admonitions. Again, his divine visionary call to the visionary heaven, where he witnessed a simulation of the handover of the sealed scroll from God to Jesus was intended to authenticate the visionary revelation narrated in 6:1—22:21. The display of God's majestic glory and divinity with the beauty of rare gemstones and lofty orations by a cast of seraphs, the twenty-four elders, and myriads of angels was intended to unequivocally show that the source of the visionary revelation was none other but God. Jesus' unmistakable portrayal as Lion of the tribe of Judah, the slain Lamb of God complemented by the oration of his divinity and messianic credentials by the host of heaven, all the more, absolved John from being seen as the source of the visionary revelation. These portrayals served to authenticate the visionary revelation and to increase its evocative efficacy.

Notably, John's heavenly visions drew their imageries from Moses' experiences on Mount Sinai, God's interactions with Israel in the tabernacle, and Isaiah's, Ezekiel's and Daniel's visionary experiences. These allusions suggest that the visionary simulations recorded in chapters 4 and 5 are a visionary version of the rhetorical authentication formulae of divine communication "thus says the Lord" (Hebrew: כה אמר יהוה; koh 'mar YHWH, Greek: Ταδε λέγει κύριος, Tade legei Kurios). In this visionary revelation, it can be rephrased as "thus shows the Lord" or "thus reveals the Lord."

REV 4

Introduction of the Repository and Outworker of God's Decrees

¹*After this, I looked, and there before me was a door standing open in heaven. And the voice I had first heard speaking to me like a trumpet said, "Come up here and I will show you what must take place after this."*

The Greek word ουρανός, ouranos (heaven), has two referents: the open sky and the perceived dwelling of God. In this scene, both referents are in view. The open door was seen in the sky. It led into a visionary stage simulating the perceived dwelling place of God. The person who had called John before was identified as Jesus Christ (1:10-18). Thus, it is Jesus who is calling him into the heavenly visionary stage. The call "come up here, and I will show you what must take place after this" suggests that Jesus was the director of the visionary revelation. This suggestion is affirmed in the visionary simulation of the handover of the sealed scroll from the right hand of the one seated on the throne to the slain Lamb in chapter 5. The call was meant to mark the shift from the personalized covering letters to the visionary revelation (4:1—22:21). It also marked a shift from a description of the earthly visionary situation of the churches to the divinely directed visionary simulations that were intended to address the identified gaps in each of the churches' historical situations. The word "must" ascertains fulfilment of the things that were to be simulated in the visionary revelation narrated in 6:1—22:21. This suggestion shows that the visionary revelation was not just John's method of relaying his message; it was a divinely inspired forthtelling and foretelling prophecy in apocalyptic genre (1:3).

The dispensationalist interpreters view the heaven to which John was called as the future abode of the victorious saints while John is viewed as a symbol of the church.[1] This view further supposes that the call "Come up here and I will show you what must take place after this" (vv.1) is Jesus' call to the church at the onset of an event known as the "rapture."[2] It also supposes that the reason for this event is to snatch the church from a seven-year tribulation that will be unleashed by the opening of the seals (chapter 6), blowing of the trumpets (chapters 8–9), and pouring of the seven bowls of God's wrath (chapter 16). This view further supposes that after a seven-year tribulation, Jesus will descend to the earth together with the previously raptured saints to reign with Christ for a thousand years.[3] Lynn R. Huber further notes:

> Dispensationalism maintains that history is divided into epochs or dispensations, each of which was marked by a specific means of salvation. For Derby and Scofield, the current age was a time between epochs, a "parenthesis" in which humanity waited for the next epoch inaugurated by the rapture of Christians from earth. These events would trigger a period of tribulation including the reign of the Anti-Christ followed by the millennial reign of Christ and the last judgment.[4]

Although a considerable number of Christians espouse this supposition, it is not supported by a faithful exegesis of the visionary revelation and its narrated version. Furthermore, the supposition does not agree with Christ's teachings on his future kingdom and the time of its consummation (Matt 25:13; Mark 13:32–33). As Ben Witherington III rightly notes, "The author of Revelation says nothing about taking Christians out of the world to escape tribulations; rather, he speaks of Christ coming and protecting Christians."[5] Craig R. Koester also ably refutes the dispensationalist position by saying, "When read in its context, God's command calls John into a temporary visionary ascent; it does not refer to the ingathering of all the faithful in heaven.[6]

The vision that John was about to be shown simulated events that were decreed by God and that would be outworked in the unfolding history. Swete avers that the statement "what had to take place after this" implies

---

1. Walvoord, *Revelation*, 103.
2. Strauss, *Revelation*, 125–29; Farmer, *Revelation*, 10–11.
3. Farwell, *Liberty*, 757.
4. Huber, *Thinking and Seeing with Women in Revelation*, 135.
5. Witherington III, *Revelation*, 107.
6. Koester, *Revelation*, 25.

SETTING OF THE HANDOVER OF THE VISIONARY REVELATION (4:1—5:14) 71

that the vision that follows is an anticipation of a future that is yet to find its accomplishment.[7] Though his observation has some merit, some happenings like the outworking of God's decrees consequent of Adam's sin, whose simulation is narrated in 6:1–8, are continuous happenings throughout human history.

²*At once I was in the Spirit, and there before me was a throne in heaven with someone sitting on it.* ³*And the one who sat there had the appearance of jasper and ruby. A rainbow that shone like an emerald encircled the throne.*

John was spiritually moved from the visionary setting in Patmos to another visionary setting in the heavens. On the new vision stage was a throne and someone sitting on it. The visionary throne and its ambience symbolize aspects of God's attributes. Depiction of God as dwelling in heaven and not on earth demonstrates his transcendence, majesty, glory, and impeccability. However, the attributes of God's infinite greatness, and omnipresence as revealed in his title *El Shaddai* stop us from imagining that he can fit in a geographical location in either the heavens or earth. Spatafora supports this supposition by saying, "The scriptures use cosmological images of 'above' and 'below' to speak of God's utter difference from human persons. They do not intend in any way to situate him in a physical location: To describe God as dwelling in heaven is to recognize the transcendence of God, God's separateness from the created order."[8]

In his description of this scene, John mentions the throne before mentioning the one sitting on it to underscore its occupant's majesty. The majestic glory and excellence of the one he saw seated on the throne was portrayed with the glitter of jasper and ruby. His deity and excellence were symbolized by a rainbow halo circling the throne whose glitter is compared with the beauty of an emerald. When expressing God's superlative holiness in speech, the Hebrew Scripture usually uses the adjective "holy" three times (*Trisagion*). However, in this visionary scene, the superlative nature of God's holiness, glory, and majesty is expressed in the beauty of highly precious gemstones.

⁴*Around the throne were twenty-four thrones on which sat twenty-four elders clothed in white garments and having golden crowns on their heads.*

John saw another visionary cast of twenty-four elders. Again, the sentence construction mentioning the thrones before the elders sitting on them shows that the twenty-four white arrayed elders represented either noble

---

7. Swete, *Revelation*, 67.
8. Spatafora, *From the Temple of God*, 252.

persons, noble themes, or noble concepts. Furthermore, "elder" is an honorary title that depicts the holder's elevated position in the community. Scripture normally uses white raiment as a symbol of inherent holiness when describing divinity (19:11, 14) and imputed righteousness when describing persons in the created order (3:4–5, 18; 4:4; 6:11; 7:9, 13–14; 19:14). These elders also had crowns (Greek: στέφανος, *Stephanos*) of gold on their heads (a symbol of bestowed honor).

James B. Ramsey identifies the twenty-four elders with God's covenant people. He supports his supposition by arguing that they used the first-person plural pronouns in their worship of the Lamb (5:9–10): "Unto him who loved us and washed us from our sins in his blood and has made us kings and priests unto God and his Father."[9] However, Mouse ably countermands this line of argument by pointing out that the manuscripts that support this view are inferior. They alter the song of the elders in 5:9–10 to read "purchased us . . . made us to be . . . we will reign." He rightly[10] notes that the better manuscripts have the pronouns in the third person, not the first, and read "purchased men," "made them," and "they will reign."[11]

First Chronicles 24:1–19 narrates how David appointed a guild of twenty-four heads of priestly families (elders) to serve God in the earthly tabernacle. A visionary simulation of service and worship in the heavenly court (anti-type of the earthly tabernacle) is more comprehendible if it is conformed to the worship in the earthly tabernacle. So, most probably, the twenty-four elders are part of the visionary cast that orate the aura, reverence, and worship that the presence of the Godhead demands. Moreover, 5:5 and 7:13–17 show that these elders are privy to heavenly things that earthly John did not know. John also calls one of them "my Lord" (7:14) showing that they represent an otherworldly reality of a higher order than John.

⁵*Out of the throne proceeds flashes of lightning, voices, and thundering. There were seven lamps of fire burning before the throne, which are the seven Spirits of God.*

The flashes of lightning, voices, and thundering are reminiscent of Mount Sinai when God gave Moses the Ten Commandments (Exod 19:16). This similarity suggests that John too was receiving the visionary revelation, from none other but God, to guide the church on her final exodus through the unfolding history to her eternal home in the new heaven and earth.

---

9. Ramsey, *Revelation*, 30.
10. Metzger, *Textual Commentary*, 738, 747.
11. Mounce, *What Are We Waiting For?*, 20.

The seven blazing lamps identified as the seven Spirits of God symbolize the fullest manifestation of the Holy Spirit. Wherever God is, his Spirit is. The Holy Spirit is the standard of God's presence. This scene supports the supposition that, similar to Moses' ascent to the mountain, John's ascent to the heaven was to authenticate the visionary revelation.

⁶The frontage of the throne was as a sea of glass like crystal. Circling God's throne were four living creatures full of eyes in front and behind.

Informed by contemporary Ancient Near East mythology concerning the negative view of the sea, Caird argues that "the glassy sea stands before the throne as a mute reminder that the whole creation is affected by the taint of evil."[12] However, a comparison of the expression "as clear as crystal" with its usage in 21:11 and 22:1 shows that it expresses exceeding purity and glory instead of chaos and evil. Thus, most probably, this glassy sea, as pure as crystal, symbolizes God's glorious footstool. It demonstrates the superlatively majestic and holy nature of the one sitting on the throne. This reading agrees with the general theme of this visionary scene—the majestic glory of the one seated on the throne.

John also saw a visionary cast of four living creatures circling God's throne. Notably and important to identifying their role, they are not sitting on thrones but circling God's throne to wait on him. This observation suggests that they role-play God's messengers. The description of the four creatures as living contrasts them with the molten gold cherubs placed on top of the mercy seat on the ark of the covenant in the earthly Tabernacle. Whereas the non-living cherubs in the earthly tabernacle symbolized God's glory, the anti-type in heaven simulate God's swift and efficient outworking of his decrees. They also orate his glory, majesty, and worship. They worship him for securing eternal salvation for humanity through the slain lamb (5:9). Their six wings and many eyes represented swift, precise, and unhindered outworking of God's decrees.

⁷The first living creature was like a lion, the second an ox, the third had a face like a man, and the fourth was like an eagle.

These living creatures are the same in number and form as the ones seen in a similar throne vision (Ezek 1:5–10). Ezekiel describes them as able to move in all directions as they are directed by the Spirit of God. This observation further supports the supposition that they role-play swift, efficient, and unhindered outworking of the decrees of God. Positively, as is used here, a lion symbolizes kingly power (Ps 22:13; 21). As a devourer of

---

12. Caird, *Revelation*, 68.

its prey, it is negatively likened to the devil (1 Pet 5:8). For its strength, an ox was used in trending corn and ploughing. Thus, it can symbolize stealth and strength (Ps 22:12, 21). A human being is, by purpose, the image and likeness of God (Gen 1:26). An eagle symbolizes God's swift and efficient care over his people (Exod 19:4). Therefore, these four living creatures may also symbolize the worship of God, and the power, strength, and swiftness in outworking God's decrees.

> [8] Each of the four living creatures had six wings full of eyes within and without. They do not rest by day and night saying, "Holy! Holy! Holy! is the Lord God Almighty, who was, who is, and who is to come."

As has been suggested, the six wings full of eyes within and without symbolize God's unhindered ability to swiftly and efficiently execute his decrees. John's audition that "they do not rest by day and night saying 'Holy! Holy! Holy!' is the Lord God Almighty, who was, who is, and who is to come," suggests that they orate God's attributes of perpetual impeccability and immutability. Such oration complements the lofty portrayal of the majestic glory of God in the beauty of gemstones. They undoubtedly prove that the source of the visionary revelation is none other but God.

> [9] Whenever the living creatures give glory, honour, and thanksgiving to the one sitting on the throne–the one who lives forever and ever, [10] the twenty-four elders fall down before the one sitting on the throne and worship, he who lives forever and ever. They cast their crown before the throne, saying, [11] "You are worthy, our Lord and God, to receive glory and honour and power, for you created all things and by your will, they were created and have their being."

The twenty-four elders complement the living creatures' worship by casting their crowns before God. This gesture expresses Ps 115:1—"Not to us God. But unto you we give glory." They ascribe to God glory, honor, and power for creating and sustaining all things by his will. As has been observed, this vision serves to authenticate that John's vision is not a figment of his imagination but is from God and therefore demands unquestionable response.

Strategic and Communicative Acts in Rev 4

God's majesty and glory were role-played by one sitting on a throne bedecked by very beautiful gemstones. His glory and majesty were also compared to the glitter of very precious gemstones. The vision was a very evocative strategic act. The role-play of God's glory and majesty was complemented by orations of his attributes in the worship by the four living creatures and the twenty-four elders. As noted earlier, this role-play was intended to authenticate the visionary revelation and to enhance the evocative efficacy of the visionary revelation narrated in 6:1—22:21.

Application of Evocations in Rev 4

As has been suggested in the preliminary observations, this scene serves to authenticate the visionary revelation narrated in 6:1—22:21. It is a visionary version of the authentication formulae of divine communication: "Thus says the Lord." It enthused and should enthuse keen reading, hearing, and response to the evocations to be generated by the visionary revelation narrated in 6:1—22:21. Secondarily, God's holiness portrayed in the glitter of gemstones and orated in the worship of the four living creatures and the twenty-four elders call upon the then and now saints to a life of holiness as their God is (1 Pet 1:15–17).

REV 5

INTRODUCTION OF THE DIRECTOR OF THE VISIONARY REVELATION

¹*Then I saw on the right hand of the one sitting on the throne a scroll written on the inside and outside sealed with seven seals.*

In this narration, John shifts his reader's attention from describing the nature and worship accorded the one seated on the throne to the sealed scroll in his right hand. The scroll is the object of the verb "saw." Old Testament visionary references to God's decreed events that are yet to be revealed to prophets are symbolized by a sealed scroll (Isa 29:11–12).

Holding something with the right hand depicts its great worth as well as the honor of the one to whom it is given.[13] A scroll that is written on the inside and outside depicts the totality of the decrees that were to be outworked in the unfolding history. This particular symbolic scroll represented God's immutable decrees that were set to be outworked throughout the unfolding history. The symbolic seven seals on the scroll signify that the decreed events were exclusively in the knowledge of God (Deut 29:29).

---

13. See note 53.

²*Then I saw a mighty angel proclaiming in a loud voice, "Who is worthy to open the scroll and to break its seals?"*

The display of the angel's might was intended to highlight the great importance of the contents of the scroll to the life of the church. His question, "who is able to open the scroll and break its seals?" aimed at drawing John's attention to what was about to be revealed and to once more emphasize the gravity of its prophetic role in guiding the church. Thereafter, John was very keen to know what the Spirit was saying to the church in the contents of this enigmatic scroll. It was also to single out and raise the ethos of the one who would be found worthy to open the scroll and break its seals.

³*And no one in heaven and on earth nor under the earth was able to open the scroll nor to look into it.*

Noting that there was no one in heaven, on earth, and under the earth who was worthy to open the scroll was a rhetorical foil to magnify the person of Jesus and his redeeming work once he is identified as the only one in all the heaven and earth who was worthy to open the seal and look inside. It was also meant to catalyze belief in Jesus, his work on the cross, and the gospel message about him.

⁴*And I wept uncontrollably because no one was found worthy to open the scroll or look into it.*

John's weeping because no one was found worthy to open the scroll and look into it highlighted its great worth, the necessity to open it, and the importance of revealing its contents to the church. It also shows how unworthy the entire created order is to be entrusted to be a repository and herald of the eternal plans of God (Deut 29:29). Even the worshipping Seraphs, the twenty-four elders, and angels were not found worthy. It reveals how far the fall of Adam alienated man from God. It also exposed the wide gap between the impeccable God and peccable creation. None is worthy to even try to pry into the secrets of God. The doctrine of the grace of God in his varied methods of rapprochements is understood more when the morass into which man fell, in the sin of Adam, is revealed.

⁵*Then, one of the elders said to me, "Do not weep! Behold the Lion of the tribe of Judah, the root of David has triumphed. He is worthy to open the scroll and its seven seals."*

The special knowledge by one of the twenty-four elders that there was one who was worthy to open the scroll, supports the earlier supposition that they do not symbolize and role-play an earthly but an otherworldly reality.

Introducing the worthy one as the lion of the tribe of Judah shows that he was the one who Jacob, the father of the nation of Israel, had prophesied about when he blessed Judah before he died in Egypt (Gen 49:9–12). He was also anticipated in Deut 18:18 and affirmed in Acts 3:22. He was the one preordained to deliver the captives in sin and lead them through the unfolding history, a final exodus of sorts, into the kingdom of God in the new heaven and earth (Isa 40:3; Mal 3:1–5; Mark 1:2–3).[14]

⁶Then I saw a Lamb, looking as if it had been slain, standing at the centre of the throne, encircled by the four living creatures and the elders. The Lamb had seven horns, and seven eyes, which are the seven Spirits of God sent out into all the earth.

Presenting Jesus on the visionary stage was deliberately delayed for dramatic effect. The depiction of Jesus as the Lamb, looking as if it had been slain, demonstrates the reason why Jesus qualified to be the only one who was worthy to take the scroll, open its seals, and look inside. He was slain, and by his blood, he redeemed men for God out of every tribe, tongue, people, and nation and made them a kingdom and priests (vv. 9). Again, the Greek verb ἐσφαγμένον, *esphagmenon* (nom. sing. neut. part. perf. pass. of the verb σφάζω, *sphazō*, to slay) describes a past activity with lasting effects.[15] It demonstrates the unquenchable efficacy of the work of Jesus on the cross. Again, portraying him using two different symbolisms, the lion of Judah which depicts his royal status, and a humbled slain Lamb which depicts his redeeming death, is a symbolic foil that demonstrates the great weight of the sacrifice in his salvific work on the cross (Phil 2:5–10).

The Lamb is seen standing next to God at the centre of throne. Positioning him at the centre of the throne that is encircled by the four living creatures and the twenty-four elders, shows that he is more exalted than those positioned a little bit further from God's throne. This exaltation is intended as a strategic act to generate evocations of honor, worship, faith and to enhance the belief value of the visionary simulations he will henceforth be directing.

A horn is used figuratively to suggest aggressive power. Likewise, it symbolizes the power of kingship.[16] As such, depicting the Lamb as having seven horns portrays the exceeding power with which he accomplishes his twin work of redeeming the world and judging the sinners. Again, the Lamb's seven horns and seven eyes are a symbolic demonstration of Jesus'

---

14. Karura, *Catalyzing Reader Response*, 178.
15. Trail, *Revelation, 1–11*, 143.
16. Perlman, "Horn," 757.

seven virtues (power, strength, honor, glory, praise, wealth, and wisdom) that are orated by the angels in vv. 12. The seven eyes described as the seven Spirits of God sent out into all the earth demonstrate Jesus' omniscience and omnipresence as he ministers in all the earth by his Spirit (John 14:15–17).

⁷*He went and took the scroll from the right hand of him who sat on the throne.*

This scene borrows its symbolism from Ezek 2:9–3:4. In Ezekiel, the scroll represented the message that Ezekiel was being commissioned to proclaim to his audience. In this scene, the scroll symbolizes the outworking of the eternal and consequential decrees of God throughout the unfolding history which, if revealed, would generate evocations that would engender patient endurance and bridge gaps in orthodoxy and orthopraxy in the seven churches and by application, to the universal church.

⁸*When he took the scroll; the four living creatures and the twenty-four elders fell down before the Lamb. Each of them had a harp and golden bowls full of incense which are the worship of the saints.* ⁹*They sing a new song saying, "Worthy are you, to take the scroll, and to open its seals because you were slain and by your blood, you redeemed men for God out of every tribe, tongue, people, and nation* ¹⁰*and made them a kingdom and priests and they will reign on the earth.* ¹¹*And I looked and heard the voice of many angels around the throne, the living creatures, and the elders and their number was myriads of myriads and thousands of thousands* ¹²*saying, in a loud voice: "worthy is the Lamb who has been slain to receive the power and riches and wisdom and strength and honour and glory and blessings.* ¹³*And I heard every creature in heaven and the earth and under the earth and on the sea and everything that is in them saying: "To the one sitting on the throne and to the Lamb, be blessings and honour and glory and might forever and ever."* ¹⁴*And the four living creatures would say, Amen, and the twenty-four elders fell down and worshipped him who lives forever and* ever.

Upon the Lamb taking the scroll from the hand of God, the four seraphs and the twenty-four elders fell before the Lamb. This act was intended to extoll the person and salvific work of Jesus. The harp in the seraph's hands symbolizes the lofty praise due to the Lamb by the heavenly host. The bowls full of incense symbolizes the saints' worship due to the Lamb. It echoes the words of Ps 141:2, "Let my prayer be counted as incense before you and the lifting of my hands as the evening sacrifice." The inclusion of one hundred trillion angels further demonstrates the superlative expression of worship due to the Lamb. The seven virtues listed in the praise: power, riches, wisdom, strength, honor, glory, and blessing portray Jesus as both the divine

Messiah and King. The heavenly choir was joined by every creature in heaven and on earth in worshiping God and the Lamb (vv. 13-14). Here, divine *latria* is extended, in equal measure, to the Lamb. This simulation demonstrates the unquestionable divinity of Jesus Christ.

The visionary simulations in chapters four and five are not necessarily revelations of the daily setting of the heavenly court and the worship that happens there. Instead, they describe the divine originator, mediator, and director of the visionary revelation in drama, descriptive gestures, and oratorial worship. These descriptions were primarily aimed at authenticating the visionary revelation just about to be shown and narrated from 6:1—22:21. They function as the authentication formula of divine communication "thus says the Lord" in visionary simulation. As said in the preliminary observations of this chapter, here it is demonstrated as "thus shows/reveals the Lord."

Strategic and Communicative Acts in Rev 5

The importance of the visionary revelation to the life of the church is shown by the symbolic gesture of positioning the scroll in the right hand of the one sitting on the throne. Highlighting the importance of the visionary revelation in this gesture drew the audience to value and respond favorably to the evocations it generates.

Portraying Jesus in the symbol of a lamb standing as having been slain demonstrates his ultimate sacrifice that qualified him to mediate the contents of the sealed scroll. This demonstration and the worship accorded him by the heavenly host elevated his ethos. Consequently, it enhanced the audience's faith and trust in the person of Jesus and his salvific work. It also enhanced the belief value in the contents of the sealed scroll.

Application of Evocations in Rev 5

This scene role-played the handing over of the sealed scroll from God to Jesus. This simulation coupled with the lofty portrayal of the person of Christ and his salvific work on the cross in the slain Lamb of God enhanced the efficacy of the strategic acts embedded in the visionary simulations narrated in 6:1—22:21. It also enthused the audience to desire to see and hear more of what was written in the sealed scroll. It further urged the saints to urgently respond to the evocations generated by the strategic and the communicative acts embedded in the ensuing visionary simulations. It would equally enthuse the present-day reader of the book of Revelation to respond to the evocations generated by the embedded strategic and communicative acts. The evocations generated by the strategic and communicative acts in the book of Revelation are ready-to-apply evocations.

Chapter 3

Outworking of God's Indiscriminate Decrees (6:1—8:1)

PRELIMINARY OBSERVATION

THIS SCENE COMMENCES A visionary simulation of the outworking of God's eternal and consequential decrees in the fallen world throughout the unfolding history. John is the only audience in the vision hall. However, he represents the entire church. The main character is feted as the Sovereign Lord, holy, true and judge of the earth's inhabitants (6:10). Though he is shown to have handed over the record and plan of outworking his decrees to the slain Lamb, they are still outworked according to his preordained plan. God's decrees are imbued with efficacy to outwork that which was decreed in its ordained time or consequential circumstance without help from other personalities.

REV 6

This scene simulates the outworking of God's decree on the present heaven and earth as a consequence of Adam and Eve's breach of the covenant they had entered with him (Gen 2:16–17). The specific events constituting the outworking of this decree were pronounced against Satan, Adam, and Eve and by extension, Adam's progeny (Gen 3:14-24). As such, they can also be identified as God's first tier judgments. Paradoxically, because they constantly remind humanity of the dire consequences of breach of God's covenants, thereby evoking abhorrence of sin leading to repentance, they also act as divine rapprochements to humanity. They include a reversal of God's blessings pronounced in Gen 1:28–30 and the divine curse on the environment (Gen 3:17–19). After Adam and Eve breached God's covenant (Gen 3:3–24) thereby earning the decreed penalty—death (Gen 2:17), God graciously decreed a redemption act (Gen 3:14–15, 31). As such, a balanced simulation of the outworking of God's decrees resulting from Adam's fall would simulate both the judgment and redemptive act.

¹*As I watched; the Lamb opened one of the seven seals. I heard one of the four living creatures saying with a voice like thunder, come!*

As opined earlier, opening the seals symbolized the act of revealing the outworking of God's decrees that were before then only in his knowledge. The call by one of the living creatures to the symbolic cast simulating each of the decreed events suggests that the four living creatures are acting as the stage crew that draws the curtains to usher in the cast simulating the decreed events. They also explain obscure aspects of the visionary revelation. Voices like thunder usually identify the voice as having God's authority (Exod 19:19; 20:18; 1 Sam 7:10; Isa 33:3). In this visionary revelation, they underscore the divine source of the simulated event.

²*I looked and behold a white horse. The rider had a bow. He was given a crown, and he went out conquering and to conquer.*

The color white has been used as a symbol of various biblical realities. It is used as a symbol for purity (Matt 17:2; 28:3, Rev 3:4; 19:8). White hair and clothes signify the wisdom and holiness of the Godhead (Dan 7:9; Rev 1:14). The white horse in Zech 6:3 represents one of the spirits/winds of heaven who outwork God's decrees. The overcomers are given white stones inscribed with a new name (2:17). In the entire visionary revelation, white color stands for an appealing entity. This observation suggests that a white cavalry horse and its rider should represent a positive aspect. However, Craig Keener suggests that the white horse and its rider represent war, especially from the Parthians who used white horses.[1] Though the Parthians humiliated the Romans in battle in 62 CE,[2] they did not take over the empire. It would not be feasible to simulate an occurrence with no evocative value to eliminate the gaps identified in the audience's historical situations (chapters 2–3).

---

1. Keener, *Revelation*, 202.
2. Desrosiers, *Revelation*, 65.

Some have suggested that this symbol signifies a false Christ.³ Such a reading seems to be a limping attempt to reconcile the visionary revelation with Jesus' eschatological teachings in Matt 24:5, Mark 13:6, and Luke 21:8. Arguing from the prevalence of the verb "conquest" in the book, Grant R. Osborne concludes that it references the general propensity of sinful humans to lust for conquest.⁴ Much as these and other scholars are entitled to their views; they must answer the question "would the simulation of their supposed reference generate evocations that would nudge the saints to work towards bridging the gaps identified in their visionary situations?" If the answer is no, then the supposed event would not constitute what the Spirit intended to say to the churches.

Moreover, the rider of this cavalry horse was given a victor's crown (Greek, στέφανος, *stephanos*), and he went out for more conquest. The crown that he receives, of course, from God, suggests that it was a reward for an interim conquest. John's audition that, "he went out conquering and to conquer," also suggests that the phenomenon personified by this symbolic cavalry horse and its rider was already conquering before it was revealed.

A question that arises is, Would God give a victor's crown to a worker of mischief? Not at all! A conquest that deserves God's commendation must have been answering to his redemptive purpose. The symbolism of the white cavalry horse, its rider with a bow, and an interim crown of conquest from God personifies a phenomenon that was already conquering before John saw the visionary revelation. Wielding a bow represents strength and conquest in battle (Gen 49:24, Ps 44:6–7, Zech 9:13). John's audition that he "came out conquering, and went out to conquer" suggests that it would also continue conquering during the unfolding history.

Therefore, it can be reasonably deduced that the cavalry white horse that goes out conquering and to conquer personifies the beginning of Jesus' conquest of the world through his death and the proclamation of the gospel (12:10–11). As such, the cavalry horse in Rev 19:11 would represent the tail-end of the conquest whereby he avenges the church by judging the beast, false prophet (19:19–21), and the dragon (20:7–10). Furthermore, no other biblical entity has been guaranteed conquest in the unfolding history except the church (Matt 16:18; Luke 10:18–19).

The conquering and everlasting kingdom of the Messiah was portended in Nebuchadnezzar's dream in Dan 2:44–45 and again in Daniel's vision in Dan 7:13–14. When the time to inaugurate it was fulfilled, Jesus, who claimed the title "Son of Man" (Mark 2:28, John 3:13), was manifested.

---

3. Strauss, *Revelation*, 155.
4. Osborne, *Revelation*, 277.

He intimated that he would build his church against which the gates of hell would not prevail (Matt 16:18).

Of all the horse riders in this visionary revelation, only this one comes out from conquest, receives an interim crown, and goes out for more conquest. An intertextual interpretation suggests that this horse rider's crown represents the Holy Spirit who gives power for gospel witness (Acts 1:8). He is also the down payment of the church's eternal inheritance (Eph 1:14) who was given on the day of Pentecost (Acts 2:1–12). Thus, she is to continue conquering until all her foes are vanquished (19:11–21; 20:1–10). The other three horses are passive symbolisms of their decreed realities. Thus, the white cavalry horse and its rider symbolize a powerful Holy Spirit-enabled redemptive work, while the other three represent the outworking of God's decreed judgments as a result of Adam's fall throughout the unfolding history (Gen 2:17; 3:14–17).

As intimated earlier, no visionary simulation of the outworking of God's providential and consequential decrees can be complete without simulating God's redemptive events and particularly the preaching of the gospel. This supposition is supported by the observation that the preaching of the gospel is also simulated by the two witnesses in the visionary scenes ushered by the trumpet blowing angel (11:1–7). Again, it is simulated by a cast of angels alongside the simulation of the preservation of the church (14:6–13). It is further simulated in the vision showing the judgment of the great prostitute (18:1–5). This position counters Aune's postulation that it is inconsistent to have this horse and its rider represent a positive event while the following three represent negative actions.[5] It is shown together with the judgments because both are different forms of God's rapprochements to humanity. Thus, the white cavalry horse represents the outworking of God's providential decree that was decreed before the foundation of the world— the victory of the church through the preaching of the redeeming death of the Lamb who was slain before the foundation of the world (13:8).

³And when he opened the second seal, I heard the second living creature say Come! ⁴And another red horse came out. Its rider was permitted to take peace from the earth so that people will kill one another, and he was given a great sword.

In the whole of the visionary revelation color red stands for entities associated with persecution, sin, and death (12:3 and 17:3). By auditioning that the rider was permitted to take peace from the earth so that people should slay one another, John shows that this cavalry horse and its rider

---

5. Aune, *Revelation 6–16*, 393.

personify a decreed judgment of wars wherein many people on earth would die (Mark 13:8a). This judgment was part of the consequences decreed for breach of the Adamic covenant: "And the Lord God commanded the man saying, "You may surely eat of every tree of the garden, but of the tree of the knowledge of good and evil you shall not eat, for in the day that you eat of it you shall surely die" (Gen 2:16–17). The outworking of this decree was activated by Adam's disobedience and continues to afflict humans throughout history. It is not necessarily a result of the victims' sin but a continuation of the judgment pronounced upon Adam's breach of God's covenant (Gen 3:14–19). Judgments that are consequences of Adam's breach of his covenant with God are irrevocable and indiscriminate. However, they can be delayed or hastened by human choices that predispose them to war, famine, and other calamities. As humanity experiences these judgments, they are reminded of God's grim view of sin. They evoke regret for sin, thereby engendering repentance. As such, paradoxically, they also function as God's rapprochements to humankind.

⁵When he opened the third seal, I heard the third living creature say, "Come!" And I looked and saw a black horse and its rider had a pair of scales in his hands. ⁶And a voice in the middle of the four living creatures said, "A choenix of wheat for a denarius and three choenixes of barley for a denarius, and do not spoil the oil.

In this scene, black color stands for the grimness of the aspect signified by the black cavalry horse. The personalities surrounded by the four living creatures are God and the Lamb. Thus, the voice that came from the midst of the living creatures must have come from either of the two. This audition was directed to John and his audience as an interpretative cue. A choenix describes a small measure. The phrase "a choenix of wheat for a denarius and three choenixes of barley for a denarius" describe decreed inflation and famines that occur in the course of history as part of the judgment for Adam's disobedience (Gen 3:14–19). Specifically, the simulated famines were decreed to happen in the unfolding history (Gen 3:17–19; Matt 24:6–7; Mark 13:8).

The order to preserve the oil has been debated without consensus.[6] The arising question is, Why would God order a preservation of oil and how would the order generate evocations that can bridge any of the gaps in the visionary situations of the seven churches? In both the New and Old Testaments, oil was used in consecration and in prayer for the sick (Jas 5:14).[7] It

---

6. Osborne, *Revelation*, 280–81.
7. Engen, "Anointing Oil," 52.

also symbolizes God's provision (Job 29:6; Joel 2:24).[8] An order not to harm the oil may show that in the midst of these judgments, God will still show his love and preserve a remnant. A strategic act from such a simulation can generate evocations that would engender reciprocal love for God.

[7]When he opened the fourth seal, I heard the voice of the fourth living creature say, "Come!" [8]And I looked and behold, a pale horse. Its rider's name was Death, and Hades followed him. And they were given authority over a fourth of the earth to kill with the sword, famine, plagues, and wild beasts.

The pale-colored cavalry horse represents a mix of decreed judgments that would result in pain and death (Matt 24:6–7; Mark 13:8). It is not clear whether the personified Hades was riding a separate horse. We can infer that wherever death is, Hades is there to receive the dead. What is clear, though, is that John must have understood the appearance of the symbolized death and Hades as symbolic parallelism that demonstrated the intensity of the decreed judgment. Notably, this plague is largely a combination of the judgments simulated by the second and third cavalry horses, plus other deadly epidemics like cancer, HIV/AIDS, and COVID-19. Being given authority over a fourth of the earth suggests that although death and Hades will continue throughout the unfolding history, the world population would continue to increase until humanity is finally judged at the white throne judgment.

The judgments simulated after opening of the second, third, and fourth seals are indiscriminate. Experience shows that death, which is the ultimate result of these judgments, can be delayed or hastened by personal choices in matters of conduct of life. For example, the effects of famine can be mitigated by prudent farming and planning. as happened in Egypt by the advice of Joseph (Gen 41:1–57). Choices of leaders can also hasten or delay some judgments. For example, some leaders can lead their nations into civil wars where many of their citizens die. Others can corruptly misuse the country's finances, leading to inadequate health services and early deaths. Others can prudently manage their countries' finances, leading to low mortality rates and high life expectancy.

This visionary revelation shows that the realities symbolized by the four cavalry horses would happen concurrently throughout the unfolding history with an intensification of their pain as history comes to a close. Thus, the gospel would be conquering amid deadly wars, famines, and deadly plagues.

---

8. Ryken, Wilhoit, and Longman, *Biblical Imagery*, 604.

⁹*When he opened the fifth seal; I saw under the altar souls of those who had been slain because of the word of God and their witness.* ¹⁰*And they cried with a loud voice saying, "Until when, O sovereign, holy and true, will you not judge and avenge our blood on those who dwell on the earth?"* ¹¹*Then, each of them was given a white robe and told to wait a little longer until their fellow servants, and brothers who were to be killed as they had been are also killed."*

This scene addresses the problem of Christian persecution that would sometimes result to martyrdom. It reveals the plight of martyrs and God's assurance of vengeance. In the temple worship, the blood of a sacrifice was poured under the altar (Lev 4:7, 18). As such, showing the souls of martyrs under the altar suggests that their martyrdom was considered to be the ultimate act of worship. It echoes Rom 12:1–2: "I beseech you, brothers, by the mercies of God that you give your bodies as living sacrifices, holy and pleasing to God, which is your act of worship to God."

The martyrs' plea for vengeance is a visionary device designed to introduce the theme of God's vengeance against the persecutors of the saints. It is an important strategic act to evoke patient endurance in suffering for faith to the point of martyrdom. As such, it could not be designed and conformed to Stephen's martyrdom which engendered the prayer "Lord do not lay this sin on them" (Acts 7:60), as some have suggested. The difference stems from the fact that this visionary revelation is simulated to evoke patience endurance in tribulations, while the narrative of Stephen's martyrdom aimed to show how martyrdom led to the spread of the gospel.

God's answer to the martyrs' plea reveals that, though the suffering believers would wish the end to come quickly, it is under God's sovereign will and that he wills that many more turn to the faith. As 2 Pet 3:9 says, "The Lord is not slow about his promise as some count slowness, but is forbearing towards you, not wishing that any should perish but that all should come to repentance." The martyrs' address to God as sovereign Lord (Greek: δεσπότες, *despotes*), holy and true, is a humble acceptance of their painful lot. They acknowledge God's sovereignty though he did not avert their persecution and eventual death.

Giving white robes to the martyrs enacted their consolation. It was a kind of wiping away of tears. It also demonstrated their prior acceptance as sons (Luke 15:22). They had already earned an unfading reward that will be given them at the second coming of Jesus Christ (2 Tim 4:8).

Finally, the consoling answer to the plea of the martyrs to be avenged speedily shows that tribulation, as a tool of suppressing the gospel and coercing the saints to apostatize, will be ongoing as long as history endures. This tribulation is simulated, albeit in different contexts in 9:15–21; 12:1–13:18;

16:12-16 and 20:7-9). Jesus said, "In this world, you will face persecution, but be of good cheer, I have overcome the world" (John 16:33).

¹²*And I saw when he opened the sixth seal, there was a great earthquake, and the sun became as black as sackcloth of hair, and the whole moon became like blood* ¹³*and the stars of heaven fell to the earth as a fig tree casts its unripe figs being shaken by a great wind* ¹⁴*and the sky vanished like a scroll being rolled up, and every mountain and island were removed from their place.* ¹⁵*And the kings of the earth, the great ones, the commanders, the rich, the powerful, every slave and free hid themselves in the caves and among the rocks of the mountains.* ¹⁶*And they said to the mountains and the rocks, "Fall on us and hide us from the face of the one sitting on the throne and from the wrath of the Lamb* ¹⁷*because the great day of their wrath has come and who can stand it?*

After Jesus opened the sixth seal, John saw a simulation of a great earthquake. He also saw the sun darken, the moon becoming like blood, and the stars falling, as a fig tree casts its unripe figs when shaken by a mighty wind. This scene simulates the events that will usher in the end of the world and the second coming of Jesus Christ (Matt 24:29). It draws its imagery from Isa 34:1-17. Isaiah foresaw the judgment of the nations that were oppressing God's people. By likening them to the starry host—a demonstration of their self-glorification—he compares their downfall to the fall of withered leaves from the vine and like shrivelled figs from the fig tree (Isa 34:4). This visionary simulation borrows Isaiah's imagery to simulate the unpreparedness of humanity for the end of the world. It uses the most gruesome symbolism that demolishes any human trust in the world and what it has to offer. This scene simulates, in gruesome details, the events that are simply described as the passing away of the present heaven and earth in 21:1.

The day of the Lord has been described in Old Testament prophecies and the teachings of Jesus Christ (Joel 2:31; Matt 24:29; Mark 13:24-25; Luke 21:25). The grouping of the victims of the wrath of God and the Lamb into their social classification (kings, great ones, commanders, rich, powerful, slaves, and free) shows that no earthly achievement or title can qualify one to escape God's final judgment except the merit afforded by the death of the slain Lamb.

Finally, humanity's slight of God's gracious rapprochement in the work of the slain Lamb is judged. Snubbing God's call for reconciliation has provoked the wrath of God against humanity. How can they escape if they neglect such a great salvation (Heb 2:3), which was first proclaimed by God himself when he said, "This is my Son, whom I love; with him, I am well pleased. Listen to him" (Matt 17:5; Mark 9:7). The weight of God's judgment for sin is demonstrated by people's preference to be killed by falling rocks than to face his wrath. Unlike the indiscriminate judgments simulated when the Lamb opened the second, third, and fourth seals, this one is discriminate. Its simulation seems to have incorporated the judgment that would have been simulated when the seventh seal was opened. Apparently, the action simulation after the seventh seal was broken only recalls the devastation of the judgment simulated when the sixth seal was opened. It also reflects on its unimaginably grim aftermath. This supposition suggests that the simulation of the passover-sealing of the saints was placed between the opening of the sixth and seventh seal to assure the saints that they would be passed over when the end of the extant heaven and earth judgment is finally executed.

In his earthly life and ministry, Jesus taught that life in the unfolding history would be normal. In Matt 24:37, he says, "As it was in the times of Noah, so it will be at the coming of the Son of Man. For in the days before the flood, people were eating and drinking, marrying and giving in marriage, up to the day Noah entered the Ark." Thus, allowed to dampen our evangelical high-octave expectation of a spectacular rapture to escape these judgments, which in some scholarly quarters are mistaken for a great tribulation, scripture states that life will be normal. "Like a thief in the night" (1 Thess 5:2), speaking of cluelessness on the part of the victims; so will it be at the second advent of our Lord Jesus Christ. As has been argued in this commentary, God's judgments are not tribulations. They are either a recompense for evil or disciplinary rapprochements to engender repentance. On the other hand, tribulations which consist of temptations, trials, and persecutions are used by God's adversaries to entice people to sin against him and to coerce the saints to apostatize.

Strategic and Communicative Acts in Rev 6

The simulation of the conquering church through the saints' witness (vv. 6:2) amidst wars (vv. 6:4), famines (vv. 6:5–6), deadly plagues, and martyrdom (6:8) demonstrated the church's invincibility. It is a strategic act that evoked hope, courage, and resilience in the saints of the seven churches as they faced opposition, trials, and persecutions to the point of martyrdom as shown by the souls of the martyred saints seen under the altar.

A visionary scene depicting the consequential judgments in the form of the havoc that had been and continues to be visited on the world because of the single transgression of Adam is also a strategic act. It evokes abhorrence of sin that engendered such painful consequences. The impact of the strategic acts embedded in the simulation of these judgments is enhanced by the saint's daily experience of the simulated judgments as and when they are outworked throughout the unfolding history.

Simulation of the martyrs' plight, their plea for vengeance, God's promise to act decisively at the appointed time, and the interim consolation, is a strategic act. It is intended to overturn the perception of martyrdom as an unwarranted shameful death to a glorious worship equivalent to a sweet-smelling sacrifice offered at the golden altar of incense—prayers and worship of God's people.

The devastating judgment on the day of the Lord that was simulated after the opening of the sixth seal is also a powerful strategic act. It was simulated in an explicit manner that highlighted the contrast between the fleeting nature of worldly glory and the painful end of those who slight God and the grace shown in the slain Lamb. It was intended to urge the audience to instead snub the allures of sin and to diligently pursue the kingdom of God and to live within its value system.

Application of Evocations in Rev 6

The strategic act embedded in the simulation of the conquering church evoked assurance of her invincibility. It must have evoked a calm assurance of eventual victory, notwithstanding the painful trials that the church was going through. The extant church faces serious opposition from a humanity that is more inclined to rationality and pluralism in claims to truth than to the only truth of the Bible. She needs to be assured of her invincibility, which is afforded by the interim crown of the Holy Spirit—the guarantee of her eternal inheritance. As such, the evocations in this simulation are applicable in total to the present-day church.

Seeing a simulation and experiencing the outworking of God's decrees in wars, famines, and deaths through plagues on fallen humanity as a consequence of Adam's sin can jolt sinners to reflect on their degree of conformity to Adam's rebellion. It can indeed reverse today's rebellion against the truth of the word of God in the Bible. The reader can reflectively imagine Satan beguiling today's church with questions like "Did God say that you shall have no other gods before me, you shall not make for yourself a graven image . . . You shall not bow down to them or worship them?" (Exod 20:3–5). Satan would continue, "No, God would not issue such a commandment. You can adore your religious, music, and political idols, and even the departed saints and ancestors." Yet another reflection question that Satan would ask is, "Did God actually say, 'If a man has sexual relations with a man, as one does with a woman, both of them have done a detestable thing and that they cannot inherit the kingdom of God?'" (Lev 20:13; 1 Cor 6:6–20). The reader would imagine Satan further saying, "No, research has shown that people who practice such are merely obeying their sexual orientation." A further reflective imaginative question would be, "Did God say that 'You shall not kill'?" The reader would again imagine Satan saying, "No, abortion is just flushing out a fetus." Such reflections, together with the simulations of God's decreed judgments would evoke repentance and resistance of today's beguiling wiles of Satan. The display of God's judgment for humanity's sin would also engender zeal in preaching the gospel, peradventure more people would be saved from its consequences (Luke 16:19–31).

Suffering as a result of the fall of Adam is an issue that has bothered believers who would envisage a God who would remove all afflictions including death. However, daily experiences, as have been simulated by the second, third and fourth cavalry horses show that this is not the case. The world continues to witness devastating wars, famines in various places, epidemics like HIV/AIDS, cancer, and COVID-19 that have indiscriminately claimed millions of lives. Apologists have tried to answer the question, Why would a loving God allow such pain upon his people? As has been argued, some of these judgments can be delayed or harried by peoples' choices. Humans should be aware that their choices have a bearing on hastening or delaying some of these judgments. For example, a country that does not put in measures to improve food security and health care may experience high child mortality rates and reduced life expectancy, thereby hastening the judgments simulated by the black and pale horses and their riders. Equally, those who keenly improve their health care can push back and delay the judgment role-played by the pale horse.

Notwithstanding the painful effect of these judgments, they paradoxically also perform a redemptive purpose. They remind humanity of their mortality, transient nature, and the grave consequences of their choices. They thus engender humility and abhorrence of sin, leading to repentance and pursuance of godliness. They also urge believers to evermore look forward to life in the new heavens and new earth where their tears will be wiped away and their mortality changed to immortality.

Showing John the souls of the martyrs under the altar, where the blood of the sacrifice was poured in the earthly temple, demonstrated that heaven considered martyrdom to be the highest form of worship. To a people going through persecution that sometimes led to martyrdom, the scene engendered patient endurance in their afflictions. The strategic act embedded in showing God consoling and assuring the martyrs that they would eventually be avenged also generated evocations of solace and enhanced patient endurance in those passing through diverse tribulations. Since tribulation of saints is a common phenomenon throughout the church age, albeit in different forms, the present-day church can also draw solace and encouragement to endure her share of tribulations.

The strategic act embedded in the simulation of the wrath of God that will be visited on the sinners at the end of the world evoked fear of being victims of such a severe judgment. The same fear should be evoked in every reader of this narration. Such fear can draw the saints to watch and pray because they do not know the day or hour when this reality will be actualized (Matt 24:42).

Just as in the churches in Asia Minor, the simulation of the outworking of God's consequential decrees generates evocations that can compel the twenty-first century church to invest in works of love that were lacking in Ephesus, shun the false teachings, immorality, and idolatry as were in the churches in Pergamum and Thyatira, cringe at the thought of being in spiritual comatose, as was in Sardis and lukewarmness in Laodicea. It urges the church to maintain orthodoxy and orthopraxy and to patiently endure tribulations as she awaits the coming of her savior.

REV 7:1—8:1

PASSOVER-SEALING OF THE SAINTS

Preliminary Observations

Structurally, the timing and setting of the scene simulating the sealing of the saints with a spiritual identifying mark appears misplaced. Its purpose suggests that it should have been simulated just before the simulation of the disciplinary judgment decrees that are simulated by the four wind-restraining angels (vv. 7:1). However, it is placed between the simulation of the execution of the sixth- and the seventh-seal judgments. A viable explanation is that the saints had to be marked out for divine protection before the destruction of the present heaven and earth whose simulation is narrated in 6:12–16. As such, this scene serves as an apt epilogue to the simulation of the outworking of God's providential and indiscriminate decrees as a consequence of Adam's fall (6:1–17). It is also a fitting prologue to the simulations of the outworking of God's redemptive decrees in divine rapprochements in the preaching of the gospel and paradoxically, in disciplinary judgments whose simulation is narrated in 8:2—11:19.

OUTWORKING OF GOD'S INDISCRIMINATE DECREES (6:1—8:1)   93

The destruction of the earth simulated after the Lamb opened the sixth seal, which resulted to the void demonstrated in a half-hour silence after breaking the seventh seal, should have quenched God's wrath against humanity's sin. There should have been no more action on the present earth. The visionary revelation should have shifted focus to simulating the new life in the inaugurated new heaven and earth. A simulation of events deemed to be happening on the present earth suggests that such events would be occurring concurrently with the events simulated when the six seals were opened. However, simulating the outworking of the different groups of decrees, i.e., indiscriminate decrees, discriminate rapprochement decrees, vindictive woes, and judgment against Satan in a single visionary scene would have overcrowded the vision, thereby introducing ambiguities that could blind interpretation. The most feasible way was, as has been done, to group together similar events and then simulate each group in a separate visionary scene.

REV 7

¹After these things, I saw four angels standing upon the four corners of the earth, holding the four winds of the earth so that no wind would blow on the earth nor the sea or any tree. ²And I saw another angel that had ascended from the east having the seal of the living God, and he cried in a loud voice to the four angels to whom authority had been given to harm the earth and the sea ³saying, "Do not harm the earth nor the sea nor the trees until we have sealed the servants of our God on their foreheads.

As observed earlier, the visionary revelation narrated in this chapter serves as an epilogue to the visionary simulation narrated in chapter six as well as a prologue to the larger visionary revelation that simulates God's rapprochements in disciplinary and retributive judgments and preaching of the gospel throughout the unfolding history (8:1—11:19). It is simulated by five angels. Four of the five simulate outworking of God's disciplinary judgments, while the fifth simulates a temporal restraining of the four angels from harming the earth until the servants of God are sealed on their foreheads. Before the simulation of each of the seven judgments, an angel would blow a warning trumpet call, peradventure the victims repent and escape this and the final judgment.

The promise of Jesus to the church in Philadelphia, "Since you have kept my command to endure patiently, I will also keep you from the hour of trial that is about to come on the whole earth to test the inhabitants of the earth" (3:10), suggests that the saints in the church of Philadelphia may have been part of the sealed saints

The imagery of four angels standing upon the four corners of the earth, restraining the four winds of the earth from blowing on the earth, nor the sea nor any tree, shows that the phenomenon being simulated would be a worldwide phenomenon. It also suggests that these four angels would simulate the first four discriminatory judgments (8:7–12). The last three woes would be simulated by a different cast. It consisted of a fallen star—signifying the devil (9:1); the one symbolized by the four horns of the altar, that is God himself; the sixth trumpeting angel and four angels who had hitherto been bound at the great river Euphrates and a host of heavenly mounted troops (9:13–17); and lastly by God and the Messiah as they take over the kingdom of the world where they reign forever and ever (11:15). The last three woes are somehow similar to the events simulated after Satan is released from the abyss (20:7–15).

The syntax in verses one and two shows that by the time John saw these four destructive angels, they were already restraining the four winds. The best explanation is that they were suffocating the earth from the life-breath from the four winds of Ezek 37:9. The urgent loud cry of the sealing angel, and the highlight that the four angels had already been given authority to harm the earth, sea, and tree, show that restraining the wind that it may not blow on the earth, sea, or any tree simulated the judgment of harming the world. As such, the simulated judgment is outworked by suffocating the earth, sea, and trees from receiving the life-giving breath. The imagery of the wind as a life-giving force could have been borrowed from Ezek 37:9, while the sealing of the righteous and the judgments of the wicked are described using imagery borrowed from the description of the destruction of sinful Jerusalem (Ezek 9:4).

Sealing of the saints so that they are not harmed when the environment, obdurate sinners, and persecutors of the saints are harmed can be described as a spiritual passover-sealing. It demonstrates that the saints would be passed over when the simulated judgments are meted against the inhabitants of the earth. The seal was placed on the saints' foreheads. Placing the visionary seal on the forehead demonstrates their spiritual recognition. They cannot be mistaken when the discriminatory judgments against the obdurate are meted.

Comparatively, the function of this sealing appears to be the same as that of binding Satan for a thousand years. The sealing of the 144,000 and the great throng from the entire world protects them from God's disciplinary judgments against the obdurate sinners and persecutors of the saints. It also guarantees them acceptance to sit with Christ on Mount Zion (14:1).

Similarly, binding Satan for a thousand years protects the saints from Satan's deception and allows them to rule with Christ for a thousand years (20:4–6). Again, the function of the simulation of sealing the saints (vv. 1–17) appears to be the same as the function of the simulation of binding Satan for a thousand years (20:1–3). Both are intended to engender encouragement of the saints in the assurance that God has sealed them for his own and that he will always care and protect them.

Furthermore, both the sealing of the 144,000 and the binding of Satan for a thousand years are engendered by the death of Jesus, the saints' testimony, and by their total commitment to Jesus to the point of martyrdom (12:11). The difference is that the former simulates the protection of the saints in the context of God's judgment against the obdurate sinners and persecutors of the saints (8:7–12), whereas the latter simulates the protection of the saints from the deceitfulness of Satan in the context of Satan's judgment (20:1–3). Notably, the events simulated after the simulation of God's disciplinary judgments (9:14–21) and the events simulated after Satan is released from the abyss (20:7–9) happen towards the tail end of the unfolding history. Though simulated using different characters and acts, they appear to be the same events.

In the last judgments against Egypt, the seal on the Israelites was the blood of the Passover lambs. Likewise, the seal on the church is the blood of Jesus, her Passover Lamb (1 Cor 5:7). The church's seal is confirmed by baptism with the Holy Spirit, who is the pledge of her eternal inheritance (Eph 1:13–14). Baptism of believers with the Holy Spirit is the only seal that is mentioned in the Christian Scripture.

⁴*And I heard the number of the sealed, 144,000 sealed from every tribe of the sons of Israel.* ⁵*Out of the tribe of Judah 12,000 were sealed, out of the tribe of Reuben 12,000, out of the tribe of Gad 12,000,* ⁶*out of the tribe of Asher 12,000, out of the tribe of Naphtali 12,000, out of the tribe of Manasseh 12,000,* ⁷*out of the tribe of Simeon 12,000, out of the tribe of Levi 12,000, out of the tribe of Issachar 12,000,* ⁸*out of the tribe of Zebulun 12,000, out of the tribe of Joseph 12,000, out of the tribe of Benjamin 12,000 were sealed.*

Though the sealing of the saints was demonstrated as a worldwide phenomenon, John's initial observation was that only 144,000 from twelve tribes of Israel were sealed. Curiously, the tribe of Dan was not named. It seems that the author of the vision wanted to maintain the number twelve due to its symbolic significance. As such, not mentioning Dan by name should not be taken as a point of theological or hermeneutical significance. After all, Dan is represented in the phrase "every tribe of Israel" (7:4).

Number twelve is normally used to represent the fullness of Israel or the initial apostles of Jesus Christ and by extension, the church. In showing the full number of the sealed in each of the tribes of Israel, the number twelve has been multiplied by a thousand to make twelve thousand. Number one thousand in Scripture has been used to hyperbolically show a multitudinous number (Exod 20:6; Ps 50:10; 84:10; Isa 60:22; Amos 5:3; Rev 20:1–3). Thus, the great number of the sealed Israelite saints is represented by the visionary 144,000 saints.

Some commentators have suggested that the 144,000 represent the Old Testament saints.[9] However, since the Lamb is not an explicit theme of the Old Testament, this suggestion is unlikely when this vision is seen together with the vision in 14:1–5, which describes the 144,000 as the ones who follow the Lamb wherever he goes. Other commentators regard the 144,000 as representing all the saints.[10] This position fails to give a convincing reason as to why John explicitly names the tribes of Israel. Moreover, there is no other place in Scripture where Christians are directly or by allusion identified with the individual tribes of Israel. Furthermore, notably and distinctly, the sealed gentile saints are enjoined with the 144,000 in the next scene as a multitude from every nation, tribe, people, and language (7:9).

In a similarly structured visionary simulation narrated in 14:1–5, the same 144,000 are seen on a visionary Mount Zion with Jesus. Similar to the throng that joins the 144,000 in 7:9, the rest of the saints in the world are later reaped and brought into communion with Jesus and the 144,000 on Mount Zion (14:15–16). This observation suggests that the visionary 144,000 saints represent the Israelite Christians who are identified as the firstfruits of the redeemed (Jer 2:3), while the throng in 7:9 and the reaped saints in 14:15–16 are the sealed gentile Christians. Together they represent the full harvest of the redeemed from all over the world (Matt 8:11).

The visionary revelation that simulated the sealing of the saints (7:1–17) and the one that showed the saints gathered with Jesus on Mount Zion (14:1–16) simulated the then and present spiritual standing of the saints. Hebrews 12:22 affirms this supposition: "We have come (Greek: προσεληλύθατε, *proseleluthate*–perfect, indicative, active of προσέρχομαι, *proserchomai* [a tense showing an abiding phenomenon]) to Mount Zion, the city of the living God, the heavenly Jerusalem." Thus, the sealing of God has an abiding effect.

⁹*After this, I looked and behold a great multitude that no one could number, from every nation, from all tribes and peoples and languages, standing before*

---

9. Walhout, *Revelation*, 81.
10. Farmer, *Revelation*, 8; Thomas and Macchia, *Two Horizons*, 167–68.

the throne and before the Lamb, clothed in white robes, with palm branches in their hands [10]*and crying out with a loud voice, "Salvation belongs to our God who sits on the throne and to the Lamb!* [11]*And all the angels were standing around the throne and the elders and the four living creatures, and they fell on their faces before the throne and worshiped God* [12]*saying, "Amen, blessings and glory and wisdom and thanksgiving and honour and power and might be to our God forever and ever! Amen."*

The phrase "after this" (7:9) shows the time sequence between the visionary audition confirming the number of the sealed Israelite saints and the manifestation of the sealed multitude from the rest of the world. Observably, the sentence and paragraph construction of John's audition (7:4-8) does not limit the sealing of the saints to only the symbolic 144,000 Israelites. Moreover, the sealing angel had gone out to all the four corners of the earth. The sealing is further described as "being sheltered by the presence of the one who sat on the throne" (7:15-17).

This multitude was part of the entire *harvest* that will be gathered when Jesus finally takes the sickle to reap his harvest from the earth (14:14-16). The two groups of the sealed saints have now become one commonwealth (Eph 2:19). Their white robes represent imputed righteousness, while palm branches represent their singular worship of God and the Lamb. They hail God and the Lamb for saving them. The four living creatures and the twenty-four elders join in a befitting doxology (7:12).

[13]*Then one of the elders asked me, "Who are these clothed in white robes, and where did they come from?"* [14]*I said to him, "Sir, you know." And he said to me, "These are the ones coming out of the great tribulation. They have washed their robes and made them white in the blood of the Lamb.* [15]*Therefore, they are before the throne of God and worship him day and night in his temple, and he who sits on the throne will tabernacle over them.* [16]*And they shall hunger no more, neither thirst any more, the sun shall not strike them nor any scorching heat.* [17]*For the Lamb in the middle of the throne will be their shepherd, and he will guide them to springs of living water, and God will wipe away every tear from their eyes.*

The elder's two-part question is dramatically framed to raise and answer the question about the composition of the church. It reveals the identity and former nationality of the victorious saints role-played by the throng on the heavenly stage. As shown in their imputed righteousness—symbolized by white robes—they are drawn from every people group in the world. Together with the 144,000, representing the redeemed firstfruits from Israel, they are united by their new identity as saints. Their catholicity informs the intended composition of the church and her future mission—to all nations.

John's address to the elder as "Lord" shows that he considered the twenty-four elders to be role-playing persons of a higher estate than he. The elder's answer shows that the twenty-four elders were privy to things that had not yet been revealed to John. This observation suggests that the twenty-four elders represented an otherworldly reality. Their explanation, "These are the ones coming out of the great tribulation," shows that the act of sealing empowers the saints to endure tribulations.

Which is the great tribulation from which the crowd emerged victorious? Some interpreters associate the great tribulation with the judgments simulated after opening the seals,[11] blowing the trumpets, and pouring the seven bowls in chapters 6, 8, 9, and 16. However, these judgments are the outworking of God's redemption and judgment decrees throughout history. Nowhere in Scripture is God depicted as the author of tribulations. Jesus said, "In the world you will face tribulations. But take heart! I have overcome the world (John 16:33). In Revelation, tribulations are simulated in chapters 11:7, 12, 13, and 20:7–9. They are orchestrated by Satan, the beast from the sea, and the beast from the land.

The great tribulation afflicts all saints in temptations, trials, and persecutions. It is visited upon them by the desires of the flesh, the machinations of the devil, competing religions, political powers, employers, parents, peers, etc. Unlike the outworking of God's decrees, tribulations are not outworked by God or his agents (Jas 1:13). The great tribulation is not just an end-time phenomenon; it afflicts the saints during their individual lifespan throughout the unfolding history (John 16:33; Acts 14:22). Whereas God's judgments are strategic acts that are intended to evoke repentance, tribulations are strategic acts by the Satan and his cahoots to coerce saints to distrust and sin against God (Job 1:11; 2:5–7).

The great throng is further described as those who have washed their robes and made them white by the blood of the Lamb. This is a different way of expressing their sealing, which qualifies them to stand before the throne of God and to serve him day and night. Since there are no nights and days in the new heaven and earth, their service is in the present world. Again, since there is no temple in the new heaven and earth, the temple in which they serve is his very presence with which he tabernacles over them as they live in the present world. Being so tabernacled and shepherded by the Lamb, they will not be afflicted by spiritual hunger, thirst, or any other want (Ps 23:1).

---

11. Walhout, *Revelation*, 8.

Strategic and Communicative Acts in Rev 7

The simulation showing the four angels restraining the four winds as a form of judgment was a strategic act. It was aimed at scaring the saints in seeing the four angels suffocating the world out of its life-breath. One would imagine the painful death out of suffocation and shudder. Seeing another angel hurriedly and urgently coming to stop the four angels from executing God's decreed judgments till God's servants are sealed is a relief-evoking strategic act.

The sealing of the symbolic 144,000 Israelites and the multitude that no one could number from all tribes, peoples, and languages is a strategic act that assured the saints of their protection from the judgments against those who slight God's rapprochements. The audition that "God will wipe away every tear from their eyes" (7:14–17) enhances the evocative efficacy of the strategic act. This audition is a communicative act that must have enthused the audience to hope in God and patiently endure tribulation.

Application of Evocations in Rev 7

The strategic act embedded in showing the visionary revelation of the four angels restraining the four winds from blowing the life-giving vitality on the earth (Ezek 37:9) must have evoked fear and trepidation. It must have engendered revival of love in Ephesus, shunning of heresies in Pergamum and Thyatira, resuscitation of the spiritually dead in Sardis, and a warming-up of the spiritually lukewarm in Laodicea lest they face such life-threatening judgments. The knowledge that God executes disciplinary and retributive judgments in the course of history should awaken today's church to evermore be vigilant, lest they fall into the trap of sin and eventual judgment.

The scene showing the speedy coming of another angel to restrain the four angels from executing God's judgment until the servants of God are sealed demonstrated God's fidelity in preserving those who trust in him, to whom he has promised, "I will never leave you nor forsake you" (Deut 31:6–8). The simulation must have evoked a sigh of relief in the primary audience. It should elicit the same evocation in the secondary readers.

The sealing of Israelite and, likewise, gentile believers, demonstrates that the death of Jesus broke the wall of partition between the Jews and the gentiles, thereby creating a new commonwealth of all believers (Eph 2:14–16). The visionary simulation of this spiritual sealing should therefore rebuke the present-day racism that is, shamefully, displayed by the presence of Black Churches and White Churches in the West. A reading and hearing of the narration of this visionary simulation should equally rebuke tribalism and the caste system, which are terrible scourges of the African and Indian contexts.

The sealing of the servants of God arouses the audience's desire to also be spiritually sealed, leading to greater surrender to God, repentance of idolatries, adulteries, and other forms of sin. It could also revive the lukewarm churches and resurrect the spiritually dead in our days. The twenty-first-century church mirrors the seven churches in virtually all ways. She can draw spiritual fervor and energy from this visionary simulation. Finally, though God's decreed disciplinary judgments are a continuous phenomenon throughout the unfolding history, the church should take courage in the knowledge that these judgments will not be meted against her. She has an unmistakable spiritual passover seal.

REV 8:1

¹*When he opened the seventh seal, there was silence in heaven for about half an hour.*

John expects to see great action when the seventh seal is finally opened. But when it happens, there is palpable silence that lasts for half an hour. Silence in a vision or cinema is also action. In this case, it has revelational significance. If not, John would not have narrated it. Informed by the Talmud (*Hag. 12b, Abodah Z. 3b*), Caird suggests that the silence is an interval when the prayers of God's people are answered after the heavenly choir sings day and night (4:8f).[12] However, Caird has not shown the connection between the events of 4:8 and the present scene, thereby consigning his position to mere conjecture. Beale and Campbell too suggest that the silence stands for the silence of the world as it awaits God's judgments.[13] This suggestion does not explain the connection between the silence and the preceding scene simulating the passing away of the extant earth.

As has been observed in the commentary of chapter six, the judgment that was simulated after breaking the sixth seal was discriminative. In actual fact, it encompasses the simulations of the end of the world that by design should have been simulated when the seventh seal is broken. However, when the seventh seal is broken, there ensued a half hour of silence on the stage. It simulated the aftermath of the events simulated after the sixth seal is broken. It was observed that the events simulated when the sixth seal

---

12. Caird, *Revelation*, 107.
13. Beale and Campbell, *Revelation*, 164.

is opened explain the reason why the sealing of the saints was, by design, placed between the breaking of the sixth and the seventh seal. It was to include the saints who were present in the judgment simulated after the breaking of the sixth seal among the sealed and therefore protected from the end-time judgments.

Observably, God's consequential decrees resultant of Adam's breach of his covenant that were to be outworked throughout the unfolding history have been simulated. The last simulation after breaking the sixth seal was the passing away of the extant heaven and earth (6:12–17). A notable silence for thirty minutes can only represent the resultant void. It is a symbolic equivalent to saying "it is done" (16:17 and 21:6). New action, predicated on a new order, is expected in the new heaven and earth. The simulation of the life in the new heaven and earth is aptly narrated in chapters 21 and 22.

Amazingly, the events simulated in the succeeding visionary revelation happen on the extant heaven and earth. This observation suggests that the events happening on the extant heaven and earth that are simulated after the seventh seal is broken happen concurrently with the events simulated upon opening the six seals. However, whereas the events simulated after the opening of the first five seals are indiscriminate and consequent of Adam's fall, the events simulated after the sixth seal and the seven trumpets are blown are discriminate and consequent of humanity's response to God's rapprochements in the gospel message and in the evocations generated by the disciplinary judgments.

Strategic and Communicative Acts in Rev 8:1

Simulating the passing away of the present world order that is contingent on humanity's fall in the symbol of palpable silence for thirty minutes constitutes a strategic act. Seeing a visionary simulation of the present world turned to nothingness exposed the grave danger and futility of sacrificing the eternally worthy and rewarding Christian witness for fleeting worldly pleasures. It was a real shock therapy that opened the spiritual and physical eyes of the readers to the reality awaiting them at the eschaton.

Application of Evocations in Rev 8:1

The evocations generated by the strategic act in this scene must have evoked shame on those who valued and trusted the allures of this transient world more than the promise of eternal life in the new heaven and earth. The simulation is a heavily loaded strategic act that generates evocations to lead those who have ears to repentance. It also engenders patient endurance in those who may be undergoing tribulations.

Though these evocations were intended to meet the needs of the seven churches, they can be applied to saints in the entire church age who likewise may be experiencing lovelessness like the church in Ephesus, the threat of heresies like the church of Pergamum, idolatry and immorality like the church in Thyatira, spiritual deadness like the church in Sardis, and spiritual lukewarmness like the church in Laodicea. Evocations from this simulation can also urge the present-day church to resist the alluring pleasures of sin, which will, after all, be turned to nothingness, and to pursue the promise of eternal life in the glorious new heaven and new earth. The African church, whose faith has been described by her own scholar, John Mbiti, as one mile long and one inch deep, can be energized by a keen reading and application of the evocations in this visionary simulation.

Chapter 4

Divine Rapprochements to the Dwellers of the Earth (8:2—11:19)

PRELIMINARY OBSERVATION

THE EVENTS SIMULATED AFTER each of the first six trumpets are blown are strategic acts. They evoke joy and hope in the assurance of God's vindication. This in turn engenders patient endurance in tribulation. Visualizing the outworking of God's judgments as a result of human obduracy can fearfully deter the saints from apostatizing. Again, since the simulated judgments were bound to happen in the course of the unfolding history, the visionary simulations were sort of a prophetic message to the audience. They are intended to evoke fear that would engender restraint to sin, repentance, and patient endurance to those who would be facing great tribulations by the inhabitants of the earth (11:7–10) and the evil trinity (11:7–10; 12 and 13).

When the simulated judgments are finally executed, they would also be strategic actions that, in addition to avenging the persecuted saints, are intended to coerce the obdurate sinners and persecutors of the saints to repent. This observation suggests that, paradoxically, they would also be divine rapprochements. Furthermore, they would also urge the persecutors to free the saints from the demands to conform to emperor worship and Romish cultural norms. Thus, they are God's instruments by which he emancipates his people from the yoke of their oppressors. Observably, the judgments would only be selectively executed on the obdurate who do not hearken to the prophetic message that would be prophesied to many peoples, nations, languages, and kings (10:11) by those who would have been given and eaten the small scroll (10:9–10).

The simulated judgments are described with the imagery of the Egyptian judgments (Exod 9:22–25; 7:20–25; 10:22–23; 10:12–15). The Egyptian judgments were planned and executed in a way that hardened the heart of Pharaoh. Hardening the heart of Pharaoh served two purposes. One, it was to foil the power of God in the eyes of the Israelites when he finally delivered them from the hands of the hard-hearted pharaoh. Thus, it was aimed at enhancing their faith and trust in their God. Second, it was to eliminate a future risk to Israel by drowning Pharaoh's forces and their superior arms in the Red Sea. Unlike the judgments in Exodus, the judgments simulated when the first, second, third, and fourth angels blow their trumpets are not meant to harden the hearts of the sinners and persecutors of the saints. Instead, they are urgent strategic acts that scream "Let my people free to worship their Lord God and savior Jesus Christ without any hindrance and coercion to worship other gods." However, the divine rapprochements in the judgments that are simulated when the fifth and sixth angels blow their trumpets would be slighted by the victims (9:20). Slight of God's grace in prophetic rapprochements coupled with disciplinary judgments would arouse God's wrath, hastening the final white throne judgment.

REV 8:2–13

DIVINE RAPPROCHEMENTS IN DISCIPLINARY JUDGMENTS

²And I saw the seven angels who stand before God, and they were given seven trumpets. ³Another angel came and stood at the altar with a golden censer, and he was given much incense to offer with the prayers of the saints on the golden altar before the throne. ⁴The smoke of the incense with the prayers of the saints rose before God from the hand of the angel. ⁵Then the angel took the censer and filled it with fire and threw it on the earth, and there were pearls of thunder, rumblings, flashes of lightning, and an earthquake.

After the thirty-minute symbolic silence, the cast of characters who were to blow the warning trumpets before the simulation of the outworking of the next set of divine judgments (8:2—9:21) appeared on the visionary stage. The cast of the four wind-restraining angels was already set to simulate the judgments. The seven angels are identified as the angels who

DIVINE RAPPROCHEMENTS TO THE DWELLERS OF THE EARTH (8:2—11:19)

stand before God. To "stand before someone" is to serve as a servant or messenger. They were given seven trumpets, of course by God, before whom they stand. Robert H. Mounce suggests that "the trumpets in Revelation are eschatological trumpets. They herald the day of God's wrath."[1] However, echoes from Jer 4:5–6, and Ezek 33:1–6 show that blowing trumpets before an impending judgment is a warning call to the victims to repent in order to avert the intended judgment. Thus, blowing of the trumpets by the seven angels, is a warning call to the victims of God's judgments to repent. It demonstrates the abundance of the grace of God, who would not wish any to perish but that all should come to repentance (2 Pet 3:9). Besides these trumpet sounds being warnings against impending judgments and as such, rapprochements, the visionary simulations, and the simulated events are also divine rapprochements. Thus, the supposition that the trumpets are God-sanctioned warnings agrees with the overriding theme of this visionary revelation being divine rapprochements.

As has been observed, these visionary revelations are also a forthtelling and foretelling prophecy. As such, they aim to call their primary audience to repentance and to engender patient endurance. However, the simulated events will be divine rapprochements to humanity living in the historical era when the simulated events are outworked. This observation suggests that both the simulations and the simulated events are effectual throughout the unfolding history. Agreeably, Beale says that "these judgments are God's judgments against unbelievers throughout the church age culminating in the last judgment."[2]

Before the seven angels began their role-play, another angel with a golden censer came onto the visionary stage. He stood at the altar and was given much incense, with the prayers of the saints to offer on the golden altar before the throne. This altar is qualified as the golden altar. Its type in the earthly temple is the altar of incense. Offering prayers mixed with incense and showing smoke rising before God demonstrates that God had received the martyrs prayers' for vengeance (6:10). Afterward, the angel took the censer, filled it with fire and hurled it onto the earth. The angel's action of hurling altar fire onto the earth after the prayers of the saints are received by God suggests that, in addition to any other purpose, the judgments to be simulated by the four wind-restraining angels would be answers to the prayers of the martyrs for vengeance against their persecutors (6:9–10).

In Exod 19:16, pearls of thunder, rumblings, flashes of lightning, and an earthquake were a warning to the people not to force their way through

---

1. Mounce, *Revelation*, 173.
2. Beale and Campell, *Revelation*, 171.

the set barrier, lest they perish (Exod 19:21–22). Here, they may be portending the severity of the judgments just about to be meted on the dwellers of the earth. This observation suggests that in addition to being retributory and disciplinary judgments, the judgments simulated by the wind-restraining angels are also paradoxically divine rapprochements, as was the case in Nineveh (Jonah 3:10). Therefore, though the martyrs prayers for vengeance are heard and answered, God is still merciful enough and willing to forgive their persecutors if they repent.

Unlike the indiscriminate judgments that are meted out on the human race for Adam's breach of God's covenant (6:3–8), these are discriminatory. They are meted only on people who do not have the seal of God on their forehead. As will be evident when the judgments are simulated, they serve both a retributive and disciplinary purpose. Again, identifying these judgments as disciplinary and retributive suggests that their primary purpose is to point the victims to their sins and to urge compliance to God's dictates. However, if the victims obtusely slight the rapprochement, then the judgment acquires a retributive function to avenge the persecuted and martyred saints and to punish the obdurate.

The visionary simulations of these judgments were aimed at coercing the seven churches in Asia Minor to urgently repent of their lovelessness, dissuade them from conforming to the teachings of the Nicolaitans and Baalam, and repent of their idolatry, immorality, spiritual death, and lukewarmness. To the persecuted saints as were in Sardis and Philadelphia, the simulations were aimed at engendering comfort and hope in the assurance that God would eventually avenge them against their persecutors. As such, it engendered patient endurance in their present sufferings. The secondary readers are equally impacted by the evocations generated by the simulations in the visionary revelation. The rest of the world is impacted by the gospel proclamation by the likes of John who have eaten the small scroll (10:9–11) and, if they do not heed, they would be impacted by the simulated judgments as they are outworked in the course of history.

⁶Now, the seven angels who had the seven trumpets prepared to blow them. ⁷The first angel blew his trumpet, and there followed hail and fire mixed with blood, and these were thrown upon the earth. A third of the earth was burned up, a third of the trees were burned up, and all green grass was burned up.

Now that the Passover-sealing of the saints is complete, the four wind-restraining angels can simulate the envisioned judgment of harming the earth, land, sea, and trees (7:1). Actually, the ensuing judgments are better described as judgments by the four cosmic angels restraining the life-giving wind. The function of the seven angels blowing the trumpets was to warn the victims of the impending judgment, peradventure they repent and are forgiven.

Observably, in some ways, the form and purpose of the judgments simulated after blowing the first four trumpets are similar to the Egyptian judgments. The Egyptian judgments were outworked progressively in terms of severity. They were so framed to reveal Pharaoh's hardness of heart and to act as a foil of God's mighty hand after he finally delivers the Israelites (Exod 7:5). On the other hand, the trumpet judgments complement one another to enhance their evocative efficacy and to heighten the perception of God's distaste of sin. Again, similar to the Egyptian judgments, they would be outworked against a recalcitrant people, to avenge the saints, and to coerce the persecutors of the saints to set the saints free to worship God and the Lamb without any hindrance.

After the first angel blew his trumpet, hail and fire mixed with blood were thrown on the earth. A third of the earth, a third of the trees, and all green grass were burned up. Earth, trees, and green grass were part of the blessings of the cosmos in the Edenic economy. A destruction of the earth, trees, and grass is a reverse of these blessings and can be regarded as a curse. However, John was seeing a simulation of events that would happen in a historical period that had not been experienced. As such, trying to identify the definite corresponding future events that would constitute this judgment would just be a speculative and futile exercise. After all, other than satisfying human curiosity, it would not enhance the evocative efficacy of the visionary revelation.

However, seeing a simulation of this disciplinary and retributive judgment that would affect humanity, livestock, and agriculture in general would generate adequate evocations to engender audience response that would bridge the gaps identified in the reader's visionary situation. Destruction of only a third of the earth, trees, and grass highlights the discriminatory nature of the judgment. This discrimination suggests that these judgments would be disciplinary in function and that their purpose is to call the victims to repentance. Secondly, they would also be retributive to the persecutors of the saints who, notwithstanding the judgment being a rapprochement, would not respond in repentance (9:20–21).

The fiery bloody hail echoes the seventh judgment meted on Egypt to punish and compel Pharaoh to set Israel free (Exod 9:13–35). Similarly, in the present vision, hail, fire, and blood represent a judgment that would be meted on the persecutors of the saints to evoke fear of God and acknowledgment that there is no other god like YHWH and to coerce the persecutors of the saints to stop forcing them to worship other gods and to let them worship their only true God and Lord, Jesus Christ. It would also be intended to avenge the martyrs over their killers.

⁸*The second angel blew his trumpet, and something like a great mountain, burning with fire, was thrown into the sea, and a third of the sea became blood. ⁹A third of the creatures in the sea died, and a third of the ships were destroyed.*

Describing the object that was thrown into the sea as "something" shows that identifying its representative reality was not considered a significant endeavour. What was significant, though, was showing the magnitude and severity of the devastation simulated by this great and fiery object. Its huge size and fiery nature represents the severity of the judgment as well as God's great revulsion for sin. Again, simulating the destruction of only a third of marine life and ships shows the discriminative aspect of the simulated judgment. Its devastating effect is compared to the effect of the first judgment against Egypt in which the Nile water was turned into blood (Exod 7:14–25). Using imagery of the exodus judgment to mirror the judgment simulated in this scene has interpretive value. The similarity suggests that this judgment was intended to punish the obstinate persecutors and avenge the saints. It was also a strategic deed to urge the persecutors of the saints to let the saints to worship Jesus and him alone as their Lord. The simulation was intended to generate evocations that would engender change in the audiences' visionary situations.

¹⁰*The third angel blew his trumpet, and a great star fell from heaven blazing like a torch, and it fell on a third of the rivers and the springs of water. ¹¹The name of the star is wormwood. A third of the water became wormwood, and many people died from the water because it had been made bitter.*

The blazing star's name is wormwood (Hebrew, *laana*, a root word for curse). Wormwood is a bitter herb in the Mediterranean lands that pollutes and poisons water. Thus, verse 11 can also be translated as "The name of the star is curse. A third of the water became accursed, and many people died from the water because it had been poisoned." This star is used in this visionary revelation to simulate God's judgment. Similar portrayals in Jer 9:15; 23:15; Lam 3:15; 19 suggest that the judgment specifically targets sinners in both the world and church. It is simulated using imageries from the first Egyptian judgment (Exod 7:14–25). This similarity suggests that the judgment would be aimed at forcing the persecutors of the saints to free them from the demands of venerating the emperor as Lord and to allow them to worship Jesus as their only Lord. Auditioning that it is only a third of the fresh water sources that became accursed suggests that the judgment was discriminatory in nature and disciplinary in purpose. As such, both the simulation of the judgment and the actual judgment were divine rapprochements. The simulation was aimed at generating evocations that would engender actions to bridge the gaps in the audience's visionary situations. Similarly, the simulated judgments would also engender actions that can bridge the gaps in the historical situations of the victims and those who witness the impact of these judgments as and when they happen in the unfolding history.

12 The fourth angel blew his trumpet, and a third of the sun was struck, and a third of the moon, and a third of the stars, so that a third of their light might be darkened and a third of the day might be kept from shining and likewise a third of the night.

When the fourth trumpet was sounded, a third of the sun, moon, and stars were struck with the intent of darkening a third of the day and a third of the night. Once again, this judgment is likened to the ninth Egyptian judgment that was meted just before the Passover judgment. The sun, moon, and stars were created to provide light during the day and night (Gen 1:16–18). As such, these illuminating bodies were created as a blessing to the heaven and the earth. Dimming them is equivalent to pronouncing a curse over the inhabitants of the earth. Night and darkness, which would result when the illuminating bodies are dimmed, are viewed eerily. Night is viewed as a time when terror strikes (Ps 91:5) and also a time of weeping (Ps 30:5). Comparatively, the present sinful world is regarded as night while Jesus is seen as the light that lights the dark world (John 1:4–5). Again, the present life is compared to the night while the incoming kingdom is compared to day (Rom 13:11-13).

These Scriptures paint a very eerie picture of night and darkness. As such, this scene simulates a terrifying, tearful, and mournful judgment as a result of the sinfulness of the dwellers of the earth. It was a rapprochement intended to engender repentance. In his eschatological teachings, Jesus predicted that, "After the distress of those days, the sun will be darkened, and the moon will not give its light; and the stars will fall from the sky, and the heavenly bodies will be shaken" (Matt 24:29). This observation may also suggest that this judgment will happen towards the tail end of human history.

¹³ *Then I looked, and I heard a vulture crying in a loud voice as it flew directly overhead. "Woe, woe, woe, to those who dwell on the earth at the blasts of the other trumpets that the three angels are about to blow.*

A new visionary character, a vulture, auditions the nature of the events to be simulated after each of the remaining angels sounds his trumpet. A vulture patiently stalks a fatally hurt or terminally sick animal to feed on its carrion once it dies. This harbinger of death is a perfect symbolic character to announce the impending woe-simulating scenes. These woes will be outworked against those who dwell on the earth—unbelievers and persecutors of the saints (6:10; 11:10; 14:6).

Strategic and Communicative Acts in Rev 8:2–13

The simulation of prayers of the saints ascending before God, symbolized as incense, is embedded with a strategic act that generates evocations of great trust in this prayer—answering God. Consequently, it could evoke desire and revival for prayer among John's audience.

Showing hail, fire, and blood raining on the earth is a strategic act that amplifies the severity of God's judgment. This vision simulated events that were to happen as history progressed. As such, both the visionary simulation and the simulated event would impact the saints. John and his audience could not imagine themselves engulfed in such a dreadful fire. It was an apt strategic act that must have evoked great fear among John's audience. It must have urged the church in Ephesus to revert to her first love, evoked repentance in Pergamum and Thyatira, and revived the dying Sardis and lukewarm Laodicea.

Showing the devastating judgment simulated by the mountain-like instrument that was thrown into the sea was also a strategic act. This scene convinced the audience that no place could offer a safe haven against God's judgments. It also demonstrated God's grim view of sin, leading the hearers of the narrated vision of the visionary revelation to repentance.

Showing the vision of a symbolic star that fell on a third of the water sources and turning them to wormwood was a strategic act. Seeing a simulation of the death of a third of humanity evoked abhorrence of sin, leading the wayward in the seven churches to repentance.

The vision showing a third of the sun, moon, and stars being dimmed was a very evocative strategic act. Seeing day turned to darkness and knowing that night and darkness portended tears and mourning must have caused a lot of fear. This fear was intended to urge the erring churches to repent of their sins. Like the message of Paul to the Romans (Rom 13:12–14) that urges the readers to put aside the deeds of darkness and to put on the armor of light, this darkness warned the saints about the dangers posed by dalliance with sin. It also awoke the Christian hope in those who were versed with the words of Jesus concerning the events that will precede his second coming.

Application of Evocations in Rev 8

The strategic acts embedded in showing the prayers of the saints being offered, accepted, and answered by God in avenging the saints must have evoked great trust in this prayer answering God. Readers down the centuries should be encouraged to watch and pray all the more in the assurance that God hears and answers their prayers. This simulation can and should kindle prayers in our churches. It should also engender patient endurance in tribulations in the assurance that God will finally avenge the saints against their tormentors.

Christianity is acknowledged as the true faith in many parts of the world. However, vices like racism, tribalism, and corruption are still rife. The events simulated in this visionary revelation reveal that disciplinary judgments are meted throughout the unfolding history. This insight should awaken the world and the erring saints against wantonness in handling their personal, civic, and religious lives.

The strategic act embedded in simulating the outworking of God's consequential decrees on sinners and persecutors of the saints throughout the unfolding history should evoke abhorrence of sin and pursuit of holiness. It would also urge those entrapped in sin to repent. However, Christians should draw comfort in the assurance that God will pass over them as he executes these judgments.

REV 9

RAPPROCHEMENTS IN JUDGMENTS TO THE OBDURATE

¹And the fifth angel blew his trumpet, and I saw a star that had fallen on the earth from heaven. He was given the keys to the abyss. ²He opened the mouth of the abyss, and smoke gushed out of the abyss as from a great furnace. The sun and the air were darkened by the smoke from the pit. ³Out of the smoke came locusts into the earth, and they were given power similar to scorpions of the earth. ⁴And they were told not to harm the grass nor any green matter nor tree but humans not having the seal of God on their foreheads. ⁵And they were not granted to kill but to torment them for five months. Their torment was like that of a scorpion when it stings a man. ⁶In those days, people seek death but do not find it, and they long to die, but death eludes them. ⁷The appearance of the locusts was like horses prepared for battle. They had golden-like crowns on their heads, and their faces were as of men. ⁸They had hair as of women and teeth as of lions. ⁹They had a breastplate of iron, and the sound of their wings was as of chariots of many horses rushing into battle. ¹⁰They had tails with stingers like scorpions, and with them was the power to injure people for five months. ¹¹Their king was the angel of the abyss whose name is Abaddon in Hebrew and Apollyon in Greek.

After the fifth angel sounded his trumpet, John saw a star that had earlier fallen from heaven to earth and remained fallen, as shown by the Greek verb πεπτωκότα (*peptōkota*), perfect participle of πίπτω, *piptō*, to fall. This star appears to be the same one called Wormwood that was seen falling from heaven (8:10). The destructive and sin-orchestrating activity of this symbolic star suggests that it could be role-playing Satan, who is once more shown falling from heaven (12:8-9). This suggestion is reinforced by the use of the pronoun "he" in the Greek verb ἤνοιξεν, *ēnoixen*, (he opened). John saw this star being given the keys[3] to the abyss—the proverbial dungeon where Satan, demons, and all manner of evil are symbolically imprisoned (20:1-3). Being given keys to the abyss, the opposite of being locked in the abyss, suggests that, most probably, this act was simulating the act of releasing Satan from the abyss after the symbolic one-thousand-year incarceration (20:1-3). To be given the key stands for being allowed to once again deceive the nations. The passive voice in the Greek verb ἐδόθη, *edothē*, and in English, "given," shows that during this time, Satan will not be restricted from deceiving humanity to sin against God. Like Balaam who taught the Israelites to sin against God in order to attract his wrath (Num 31:16), so will Satan try to deceive men to apostatize and harden their hearts towards God and the gospel in order to arouse his anger. The resulting obduracy will attract the white-throne judgment (20:10-15).

After the star opened the abyss, smoke gushed out of its mouth, darkening the sun and the air. The symbolism of smoke that darkens the sun and air represents sin—a pollutant of the world. In John's other texts, he describes sin as darkness (John 1:5; 1 John 2:9-11). Out of the darkening smoke (sins) came locusts (judgments) on earth. Some have interpreted this

---

3. See commentary on Rev 1:18.

scene to have simulated Satan being used by God as an agent of judgment.[4] However, judgment (symbolized by locusts) resulted from sin (symbolized by smoke from the abyss); it is not directly engendered by Satan, who is symbolized by the fallen star. The star induced sin whose consequence is the judgment of God (Rom 6:23). The use of locusts as a symbol representing judgment may have been borrowed from Exod 10:15 and Joel 1-2. John auditions that the locusts-judgments were given power like that of scorpions of the earth (9:3). This audition demonstrates that obduracy and rebellion against God attracts very severe and painful judgment.

The locusts were told not to harm the grass, plants, or trees but only those people who did not have the seal of God on their foreheads. They were further not allowed to kill but to painfully afflict the victims for five months. This command suggests that the judgments were essentially discriminatory. The description also suggests that they were a kind of purposeful disciplinary torture. It also suggests that they were retributive judgments to avenge the martyrs. Paradoxically, they were a last chance rapprochement to those who did not have the seal of God on their foreheads. The limited period of five months appears to have been used synonymously for the "little while" when Satan will be set loose to instigate obduracy and rebellion against God (20:3b, 7-9).

John auditions that in those days, people will seek death but will not find it; they will long to die but death will elude them. In addition to showing that this judgment is a kind of torture, this expression highlights the severity of the pain during the duration of the judgment. Use of the demonstrative adjective "those" in the phrase "those days" and modal auxiliary verb, "will," in the phrase "men will seek" (9:6), suggests that the simulated woe was situated in the future of John's time. This suggestion reinforces the supposition that this woe would happen at the tail end of history.

The symbolism depicting these end time woes in form of locusts looking like cavalry horses is borrowed from Joel 2:4. It demonstrates swiftness and severity of this woe. The symbolism of golden crowns (Greek: στέφανος, *stephanos*) upon their heads symbolizes their indomitable nature. In addition, the locusts' human-like faces and women's hair may symbolize the human factor in execution of the woe (11:13; 16:12-17; 19:11-19; 20:7-8). Depiction of their teeth as those of a lion is a parallelism that demonstrates the severity of the judgment. The breastplates of iron, a symbol of impenetrability, show how hard it will be for the victims to escape the woe. Description of the rattling of the locusts' wings as like chariots of war demonstrates the fast, furious, and wide spread of this end-time woe. Finally,

---

4. Beale and Campbell, *Revelation*, 188.

the symbolism in the locusts' tails resembling scorpions' tails demonstrates the intensity of the pain inflicted by this woe. In identifying that the king of the locusts was the king of the abyss, John infers that the star that had fallen was role-playing Satan. His dominion is exercised through enticing humanity to sin, thereby attracting God's severe judgments. Saying that the king of the abyss was known in Hebrew as *Abaddon* (destruction) and in Greek as Ἀπολλύων, *Apollyon* (destroyer), further affirms that the star that had fallen was role-playing Satan who, according to John 10:11, "came to kill, steal, and destroy." This chilling description enhanced the efficacy of the embedded strategic act.

The readers were not expected to decode the referents of every symbol. The visionary simulations were essentially strategic acts that were intended to evoke fear that would engender repentance by the sinner, and patient endurance in the saints. They were also meant to stir the saints to greater faith and evangelism, peradventure some of the sinners would be saved.

[12] The first woe has passed; behold, two more woes are coming after this. [13] And the sixth angel blew his trumpet, and I heard a voice from one of the four horns of the golden altar before God [14] saying to the sixth angel having the trumpet, "Release the four angels bound at the great river Euphrates. [15] And the four angels who were prepared for the hour and day and month and year were released so that they might kill a third of humanity. [16] And the number of the armies of the cavalry was two hundred million (200,000,000). I heard their number [17] and saw in vision the horses and their riders having breastplates that were fiery red, dark blue, and yellow as sulfur. The heads of the horses were like lions' heads, and out of their mouths proceed fire and smoke and brimstone. [18] By these three plagues of fire, smoke, and brimstone proceeding out of their mouths, a third of humanity was killed. [19] The power of the horses was in their mouths and tails, for their tails are like serpents having heads with which they injure. [20] And the rest of humanity who were not killed by these plagues did not repent of the works of their hands nor stop worshipping demons and idols made of gold, silver, bronze, stone, and wood which cannot see, hear or walk. [21] And they did not repent of their murders, sorceries, sexual immorality, and thefts.

After the sixth angel blew his trumpet, John heard a voice from one of the four horns of the golden altar before God. This is the altar where worship and petitions are offered. Depicting the voice emanating from one of the horns of the altar, under which the praying souls of the martyrs were last seen, suggests that in addition to the simulated woe being visited on the obdurate sinners, it may also be an answer to the saints' plea for vengeance (6:10). Depicting inanimate horns of the altar speaking, such as had happened when a donkey spoke to Baalam (Num 22:28–30), demonstrates the sinners' stubbornness to God's relentless rapprochements.

The voice from the horn of the altar ordered the angel who had blown the sixth warning trumpet to release the four killer angels bound at the great river Euphrates. The order to release the four killer angels after the warning trumpet had been sounded suggests that the victims had slighted the warning and judgment had to be executed. The symbolism of four angels held at the river Euphrates derives its imagery from the extant belief that every locality was under an angelic prince (Dan 10:13). Daniel 10:12–14 suggests that the angel who was bringing an answer to Daniel's prayer for their emancipation was held up by an opposing demonic prince of Persia for twenty-one days until Michael, the chief prince, came to help the restrained angel. Informed by Daniel's vision, the four angels in Revelation can be construed to be God's messengers who were bringing judgment in answer to the pleas of the martyrs mentioned in 6:9 but were held up just as the angel in Daniel's time was restrained when delivering the answers to his prayer. However, because the hour, day, month, and year of the martyr's vindication, which was predetermined through God's immutable decrees, had now come, their release could not be delayed any longer (6:11).

John auditions that the four angels were released to kill a third of humanity using a two-hundred-million-member, plague-inflicting army. The horse riders were girded with breastplates that were fiery red, dark blue, and yellow as sulfur. The colors of these breastplates represent the hottest form of flame of fire. Therefore, these fiery breastplates demonstrate the severity, invincibility, and unavoidability of God's vengeance against sinners and persecutors of his saints who, notwithstanding his grace rapprochements, slighted it.

Depicting the army as an enormously large number of soldiers with fiery armor demonstrates the vast reach of the simulated woe. The description of their cavalry horses as having heads like lion heads with fire, smoke and brimstone gushing out of their mouths, and their equally lethal serpent-like tails demonstrates how vicious and deadly the woe would be. This woe is a last resort rapprochement that, if not responded to, would attract God's retributive final judgment. It is intended to urge people to repent of their murders, sorceries, fornication, and thefts. Sadly, John notes that the victims did not repent of their worship of devils, gold, silver, brass, stone, and wood idols. Idolatry is an affront against God that attracts his wrath. This hardening of heart may be the work of Satan, who is shown as having been released from the abyss after the thousand-year incarceration (20:7–8).

Strategic and Communicative Acts in Rev 9

The horrifying symbolism in the scenes simulated after the fifth and sixth angels blew their trumpets cannot be adequately matched to anything that was and is currently known. They are embedded with strategic acts that evoke fear of ever being victims of the simulated woes. It was meant to jolt the seven churches to work towards eliminating any gap in their visionary situations.

The expectation of repentance by the victims of these two woes reveals the manifold grace of God. They also show that God uses all manner of ways to awake humanity to their need for repentance. The audition that the victims of these woes did not repent is a communicative act that is meant to justify God for meting these and further judgments.

Application of Evocations in Rev 9

The simulated woes further buttress the supposition that though the woes poured on the world before the final judgment have an element of retributive justice, they are majorly divine rapprochements that are intended to call sinners to repentance. Their simulation evoked fear in the saints of ever slighting God's rapprochements.

The horrifying symbolism and severity of the woes simulated in this scene would similarly generate evocations of fear in the secondary audience. The gap between the present day's historical situation, governed by unrestrained human rights, plurality, and unbridled sensuality and the historical situation demanded of the faithful by the word of God can be abridged by repentance that is ably engendered by the evocations generated in this visionary scene.

God's great mercy that is shown to the very obdurate should call the saints to exercise the same mercy in forgiveness and works of love. God's justice should also call us to exercise justice in dealing with fellow human beings. The world is reeling with problems of low remuneration in workplaces, economic exploitation of the weak nations by the militarily mighty and economically rich, gender discrimination, and many other types of human rights abuses. The communicative act revealing God's justice should evoke a desire, especially to those wielding authority and power to exercise mercy and justice to the subjugated peoples.

REV 10:1—11:19

RAPPROCHEMENTS IN CHRISTIAN WITNESS

Preliminary Observation

The following two chapters narrate simulations of divine rapprochements in Christian witness. It is led by the church which is guaranteed success, though it thrives in a very hostile world—outer court. John, who has all along been a passive seer and amanuensis to all that he sees and hears, is incorporated not only as part of the cast but a prophet to prophesy to many peoples, nations, languages, and kings (10:8-11). After incorporation as both a cast and prophet, he simulates the assured success of the church throughout the unfolding history—forty-two months—in the symbolic measurement of the temple (11:1-2). The placement of the simulation of the centrifugal and centripetal missions of the church amidst rapprochements in disciplinary judgments suggests that God designed both to complement each other in calling a recalcitrant and obdurate world to obedience in faith.

REV 10

COMMISSIONING OF JOHN TO PROPHESY TO MANY PEOPLES

¹*And I saw another mighty angel descending out of heaven clothed with a cloud, and a rainbow on his head and his face was like the sun, his feet like pillars of fire,* ²*and he held a little open scroll in his hand. And he placed his right foot on the sea and the left on the earth* ³*and he cried out in a loud voice like the roar of a lion. When he cried out, the voice of the seven thunders spoke.* ⁴*And when the seven thunders spoke, I was about to write, but I heard a voice out of heaven saying, "Seal what the seven thunders have said and do not write it."* ⁵*And the angel whom I saw standing upon the sea and the earth lifted up his hand to heaven* ⁶*and swore by the one who lives forever, who created heaven and earth and the things in it and the sea and the things in it. "There will be no more delay."* ⁷*But in the days of the voice of the seventh angel when he is about to blow the trumpet, the mystery of God as he himself proclaimed by his servants the prophets will be fulfilled."* ⁸*Then the voice that I had heard from heaven spoke to me again, saying, "Go take the little open scroll in the hand of the angel standing on the sea and the earth."* ⁹*So I went to the angel, saying to him, "Give me the scroll." And he said to me, "Take and eat it, and it will make your stomach bitter, but it will be as sweet as honey in*

your mouth." ¹⁰And I took the little scroll out of the hand of the angel and ate it, and it was as sweet as honey in my mouth, but when I had eaten it, it was bitter in my stomach. ¹¹And he told me, "You must prophesy again concerning many peoples, nations, tongues, and kings"

A new character appears out of heaven. John identifies him as a mighty angel. Beale and Campbell identify him as either Yahweh or Christ.[5] The observations that he swore by him who lives forever, who created the heavens and all that is in them, the earth and all that is in it, and the sea and all that is in it (vv. 6) eliminates the suggestion that he was role-playing God the Father. The adjective "mighty" highlights the exalted persona of the person the angel role-plays. His costume of a heavenly cloud, a rainbow halo over his head, a face shining like the sun, and feet like pillars of fire identify him with the son of man in Dan 7:13–14 and the Christ in 1:16. He also resembles the soon-coming Christ described in Acts 1:9–11. These observations suggest that this mighty angel was role-playing Jesus. Use of the number seven to describe the mighty angel's dialogue partner suggests that the one represented by the seven thunders, in synecdoche of voice standing for the speaker, is Yahweh.

Describing the scroll in the mighty angel's hand as little contrasts it with the scroll shown earlier in the right hand of God (5:1). While the former was a repository of God's decrees that would be outworked in the unfolding history, the latter contained aspects of the manifold outworking of God's decrees that were to be incorporated in the gospel message that John and by extension the church was to prophesy to many peoples, nations, tongues, and kings (10:11 and 11:1–7).

Standing on both the sea and the land, the domain of the dragon, beast from the sea, and the beast from the land (12:1, 11), shows that the intended audience of the gospel that John was to be commissioned to prophesy are the dwellers of the domain of the evil trinity of the dragon and the two beasts. It also demonstrates the intended global reach of the prophecy (Matt 28:19-20). Likening the angel's voice to the roar of a lion identifies him with the lion of the tribe of Judah (vv. 3). The phrase "when he cried out" coming before the phrase "John heard the seven thunders speak" suggests that the voice of the seven thunders was answering to the voice of the mighty angel. The description of the thunders as seven emphasizes the completeness, finality, gravity, and supreme source and value of their message. It appears that the seven thunders were not foreign to John as they are to us, as evidenced by his use of the definite article "the." Most probably, the seven thunders stood in synechdoche of voice for the one who spoke the message.

---

5. Beale and Campbell, *Revelation*, 201.

Alternatively, since thunder is associated with God, then the seven thunders may be standing in metonymy to the almighty God (1 Sam 2:10; Job 37:4–13; Ps 18:13; Isa 29:6).

John was about to write down what the seven thunders had said but heard a voice from heaven say, "Seal up what the seven thunders have said and do not write it down." James B. Ramsey observes that John was told not to write matters not to be revealed at all to the church on earth.[6] Robert H. Mounce opines that "it is more plausible that the seven thunders, like the seal and trumpets, formed another series of warning plagues. The adamant decision of the human race not to repent (9:20–21) would render another series useless . . . so it was too late to record any further warnings."[7] Though these great scholars are entitled to their opinions, an interrogation of the discourse between the three speakers—the mighty angel, the seven thunders, and an obscure prohibitor to the writing of the words spoken by the seven thunders—shows that the seven thunders were answering to the voice of the mighty angel. Notable too is that the obscure prohibitor is presented as oblivious of the imminency of the day of the Lord and thus the urgency to proclaim the message in the small scroll to humankind. This supposition suggests that the obscure character may have been one of the characters who wait on God—one of the four living creatures—who did not know the day or hour when the son of man would come (Mark 13:32). However, Jesus knew the day and hour from the scroll that he had received from the one seated on the throne. This supposition explains his urgency of handing over the small scroll to John to prophesy its contents.

The obscurity of the person prohibiting John from writing what the seven thunders had said is suggested by the lack of a definite article before the word "voice" φωνη (*phone*). The voice stands in synecdoche of voice for the person who spoke it. Moreover, if to unseal is to reveal, then to seal is to conceal. Sealing a prophecy or vision after it has been shown to a prophet is usually ordered if it is for private consumption (2 Cor 12:1–4) or if its fulfilment is due after a very long period (Dan 12:4). But according to 1:3, the time for the fulfilment of the prophecy simulated in Revelation is imminent. Furthermore, it is not stated that John needed to be exclusively given the message of the seven thunders for his private use. Therefore, the prohibition not to write what the seven thunders had said is inconsistent with similar episodes in the rest of the Christian Scripture. It must have been spoken loosely for another purpose, other than to be bluntly obeyed.

---

6. Ramsey. *Revelation*, 426.
7. Mounce, *Revelation*, 204.

Most probably, the prohibition is part of a visionary foil that served to raise the ethos of the person being role-played by the mighty angel once he countermands the prohibition. The countermand would also highlight the gravity and urgency of the message spoken by the seven thunders. Since the command "do not write but seal what the seven thunders have said" was synonymous with being told that the event that had been auditioned would be delayed (Dan 12:4), then the mighty angel's countermand meant that there will be no more delay (10:6), which means that the message should not be sealed. Use of the word "will" shows the irrevocable nature of the mighty angel's countermand. The obscure heavenly speaker, who had initially stopped John from writing and therefore, revealing the message of the seven thunders, gave in to the countermand of the great angel and told John to take the small scroll from the hand of the mighty angel.

The use of the conjunction "but" in the mighty angel's countermand explaining what instead should happen, shows that the seven thunders had spoken something concerning the imminent fulfilment of the mystery that was to be simulated when the seventh angel blows his trumpet. The visionary scene ushered by the blowing of the seventh trumpet announced the takeover of the kingdom of the world by God and his Messiah (11:15–19). It will later be simulated in the vision showing the passing away of the extant world and the incoming of the new heaven and earth (21:1–4).

The Greek conjunction *kai* that starts verse 8 should be translated as "then" to show continuation. As such, John's use of the word "then," which points the audience to the event that occasioned his being allowed to take the scroll, shows that the message that he had been told to seal was the one written in the small scroll (10:8). John and his audience were familiar with prophets being commanded to eat scrolls (Jer 15:16; Ezek 2:8–3:3). Eating the scroll was a visionary simulation demonstrating receipt of a divine prophetic message. Describing the scroll as sweet in the mouth demonstrates the prophet's ease at receiving God's prophetic word, while describing it as bitter in the stomach demonstrates the risky but inevitable compulsion to prophesy it. Prophesying God's message sometimes resulted in the rejection, persecution, and at times martyrdom of the prophets. The gospel message is not meant to be retained in the knowledge of the prophet; it should be vomited out. In other words, against all odds, it should be prophesied to the intended audience. After eating the small scroll, John was commissioned by the mighty angel to prophesy to many peoples, nations, languages, and kings. In the gospel by his name, John describes the gospel as flowing out of the bellies of those who believe (John 7:38).

All along, John has been a spectator, a keen observer, listener, and scribe of what he had seen and heard. But from this point in the visionary revelation, he is incorporated as part of the cast. He is also commissioned to proclaim the things written in the little scroll. The next visionary revelation will simulate how the prophecy will be proclaimed—through the centrifugal and centripetal mission of the church.

Strategic and Communicative Acts in Rev 10

The voice of the seven thunders, the prohibition not to write their message, and the mighty angel's countermand of the prohibition constitute a foil. It enhanced the persona of Jesus Christ who is role-played by the mighty angel. He is portrayed as the heir of God's decrees and divine plans. The foil also increased the gravity and belief value of the message of the imminent end of the world and establishment of the kingdom of God (11:15).

The act of giving John the scroll and telling him to eat it is a strategic act. It was followed by an audition that the scroll was sweet in the mouth and bitter in the stomach. It draws its evocative efficacy from the audience's knowledge of similar occurrences in the Hebrew Bible (Jer 15:16; Ezek 2:9–10). It was intended to encourage John and the preachers who would come after him, in the risky but inevitable task of preaching the gospel. It also prepared John's audience to interpret the succeeding visionary simulation (chapter 11).

Application of Evocations in Rev 10

The visionary revelation was explicitly aimed at urging John to proclaim the things he had seen and heard. In addition, the act of handing over the small scroll to John and ordering him to prophesy its message to many nations, peoples, and tongues was also aimed at urging John's audience to adopt the commission.

The twenty-first-century world is driven by the quest for economic success. Moral, ethical, and religious values have been sidelined as the world pursues the god of money, power, and hedonism. More than ever before, the present world needs an energized church that would rebuke its waywardness and point it to Jesus. It should also be redirected from its trust in economic, military, and technological might to trust in the living God and his saving grace. The symbolic handover of the scroll urges the church of all time to zealously preach about the imminent end of the present world and the establishment of the everlasting kingdom of God.

REV 11

CHURCH'S MINISTRY IN THE WORLD AND ATTENDANT TRIBULATIONS

¹Then I was given a measuring rod like a staff and was told, "Rise and measure the temple of God, the altar, and those who worship there, ²but do not measure the court outside the temple; leave that out, for it is given over to the nations. They will trample the holy city for forty-two months.

John has now been incorporated as one of the cast, simulating how the message of the little scroll is to be prophesied to many peoples, nations, tongues, and kings. He is given a measuring rod and told to go and measure the temple of God, the altar, and those who worship in it. The imagery is borrowed from similar symbolisms in Ezek 40–44 and Zech 1:16–17; 2:1–2. Ezekiel, an exilic prophet, saw visions of a man measuring the walls of Jerusalem and the temple fourteen years after they were destroyed by the Babylonian army in 586 BCE. His vision portended God's aided restoration of Jerusalem and the temple after Judah's seventy-year exile.

In a similar vision, Zechariah was also shown a vision of the reconstruction of the city and temple to assure the returnees from exile that its construction, which had stalled, would be completed notwithstanding serious opposition (Zech 1:16–18; 2:1–2). This reading agrees with Andrea Spatafora's opinion that "measuring often has a symbolic sense—a meaning other than the obvious one of determining the measurements of an object, possibly to serve as a blueprint for construction. It can signify that something is marked out as someone's possession or that it is destined for destruction."[8] In this visionary revelation, these Old Testament visions are reused to assure John and the seven churches that the work of building the church through prophesying before many nations, tongues and kings had God's backing and would therefore be certainly accomplished (chapters 10 and 11).

The command "Do not measure the court outside the temple but leave it out, for it is given over to the nations, and that they will trample the holy city for forty-two months" explains the church's sojourn throughout the unfolding history. She subsists amid an obdurate people (herein envisioned as the outer court).[9] However, through many tribulations (Acts 14:22), she will overcome and be ushered into a life of bliss in the new heaven and earth.

---

8. Spatafora, *From the Temple of God*, 163–64.
9. Charles, *Revelation*, 274.

The description of this sojourn draws its imagery from the prophetic words of Jesus in Luke 21:24: "Jerusalem will be trampled on by the Gentiles until the times of the Gentiles are fulfilled." To date, the Dome of the Rock, a Muslim mosque, stands on the ground where the Jewish temple stood before 70 CE. Thus, forty-two months is a litotic expression of the unfolding history from the time of John to the establishment of the kingdom of God in the new heaven and earth. It is compared to the time of Elijah's outlawed life whereby he was divinely sustained (1 Kgs 11; Luke 4:25; Jas 5:17).

> ³*And I will grant authority to my two witnesses, and they will prophesy for 1260 days clothed in sackcloth.* ⁴*These are the two olive trees and the two lampstands that stand before the Lord of the earth.* ⁵*And if anyone would desire to harm them, fire proceeds from their mouths and consumes their enemies, and if anyone would desire to harm them, this is how he is doomed to be killed.* ⁶*They have the power to shut the sky, so that no rain may fall during the days of their prophesying. And they have power over the waters to turn them into blood and to strike the earth with every kind of plague as often as they desire.* ⁷*And when they have finished their testimony, the beast that rises from the bottomless pit will make war on them and kill them* ⁸*and their dead bodies will lie in the street of the great city that figuratively is called Sodom and Egypt, where their Lord was crucified.* ⁹*For three and a half days, some from the peoples, tribes, languages, and nations will gaze at their dead bodies and refuse to let them be placed in a tomb,* ¹⁰*and those who dwell on the earth will rejoice over them and make merry and exchange presents because these two prophets had been a torment to those who dwell on the earth.*

John and the church's prophetic work is simulated by a cast of two witnesses (vv. 3). In Jewish culture a matter was authenticated by two witnesses (Deut 19:15; John 8:7). Mounce opines that the two witnesses "are not two individuals but a symbol of the witnessing church in the last tumultuous days before the end of the age."[10] This commentary agrees with Mounce's opinion to the extent that the two witnesses are a visionary cast simulating the witness of the church. However, it differs in his opinion that the witness will happen in the tumultuous days before the end of age. John's—and by extension the church's—preaching ministry was to commence immediately and run for the entire church age.

In this scene, the two witnesses are depicted in the symbol of two olive trees and two lampstands (vv. 4). This symbolism stands for a Holy Spirit-enabled church that was to preach to the world in the unfolding history which here is depicted litotically as 1,260 days. John Sweet rightly avers that

---

10. Mounce, *Revelation*, 217.

the 1,260 days, approximately three and a half years, in Daniel represents a limited time of tyranny and suffering for the faithful in Israel before vindication.[11] The comparison between this time of tyranny and eventual vindication and the church's sojourn throughout the unfolding history is a litotic presentation of time to assure the church that just as happened to Israel, her vindication is imminent.

This visionary symbolism is borrowed from Zechariah's vision, in which he saw a similar vision (Zech 4:2–7). Two olive trees were supplying oil to a lampstand. An angel told Zachariah that the symbolic lampstand and the two olive trees were a semiotic word of the LORD to Zerubbabel. It signified that the work of building the temple would "not be accomplished by Zerubbabel's might, nor by his power, but by the Spirit of God" (Zech 4:6). It assured Zerubbabel that though the work had stalled because of serious opposition, it would be fully accomplished by the help of God. Using similar symbolism, John's visionary revelation assured him and the church—the lampstands (1:20)—that their mission will certainly be accomplished by the enablement of the Holy Spirit.

John's and the church's mission to the world is simulated by a cast of two witnesses clothed with sackcloth. Wearing sackcloth is a gesture signifying obeisance and contrition of body, spirit, and soul before God. The two witnesses were to preach for a period of three and half years; again, the entire unfolding history expressed in litotes. The symbolic one thousand two hundred and sixty days or three and half years seems to have been borrowed from the "a time, times and a half a time" of Dan 12:7, which signified the unfolding history.

The audition in verse 5 shows that the church is ordained to preach and judge the world with the agency of the word of her testimony (12:11). The audition in verse 6 shows that the church is expected to have the power and Spirit similar to Elijah, who in his heyday shut heaven as a form of judgment against sinful Israel and her king for three and a half years (1 Kgs 17:1; Jas 5:17–18). She is also expected to have the spirit and power of Moses, who turned water into blood as a judgment miracle against Pharaoh to compel him to let Israel go (Exod 7:17–25).

John's audition in verses. 7–9 shows that nothing can halt the advance of the gospel. Two scenarios can be deduced in this scene: the individual's and the church's witness. After a successful witness, albeit through many tribulations, the individual dies either naturally or through martyrdom. Their bodies are shown lying in the streets of the great city that is symbolically known as Sodom and Egypt, where their Lord was crucified. Sodom

---

11. Sweet, *Revelation*, 8.

represents debauchery, Egypt represents bondage and Jerusalem represents martyrdom of God's prophets. This symbolic city could be a representation of the world where the church is vexed by debauchery similar to that of Sodom, experiences spiritual and physical bondage just as Israel experienced in Egypt, and her saints are martyred just as God's prophets were martyred in Jerusalem (Matt 23:37; Luke 13:34).

The scene showing the witnesses' unburied bodies lying on the streets for three and a half days demonstrates that their shameful death would surely be vindicated by their resurrection. It also simulates their intermediate state that is litotically expressed as three days. However, to the unbelievers, represented by the cast of people from all nations, tongues, and languages who gaze scornfully at the bodies of the dead witnesses, their shameful unburied state proved their long-held view of the futility of faith. According to Peter, they mockingly ask, "Where is the promise of his coming? For ever since the fathers fell asleep, all things are continuing as they were from the beginning of creation" (2 Pet 3:4).

The second scenario depicts the corporate church's witnesses during the unfolding history. In this scenario, the two witnesses are a visionary cast role-playing the witness of the church throughout the unfolding history. The death of the two witnesses shows an end-time apostasy that is expected to happen throughout the whole world (2 Thess 2:3–12). This end-time apostasy is also simulated as the battle of Armageddon (16:12–16). It is again simulated in the scene showing Satan being set loose from the bottomless pit (9:1–21; 20:3, 7–9) who would then deceive the whole world (Gog and Magog) to fight against God's people, the city he loves (20:9). Using the words of Poythress, the three and half days are a period of such intense persecution that the witness of the church seems to be completely snuffed out.[12] Jesus spoke about it, saying, "If those days had not been cut short, no one would survive, but for the sake of the elect those days will be shortened" (Matt 24:22).

¹¹But after three and a half days, the breath of life from God entered them, and they stood up on their feet, and great fear fell on those who saw them. ¹²Then they heard a great voice from heaven saying to them, "Come up here!" And they went up to heaven in a cloud, as their enemies watched them.

After the litotic three and half days of great obduracy and apostasy of the saints, which will be evoked by tribulations by the loosed Satan and his earthly cahoots, the breath of life from God entered the dead witnesses. They stood on their feet and terror struck those who saw them dead (vv. 11).

---

12. Poythress, *Returning King*, 130.

Their resurrection can be construed as God's intervention to end the Satan-instigated tribulation that would foment obduracy and was also likely to engender apostasy (20:9b–10). This visionary simulation agrees with Jesus' eschatological discourse in Matt 24:22—"For the sake of the elect those days will be shortened."

After the symbolic two witnesses are resurrected, they heard a voice from heaven calling, "Come up here." And they went up to heaven in a cloud, while their enemies looked on (vv. 12). This episode is similar to the one narrated in 1 Thess 4:14–17. These parallel texts suggest that after the end-time apostasy is brought to an end, the events that will bring about the passing away of the extant heaven and earth will commence. The dead saints will be resurrected while the living saints are changed, and the two, in similar new bodies, will be translated to the new heaven and earth (1 Cor 15:52–53). The resurrection of the dead is described with the words "The sea gave up the dead that were in it, and death and Hades gave up the dead that were in them" (20:13). The saints will be called up to heaven while the sinners face the final white-throne judgment (20:13–16).

[13] And at that hour, there was a great earthquake, and a tenth of the city fell. Seven thousand people were killed in the earthquake, and the rest were terrified and gave glory to the God of heaven. [14] The second woe has passed: behold, the third woe is soon to come.

"At that hour" points to the time the dead witnesses are called to heaven. Simultaneous to the resurrection and translation to the new heaven and earth, a new visionary scene simulated a great earthquake whereby a tenth of the city fell and seven thousand people died. The felled city seems to be Jerusalem, whose people killed their prophets, Jesus and the Apostles of the Lord (11:8). Here it symbolically stands in synecdoche of part for for the whole world. The earthquake signalled the passing away of the extant heaven and earth. Just as after the earthquake that followed the death of Jesus Christ, whereby the onlookers were terrified and exclaimed, "Surely he was the Son of God!" (Matt 27:54; Mark 15:39; Luke 23:47), in this visionary vision, the onlookers were terrified and gave glory to the God of heaven (11:13). The resurrection, the translation of the saints, and the destruction of the extant earth and heaven will be witnessed by all, even those who pierced him (1:7). Then they will glorify the one they had previously mocked and slighted.

[15] The seventh angel blew his trumpet, and there were great voices in heaven saying, "The kingdom of the world has become the kingdom of our Lord and his Christ, and he will reign forever and ever." [16] The twenty-four elders who

were sitting on their thrones fell upon their faces before God sitting on his throne and worshipped him [17]*saying "We give thanks to you, Lord God Almighty, the one who is and who was because you have taken your power and have begun to reign.* [18]*The nations raged and your wrath has come. The time has come to judge the dead and reward your servants, the prophets, and your people who revere your name, both great and small, and destroy the destroyers of the earth."* [19]*Then God's temple in heaven was opened, and the ark of his covenant was seen within. And there appeared flashes of lightning, rumblings, thunders, an earthquake, and a severe hailstorm.*

The voices that John finally heard after the seventh trumpet was blown announced the complete overthrow of the kingdom of the world and the establishment of the eternal kingdom of God. This episode was foreboded in 10:7 in the mighty angel's words: "In the days of the voice of the seventh angel when he is about to sound the trumpet, the mystery of God will be fulfilled, just as he announced to his servants the prophets" (10:7). This prophecy was announced to Daniel (Dan 12:3–12).

The scene that follows is hope-inspiring. It is simulated by the twenty-four elders who were earlier identified as curtain-raisers and orators of the attributes and majesty of God through their worship. Here, they are heard extolling God for taking his place as king. They scornfully look back to the past, when the kings of the earth gloated with rage against God and his people by using imagery and language used in the second Psalm. They audition that the everlasting kingdom of God would be preceded by a judgment of the dead and the destroyers of the earth and a rewarding of God's servants, the prophets, and all who revere his name (vv. 18).

The scene closes by showing God's temple in heaven being opened. John saw the ark of God's covenant and flashes of lightning, rumblings, and peals of thunder, an earthquake, and heavy hail (vv. 19). Parties to a covenant would deposit their copies of the covenant in the temples of their gods (Exod 25:21–22). This gesture was a form of swearing in the name of their gods that they would live by the terms of the covenant. The swearing parties would visit the temple and read the covenant to ensure they keep it as a living document. A scene showing the ark of God's covenant in the heavenly temple shows that the time to outwork the eschatological blessings and curses stipulated in it had been fulfilled (10:7). Hereafter, the end of the world is simulated by flashes of lightning, rumblings, pearls of thunder, and severe hailstorm.

Strategic and Communicative Acts in Rev 11

The scene in which John measures the dimensions of the temple, altar, and those who worship in it, plus the audition that he was told to leave the outer courts to be trodden by the gentiles for forty-two months, is embedded with strategic acts. For an audience who understood that the symbolic measuring of the temple was an assurance of its construction, this strategic act assures them that, notwithstanding the various tribulations by the world in the outer court, the church's mission would not be thwarted.

The scene showing the divine commissioning, empowerment, tribulations, vindication, and eternal rewards to the two witnesses is a strategic act that is intended to evoke encouragement and endurance among the audience as they preached in the context of serious opposition. The audience's familiarity with the prophecy of Zechariah served to enhance the efficacy of the strategic act to evoke zeal in the knowledge that the work that they are being called to do in 10:11 has the steady backing of the Holy Spirit.

Simulating the fate of the preachers in the killing of the two witnesses, not being buried for three days, and the scorn expressed by the world exhorted the church that tribulations are their lot in this world (John 16:33). However, they were assured of great success in their mission and at the end of their earthly life, a better resurrection. The resurrection of the witnesses and being called up to heaven was a strategic act that evoked hope, endurance, and greater fervency in John's audience.

The scene simulating the complete overthrow of the kingdoms of the world and their takeover by God and his Christ constitutes a hope-inspiring and fervency-generating strategic act. The audience is drawn to esteem God and his work and to despise the pursuit of this world's fleeting and temporal pleasures. These evocations would lead to repentance of lovelessness in Ephesus, heresies in Pergamum, idolatry in Thyatira, spiritual death in Sardis, and lukewarmness in Laodicea. They would also enthuse Sardis and Philadelphia to uphold their faith.

The scene showing the open temple in heaven and the ark of the covenant shows that God is a covenant keeper. The saints can, thus, hopefully wait for their reward and vindication. Showing this scene evokes a desire to keep God's word.

Application of Evocations in Rev 11

The strategic act embedded in the symbolic measuring of the temple assured the saints that the church's mission cannot be thwarted by any earthly power.

Comparison of her mission with that of Joshua and Zerubbabel assures the church of great success notwithstanding present and looming tribulations. She was encouraged in the knowledge that the Holy Spirit will empower her proclamation just as he had empowered Joshua's and Zerubbabel's mission.

The twenty-first-century church, which trusts more in monetary might and organizational skills, risks building towers of Babel in the name of cathedrals and programs as opposed to vibrant Holy Spirit-led, Scripture-teaching, and gospel-preaching churches. The strategic acts embedded in this visionary revelation should evoke fervency in God's mission. Ministry faces a shortage of human resources due to competition with other careers that promise better pay perks. The church's victory and eventual vindication simulated in these scenes should encourage more people to join the ministry.

The assurance that God has availed the ability to perform strategic miracles to authenticate the gospel and that no one can thwart God's purpose until it is accomplished is an encouragement to the present-day church to continue in her witness. Similarly, the simulation of martyrdom and an assured resurrection after an intermediate period litotically expressed as three and a half days should evoke hope and greater endurance among the persecuted saints.

The simulation of God's takeover of the world's kingdoms should speak to the church and the world in the twentieth century. The central human pursuit today is maximum happiness. The entertainment and fashion industries, which offer worldly and sensual enjoyment, are currently the most attractive ventures. Values and moral-based sectors such as teaching and religion are scorned at and cash-starved. Money initially donated for Christian missions has been diverted to human rights and social programs. This simulation should arouse greater esteem and investment in the mission of God.

Chapter 5

Tribulation of the Church by the Evil Trinity (12:1—14:20)

PRELIMINARY OBSERVATIONS

THE VISIONARY REVELATION NARRATED in chapter twelve and thirteen narrate the tribulation of the church throughout the unfolding history that is perpetrated by an evil trinity of Satan, the beast from the sea (the imperial power), and the beast from the land (the imperial vassals and cult leaders). It echoes Jesus' words "In this world, you will suffer tribulation but be of good cheer, I have overcome the world" (John 16:33). Notwithstanding these Satan-led tribulations, the church's victory is assured as simulated in Rev 14, where the triumphant church is seen sitting with the Lamb on Mount Zion. Here, they are joined by the harvested saints from the earth (14:15-16).

REV 12

TRIBULATION OF THE CHURCH BY SATAN

Chapter twelve highlights and evokes the need for the church's vigilance by a demonstration of her vulnerability using imagery drawn from Jer 4:31. In this scriptural text, the vulnerability of the daughter of Zion (Jews) is depicted in the image of a woman in labour pains giving birth to her first child and fainting in the presence of her murderers. Similarly, the ensuing scene gives us an esoteric[1] view of Satan's work against the saints in the unfolding history by taking the reader back to his rebellion and deportation from heaven. It introduces Satan as the force behind the opposers of God and persecutors of his saints. The visionary scene assures the church of God's help in the portrayal of her earthly struggles and assured deliverance using a mosaic of imageries from the age-old contention between Satan and Eve's seed (Gen 3:15), Israel's bondage in Egypt, her deliverance through the Red Sea, the wilderness wanderings, and entry into Canaan.

¹A great portent appeared in the heavens; a woman clothed with the sun was standing on the moon, and on her head was a crown of twelve stars. ²She was pregnant. She cried in pain as she was about to give birth.

In this visionary scene, John sees a great portent in the heavens. A portent is an animate or inanimate symbol in whose configuration aspects of the signified entity are embedded. As such, a portent communicates messages about its signified entity to its beholders. Portents can be used in a visionary revelation to generate evocations that can engender intended actions to bring positive change to their beholders' visionary situations. The adjective "great" describing the portent that John saw highlights its efficacy to represent its signified entity, communicate the right message, and evoke the desired responses.

An aspect that may help identify the portent's signification stands out: the glorious sun attire, the moon footstool, and the crown of twelve stars. The passive voice of the Greek word περιβεβλημένη, *peribeblēmenē*, a perfect participle of περιβάλλω, *periballō* (to clothe) with the sun, standing on the moon footstool, and having a crown of twelve stars stands for an entity that has been clothed by a higher being with glory. The symbol of twelve stars, which has at times been used to stand for the twelve tribes of Israel and at times for the twelve apostles of Jesus, and the description of the fate of her son in the succeeding scenes suggest that this portent stands in metonymy for Israel and in metalepsis the church. According to Bullinger, a metonymy is a figure of speech by which one name or noun is used instead of another to which it stands in a certain relation while a metalepsis is a double metonymy or a compound metonymy, or a metonymy in two stages, whereby only one of which is expressed [2]

³Then another sign appeared in the heavens, an enormous red dragon with seven heads, ten horns, and seven crowns on its heads. ⁴Its tail swept a third of the stars out of the sky and flung them onto the earth. The dragon stood in

---

1. Bullinger, *Figures of Speech*, 708.
2. Bullinger, *Figures of Speech*, 538, 609.

front of the woman who was about to give birth so that it might devour the child the moment he was born.

The posture of the dragon suggests that it role-plays Satan, the archenemy of the church. "Red," the color of blood, demonstrates Satan's infamy as a killer, thief, and destroyer (John 10:10). An observation of this scene together with chapter thirteen and seventeen suggests that the beast's seven heads, ten horns, and seven diadems demonstrate that it uses the Roman Empire—the fourth fierce beast of Dan 7:7, its emperors, and vassal kings to vex the church. In John's lifetime, Rome had persecuted the Jews, more so in the war that culminated to the destruction of the Jewish temple in CE 70.[3] By the time of writing this text she was persecuting the saints (1:9 and 17:6). In the minds of believers, Rome's deeds were indeed satanic. She could be described as Satan incarnate. As such, it was apt to use this imagery to depict the heinous work of the devil against the Jews and the nascent church through the agency of Rome, her emperors, and vassal kings. Sweeping a third of the stars of heaven with the dragon's tail shows Satan's ability to engineer martyrdom of some of the saints. The scene uses imagery drawn from Dan 8:10, where throwing some of the stars to the ground stood for the martyrdom of God's saints. It also shows the devil's subtility in luring some of the lukewarm saints to deny their faith.

[5]*She gave birth to a son, a male child, who will rule all the nations with an iron sceptre. And the child was snatched up to God and his throne.* [6]*The woman fled into the wilderness to a place prepared for her by God, where she might be taken care of for 1,260 days.*

One can hurriedly identify the child born to the woman as Jesus, in which case the woman would be identified as Mary. In this scenario, Herod's desire to kill baby Jesus, Jesus' temptations by the devil, and his death could be construed as the dragon waiting upon his birth to devour him while his resurrection and ascension would be construed as God's act of taking him to heaven. Such an inference would demand an interpretation that the woman's offspring are Mary's other children. This position would not be tenable in the first-century belief economy where Mary was not considered to be the mother of the church but a follower of Jesus (Acts 1:9–14).

The scene showing the woman's flight into the wilderness narrows the probable identity of the signified reality of this portent. Most probably, the scene compares the church's pilgrim on earth throughout the unfolding history with the contention between good and evil that started in the garden of Eden (Gen 3:1) and Israel's pilgrimage in Egypt from where she is delivered,

---

3. Josephus, *Complete Works*, 887.

led through the waters of the Red Sea, where Leviathan, the sea monster in post-Exodus imagery, would have drowned her, but God dried up its waters to have her pass through to safety (Ps 74:13–15; Isa 27:1). The enemy retreated but continued to vex Israel over the centuries. The unfolding history is expressed in a litotes (1260 days), comparable to Elijah's time of vexation by Ahab and the days of Israel's vexation by Antiochus Epiphanes (*Antiq.* 12.5.3–7.7), to minimize the despondency that could result from envisioning a long period of tribulations.

> [7] Then war broke out in heaven, Michael and his angels fought against the dragon, and the dragon and its angels fought back. [8] But he was not strong enough, and they lost their place in heaven. [9] The great dragon was hurled down, that ancient serpent called the devil, or Satan, who leads the whole world astray. He was hurled to the earth and his angels with him. [10] Then I heard a loud voice in heaven say, "Now have come the salvation and the power and the kingdom of our God, and the authority of his Messiah. For the accuser of the brethren, who accuses them before our God, day and night has been hurled down. [11] They triumphed over him by the blood of the Lamb and by the word of their testimony and did not love their lives so much as to shrink from death. [12] Therefore rejoice you heavens and you who dwell in them! But woe to the earth and the sea because the devil has come down to you! He is filled with fury because he knows that his time is short."

Chapter 12:7–12 narrates a visionary revelation that simulates the devil's overthrow from his former exalted status in heaven way before the fall of man. His self-exaltation and overthrow are reflected in the taunt extended to Babylon for her self-exaltation (Isa 14:12–16) and the lament against the king of Tyre (Ezek 28:12–19). The angels of God led by archangel Michael, the presumed guardian angel of God's people (Dan 12:1), are credited for fighting and overcoming Satan and his angels. They were expelled from heaven and thrown into the world (12:8–9). Before the fall, Satan is reputed to have been the accuser of the saints before God (Job 1:6–12; Zech 3:1–2). His defeat ushered in salvation, strength, the kingdom of God, and the power of his Christ into heaven, from where Satan accused the brethren every day before God (vv. 10). The good news is that, as a follow-up to Satan's defeat in heaven, Jesus' incarnation into the world, his death, resurrection and the saints' surrender to him, even in the face of death, have completely overcome him (vv. 11).

The heavens and those who dwell in them are urged to rejoice because the accuser of the brethren is debarred from accessing the presence of God where he initially accused them day and night (vv. 12). However, woe is pronounced upon the earth and its dwellers because Satan has come to them in fury because he knows his time is short. Thus, now, he prowls around like a roaring lion, seeking someone to devour (1 Pet 5:8).

¹³ *When the dragon saw that he had been hurled to the earth, he pursued the woman who had given birth to a male child.* ¹⁴ *The woman was given the two wings of a great eagle so that she might fly to the place prepared for her in the wilderness where she would be taken care of for a time, times and a half time out of the serpent's reach.* ¹⁵ *Then from his mouth, the serpent spewed water like a river to overtake the woman and sweep her away with the torrent.* ¹⁶ *But the earth helped the woman by opening its mouth and swallowing the river that the dragon had spewed out of his mouth.* ¹⁷ *Then, the dragon was enraged at the woman and went off to wage war against the rest of her offspring, those who keep God's commands and hold fast their testimony about Jesus. The dragon stood on the shores of the sea.*

After being debarred from accessing heaven (Isa 14:12-16), the devil focused on pursuing the woman and her seed (Gen 3:15; Rev 12:13). The imagery used to simulate the church's final exodus in vv. 14 appears to have been borrowed from Israel's flight and exodus from Egypt. After being delivered from Pharaoh's bondage, Israel was divinely nourished with manna for the entire exodus period. The Bible refers to the flight of Israel from Egypt as being carried on eagles' wings (Exod 19:4). This simulation assures the saints that similarly, the church is unassailable, notwithstanding the trials, temptations, and persecutions orchestrated by Satan.

The scene showing the dragon following after the woman and spewing water like a river to trap the woman and God's countering act of opening up the earth to swallow the water (vv. 15) looks back to the story of Israel's deliverance in the Red Sea, where God dried up a way for her to cross on dry ground (Exod 14:29). Her pursuers were swallowed in the sea (Exod 14:28). This recall mirrors the devil's relentless assault against the church through tribulations by the evil trinity that were vexing the church in John's days and God's countering acts of deliverance. After the devil failed in his schemes against the woman, he pursued her offspring—the church sojourning in the unfolding history (vv. 17). How is the devil going to wage war from this time onwards? He will use the political powers and competing cultic systems, as will be shown in the succeeding visionary simulation narrated in chapter thirteen.

In summary, this visionary scene simulates the nature of the church's exodus throughout the unfolding history. It shows the church's birth, mission, tribulations, and divinely aided triumphs using a mosaic of imageries borrowed from the storylines of Satan's fall from his former exalted state in heaven, Israel's bondage and deliverance from Egypt, and her Exodus through the wilderness into Canaan. The dragon is portrayed pursuing the church just as Pharaoh, the king of Egypt pursued the children of Israel. Again, just as God protected and nourished Israel with manna throughout her wilderness wonderings, he too sustains the church by his word throughout the unfolding history (John 6:32–58). The visionary scene is structured using litotes and foils to enhance the efficacy of the evocations generated by its strategic acts.

Strategic and Communicative Acts in Rev 12

Generally, showing this visionary scene constitutes a strategic act. It reveals the church's vulnerability to Satan's evil schemes. However, it also displays the latent work of God in aid of the church. Seeing the simulation of the devil's schemes evoked dread but the simulation of the countering work of God evoked faith and greater trust in God.

The simulation of the devil's unrelenting assault against the saints (a third of the stars of heaven) also constitute a powerful strategic act. It must have evoked heightened vigilance among the saints. It brought home the reality that their adversary, the devil, prowls around like a lion looking for someone to devour (1 Pet 5:8). It is also a foil that magnifies God's salvific work.

The simulation of God's care and preservation of the church in the scene showing the woman being led to the wilderness where she is nourished for 1,260 days is a strategic act. It serves to calm the saints in their persecutions by the evil trinity. It also evoked adoration of God for his love and grace.

The strategic act embedded in the simulation of Satan being chased out of heaven by Michael and his angels assured the saints that the devil could no longer accuse them before God. However, the Devil's ejection from heaven into the earth is a scare that evokes greater vigilance.

The simulation of Satan's relentless pursuit of the church and the countering work of God's constant care is a strategic act that evokes great assurance of God's care. It must have fortified the faith of the saints in Smyrna and Philadelphia who were passing through tribulation.

Application of Evocations in Rev 12

The evocations generated by the strategic act embedded in the visionary scene showing the woman in birth pains with the devil waiting to devour her child must have jolted the audience to greater vigilance. God's deliverance of the woman and child evokes trust in his ever-caring nature. The evocations generated by the strategic act embedded in showing the devil following after the woman and spitting water to overwhelm her urges believers to pray always that they may overcome the devil's ceaseless and ferocious attacks. The simulation must have jolted the lukewarm, dying, and dead churches in Asia Minor to desire revival. It also must have evoked greater trust in God's fidelity among the suffering saints in Smyrna and Philadelphia.

The scene showing Satan's inability to get hold of the woman and instead choosing to pursue her offspring shows that he does not relent. Like a roaring lion, he looks for someone to devour (1 Pet 5:8). He aims to stop the church from growing through self-edification and witness of Christ. Today's scheme of stopping the church is to subtly convert her from being an army of the Lord into a social club. Observably, the success of today's church is no longer measured by the conversion of souls but by the number of congregants, luxury displayed in the beautiful cathedrals, choir shows, and motivational speeches. Liturgy is more skewed towards entertainment of the congregants than the worship of God and inculcation of Christian morals and ethical character. This visionary revelation should urge the church to travail in childbirth until faith and witness of Christ and Christ alone become the object of her mission.

REV 13

TRIBULATIONS OF THE CHURCH BY THE IMPERIAL POWERS

¹*Then I saw a beast coming out of the sea. It had ten horns and seven heads and ten crowns on its horn and on each head a blasphemous name.* ²*The beast resembled a leopard but had feet like those of a bear and a mouth like that of a lion. The dragon gave the beast his power and his throne, and great authority.* ³*One of the heads of the beast seemed to have had a fatal wound that had been healed. The whole world was filled with wonder and followed the beast.* ⁴*People worshipped the dragon because he had given authority to the beast, and they also worshipped the beast and asked, "Who is like the beast? Who can wage war against it?* ⁵*The beast was given a mouth to utter proud and blasphemous words and to exercise authority for forty-two months.* ⁶*It opened its mouth to blaspheme God and slander his name and dwelling place and those who live in heaven.* ⁷*It was given the power to wage war against God's holy people and to conquer them. And it was given authority over every tribe, people, language, and nation.* ⁸*All inhabitants of the earth will worship the*

beast—all whose names have not been written in the Lamb's book of life, the Lamb who was slain from the foundation of the world. ⁹*Whoever has ears, let him hear.* ¹⁰*If anyone is to go into captivity, into captivity, they will go. If anyone is to be killed with the sword, with the sword, they will be killed. This calls for patient endurance and faithfulness on the part of God's people.*

The previous visionary revelation paused at the scene showing the red dragon standing on the sands of the sea (12:17). The sand of the sea is an idiom describing the countless number of people in the world (Gen 22:17). The current scene simulates a fierce contention between the church and an unholy alliance of Satan, the beast from the sea (the Roman imperial power that ruled the then-known world), and the beast from the land (imperial cult leaders—and hence the tag "false prophet"). It answers the question, What was the nature of the duel between the dragon and the woman's offsprings mentioned in 12:13? A visionary simulation of how Satan uses the existing political, economic, and religious systems to oppose the Christian faith and work of the church is intended to generate evocations that would awaken greater faith, vigilance, prayer, and endurance among the saints.

As the scene opens, John sees a beast coming from the sea. Echoes from the book of Daniel identify beasts with world empires that colonize and persecute God's people. Its description shows that it is similar to the beast on which the great whore Babylon sits (17:3, 9–12). Its ten horns were same in number with the beast of Dan 7:7. This observation suggests that it is the same beast described in Dan 7:7–8 and in Rev 17:3, 8, 9–12. In Daniel, as in Revelation, this beast symbolized the Roman Empire.[4] In addition to the ten horns of Daniel's beast, Revelation's beast from the sea had seven heads that had blasphemous names. The seven heads that had blasphemous names symbolize the Roman Emperors some who were posthumously deified by the state and others deified themselves in their lifetime and hence the tag of being blasphemous. The ten horns with ten crowns may represent ten vassals of Rome's reigning monarch during the time of John. During the time of Domitian, the province of Asia had been governed by eleven successive governors. The eleventh governor (Rufus) was appointed circa 95/96 CE.[5] Perhaps, Revelation was written before the eleventh governor was appointed, and hence the ten horns instead of eleven. Resemblance to a leopard (the Greek Empire [Dan 7:6]), bear (the Medo-Persian Empire [Dan 7:5]), the lion (the Babylonian Empire [Dan 7:4]) suggests that the Roman Empire espoused these former empires' values. Indeed, it espoused

---

4. Josephus, *Complete Works*, 341.
5. ECK, *Prokonsul Von Asia*, 151.

the philosophy, art, and learning of the Greeks, the splendor of Persia, and the boasting of Babylon.

One of the beast's seven heads had a fatal wound that had healed. There was a rife speculation that Emperor Nero, who had died in 68 CE, would resurrect (*Nero redivivus*[6]). As such, some scholars have suggested that the injured head stood for Emperor Nero. The beast's fatal wound was identified with his death and its healing with his speculated resurrection. Such a fallacious interpretation may not be tenable in a visionary revelation whose seer was wholly pliable to the omniscience of the Holy Spirit. Mounce convincingly argues that perhaps the beast's mortal wound may refer to the near-collapse of leadership while its healing refers to the re-establishment of order. These chaotic scenes began just before the death of Nero until the ascension to power by Vespasian (69–79 CE). He also suggests that perhaps no historical allusion is intended and the purpose of the figure is to underscore the tremendous vitality of the beast.[7] The symbolism of the fatal but healed wound could also represent the lingering persecution similar to the one unleashed on Christians by Emperor Nero.[8] Whichever the reference, it served to show the recurrent nature of the persecution of Christians by the beastly emperors and their minions.

Because of the authority wielded by the beast over the affairs of men, people were given to worship both him and the dragon who was the power behind the beasts' throne (vv. 4). The people's amazement expressed in the questions "Who is like the beast?" and "Who can wage war against it?" shows the great awe in which the emperor was held by his vassals and their subjects. Indeed, Rome had conquered the known world and restored peace in a troubled region no wonder the awe with which she was held. The phrase "being given" (vv. 5) suggests that the beast performed his heinous acts using the power of the dragon. However, the unfolding history in which the beast was to vex the saints is litotically diminished to forty-two months. Christians were aware of the forty-two months in which the Jews withstood great persecution by Antiochus Epiphanes IV, who had also deified himself, during the Maccabean revolt after the abomination that caused the desolation of the second temple between 167 and 164 BCE. They could easily compare their present persecution by Rome with the persecution of the Jewish nation during Antiochus' heinous rule. The visionary revelation evoked hope that just as God delivered the Jewish nation to later establish

---

6. Keener, *Bible Background*, 796.
7. Mounce, *Revelation*, 248.
8. Koester, *Revelation*, 523–637.

the Hasmonaean rule,[9] he would similarly deliver the Christians from their present persecution by the evil trinity.

The proud words uttered by the beast and his blasphemies are described in 12:6 as blaspheming against God (deifying her emperors) and slandering his name, his dwelling place (the temple, which Rome had already destroyed in 70 CE), and those who live in heaven-Godhead (vv. 6). The phrase "and he was given authority over every tribe, people, language and nation" (vv. 7) shows that the beast was an earthly ruler who had been allowed, of course by God, to rule the entire known world.

Other than those written in the book of life, the rest of humanity is prone to worship the beast (vv. 8). Describing people as having their names written in the book of life is an incarnational way of describing a heavenly reality using an earthly conceptualization to aid earthly people to fathom heavenly realities. Indeed, the use of books in the vision does not mean that God needs a book of records to aid his memory. Such a notion would contradict his attributes of omnipotence, omniscience, and omnipresence. Describing Jesus as "the Lamb that was slain from the foundation of the world" assured the saints that their salvation was not an afterthought. It was indeed decreed before the foundation of the world but outworked in Christ's death.

The saying "if anyone has an ear, let him hear" (vv. 9) directs the audience to note the gravity of the succeeding statement and to urge the seven churches to brace themselves for the possibility of captivity and martyrdom alluded to in the audition: "If anyone is to be taken captive, to captive he goes; if anyone is to be slain with the sword, with the sword must he be slain. Here is a call to endurance." Koester rightly notes that this statement exhorts readers to bear suffering faithfully.[10] This audition stresses that the beast would surely take some to captivity and kill others for their faith, but so be it. It is an exhortation aimed at engendering determination to endure tribulations by the evil trinity.

> [11] *Then I saw a second beast coming out of the earth. It had two horns like a lamb, but it spoke like a dragon.* [12] *It exercised the authority of the first beast on its behalf and made the earth and its inhabitants worship the first beast whose fatal wound had been healed.* [13] *And it performed great signs, even causing fire to come down from the sky to the earth in full view of the people.* [14] *Because of the signs it was given the power to perform on behalf of the first beast, it deceived the inhabitants of the earth. It ordered them to set up an image in honour of the beast who was wounded by the sword and yet lived.*

9. Josephus, *Complete Works*, 403–38.
10. Koester, *Revelation*, 523–637.

> ¹⁵*The second beast was given the power to give breath to the image of the first beast so that it could speak and cause all who refused to worship the image to be killed.* ¹⁶ *It also forced all people, great and small, rich and poor, free and slave, to receive a mark on their right hand or on their foreheads,* ¹⁷*so that they could not buy or sell unless they had the mark, which is the name of the beast or the number of its name.* ¹⁸*This calls for wisdom. Let the person who has insight calculate the number of the beast, for it is the number of a man. That number is 666.*

Showing the second beast coming from the earth identifies its representative entity as native to Asia Minor. It should not be lost on the interpreters that the beasts are symbolic visionary characters. They represent entities, persons, and ideologies in the real world. They also simulate extant and future human experiences. This beast's two horns like a lamb's show that it role-plays an entity that, like the Lamb of God who was propagating the Christian faith, was propagating the emperor cult. The audition that "it exercised all the authority of the first beast to compel the inhabitants of the earth (the jurisdiction of its representative reality) to worship the first beast" (vv. 12) suggests that the second beast was role-playing the first beast's vassal kings who zealously propagated emperor worship on behalf of the self-deified emperor. Showing the second beast causing fire to come down from heaven into the earth in full view of the people (vv. 13–15) simulates the false prophet's great subtilty in turning the hearts of the populace, including the elect (Matt 24:24) to worship the Roman emperor.

As John watched on, he saw the beast ordering the inhabitants of the earth to make an image of the beast who was wounded by the sword yet lived (vv. 14). Carving images of emperors was a common practice. This visionary scene may be a simulation of a real happening where an image of the ruling emperor was carved and erected on a shrine. However, to give breath to the image of the beast may be describing offering of *latria*, which is the reserve of the living God to a non-living image. There is evidence of the execution of Christians for refusing to worship the emperor's statue just a few decades after the writing of Revelation (Pliny, *Ep.*, 10.96). The book of Revelation was perhaps written after Domitian dedicated an imperial statue nearly five meters high in the imperial temple in Ephesus."[11] This image could be in reference here.

As the visionary scene unfolded, John saw the beast putting the mark of the name of the first beast on the right hand or forehead of all the inhabitants of the earth. As in many world cultures, in the audience's culture, a person's name signified the values and character traits of the named person.

11. Keener, *Revelation*, 351.

This scene simulated a forced adoption of the beast's value systems on the entire populace. No one could buy or sell unless they adopted the value systems of the beast. This adoption of value systems is described as receiving the mark of the beast (vv. 17). John divides the victims into a pair of opposites, "small and great, rich and poor, free and slave," to emphasize the proliferation of the inevitability to adopt the value systems of the beast.

An alternative view is suggested by the words written on the coinage minted in the Eastern Mediterranean region. Keener notes that "Roman coins in the Eastern Mediterranean announced that the emperor was "son of god" and "god." Domitian demanded the title "Our Lord and God" (*Dominus et Deus Noster*).[12] Anybody willing to engage in trade had no choice but to use such blasphemous coins that proclaimed that the ruling caesar was a god. Subtly, the provincial governors were coercing every user of the coins to proclaim the caesars as their Lord and God. In shedding light on the connection between the mark of the beast and commerce, Beasley-Murray notes, "One could hardly refuse to use the money, either to accept it or give it for that would put one out of business and lead to starvation. There is no doubt that the net was tightening for the Christians in Asia Minor in John's days."[13] As such, Christians not willing to hold coins promoting the emperor's divinity in their hand would find it very difficult to buy or sell. Either view, Christians are being called upon to decisively resist being entangled in sinful practices.

The audition "this calls for wisdom: let the one who has understanding calculate the number of the beast, for it is a man's number, and his number is 666" (vv. 18) suggests that finally, John cautiously and wisely names the beast from the sea. Wisdom and caution dictated that he uses its name's numerological equivalent. The phrase "this calls for wisdom" also implies that it was not prudent and safe to explicitly name the then-extant beast from the sea. Wisdom also dictated that he discreetly does so to shield the book of Revelation from being seen as an affront to the person so named, thereby jeopardizing the Christian course.

Whereas it was easy for John's primary audience to match the number of the beast with his name, the inability to undoubtedly ascertain the dating of the visionary revelation makes it very difficult for the secondary audience of the twenty-first century to undoubtedly identify the beast from the sea through numerology (*gematria* in Hebrew or *isopsephism* in Greek).[14] Gematria is the practice of "assigning a numerical value to each letter of a

---

12. Beasley-Murray, "Premillennialism," 18; Keener, *Revelation*, 336.
13. Beasley-Murray, "Premillennialism," 21.
14. Marshall, Travis, and Paul, *New Testament*, 322.

name—adding the numerical value of the letters of a person's name, adding up the totals, and getting a number that is supposed to be significant."[15]

A question that baffles every secondary reader is, Does textual and historical evidence suggest that future world leaders who exhibit the beast's characteristics will have the numerological equivalent of their names or titles adding up to 666? Since the number was dictated by the name and therefore coincidental, the answer is no. This deduction shows the futility of trying to identify subsequent world leaders as the beast by matching the sum of their numerological equivalents with 666.

Whereas the mark of God is holiness, the devil's mark is sin. Sin is the real mark of the beast who uses the dragon's power (devil) to work out iniquity. Again, since the devil came to steal, kill, and destroy, while Jesus came to give life and to give it more abundantly (John 10:10), the devil can be regarded as the chief antichrist. Any leader who, in cahoots with the devil, works out that which is against Christ's purpose is therefore an antichrist. Furthermore, Rev 14:9 and 16:2 suggest that having the mark of the beast is equated to worshipping the beast. As explicitly shown, having the mark of the beast can be repented and forgiven (9:20; 11:13; 16:2–11). Mechanical marks on the body, tattoos, or computer chips inserted in body parts cannot be repented. Therefore, the mark of the beast may not be identified with a physical mark on the body or a technological identifier inserted in the body.

The mark of the beast has caused great consternation throughout Christian history. In every Christian age, people have vainly tried to compare world and religious leaders with the description of this fearsome figure.[16] Suffice it to say that the narration of this visionary revelation was aimed at solving the needs in the historical situations of the seven churches. It was not primarily a message for us now; it was theirs then. We own and apply it by contextualizing it to our situations. As such, the name of the particular antichrist in their time had a numerological total of 666. The numerological totals of the names of antichrists are not similar in the different historical eras and geographical locations. It is possible to consider Mohamed, Jihadist groups, communist leaders who persecute Christians, some popes who persecuted Christian reformers, and even Protestant leaders who pervert the cause of Christ as antichrists, even though their names' numerological equivalents do not add up to 666.

From the time of John, not having the mark of the beast identifies the elect (14:9; 14:11; 16:2; 19:20; 20:4). However, having the mark identifies those sold out to the devil and the sinful worldly systems all over human

---

15. Walhout, *Revelation*, 142.
16. Koester, *Revelation* (eBook), volumes 25, 27, and 28.

history (Gen 4:15). The mark of the beast contrasts with God's seal on the foreheads of the saints of God (Ezek 9:4–6; Rev 7:2; 9:4). Thus, the mark of the beast is nothing more than being enslaved by sin, whereas God's seal, baptism with the Holy Spirit, identifies the saints as his own so that they are passed over when God metes disciplinary judgments, sin is the mark that identifies those to be judged.

As the church and commentators grope in the dark, speculating that the mark of the beast is a physical tattoo or technological microchip that will be implanted in the body or the bloodstream, the devil and his minions are busy putting the mark of the beast on millions by imprisoning them in the grip of sin. Today, there are businesses, job opportunities and loan facilities that the elect cannot enjoy unless they succumb to sinful ways such as supporting perversions like homosexuality, the right to abort, racism, corruption, or giving in to other sinful seductions. Notably, any person who overtly or covertly causes people to deny Jesus and his salvific work is the antichrist and qualifies to be so identified.

Strategic and Communicative Acts in Rev 13

This scene highlights the tribulation of the church by the Roman Emperors and their provincial kings. Highlighting Rome's tribulation of the church was a powerful strategic act. It evoked caution, prayer, patient endurance, vigilance, and an enhanced witness of Christ by the churches (vv. 10).

Referring to the beast from the land as a false prophet, whose power to deceive is simulated in a hyperbolic act of showing him calling fire from the sky, is also a strategic act. He is referred to as a false prophet because he was the mouthpiece and enforcer of the dictates of the beast from the sea, the Roman Emperor. The works of this beast are highlighted to forewarn the saints of the subtle devices of the evil trinity (2 Cor 2:11).

Auditioning that the evil trinity will vex the church for only forty-two months is a litotes. This figure of speech is used to soften the impact of tribulations by the evil trinity. The churches drew comfort in the assurance that their persecutions are temporal in comparison with their eternal reward.

Application of Evocations in Rev 13

This visionary revelation was meant to spur the saints in the seven churches to be wary of the schemes of the antichrists in their historical situations. Unlike us, they could explicitly identify the dragon and the beasts. They were not wondering and asking questions such as, Who or what is represented by this or that beast? Moreover, answering such questions may not be as helpful as answering the question, Which are the communicative and strategic acts in this visionary revelation and which evocations do they generate? Finally, but more importantly, how did these evocations eliminate the gaps in the primary audiences' visionary situation, and how would they eliminate gaps in our situations? The visionary revelation awakened the primary audiences to the fact that they were being opposed by a nefarious unholy trinity. It prompted the church to watch, pray, and be strong in the Lord as she faced tribulations in her earthly sojourn.

Every geographical region and Christian generation have their share of tribulation from the devil, antichrists, and false prophets. They may be in the form of political leaders who oppose the propagation of the Christian faith, other competing religions, or even ideologies like communism or unbridled human rights. The present-day Christian should identify the subtle ways these antichrist persons and ideologies use to oppose the Christian faith and the gospel and to mark Christians with the mark of the beast—sin. These should be countered by greater vigilance, more prayer, mission, and enthusiasm in witnessing Christ in the social, economic, and political arenas, and to people yet to be reached.

REV 14

ENTHRONING THE LAMB AND SAINTS IN ZION

Preliminary Observations

The visionary simulation narrated in this chapter is a fitting epilogue to the visionary simulations narrated in chapters 12–13 and a fitting prologue to the simulations narrated in chapters 15–20. It looks back to and counters the evil trinity's opposition to Jesus and the church in chapters 12 and 13. It compares this opposition to King David's opposition by Israel's vassals—the Jebusites—when he went to set up his headquarters at Jerusalem and afterward by the Philistines when they heard that he had taken over Jerusalem and established Zion as his headquarters (2 Sam 5:6–25). David's recall of this victory is celebrated in Ps 2:1–12. In this psalm, the opposition of David by these nations' kings is interpreted as an affront against YHWH and his anointed one. These vassals are reported to have said this about King David and his God: "Let us burst their bonds asunder and cast their cords from us" (Ps 2:2–3).

The psalm shows that God in heaven will put the enemies of his anointed one in derision, for he is the one who had established David on "Zion, my holy hill" (Ps 2:6). Using the same imagery, albeit in visionary simulations, the visionary revelation narrated in chapter 14 interprets the evil trinity's affront against the church in chapter 12 and 13 as an anti-type of King David's experience. Similarly, the evil trinity's affront is seen as laughable and futile since it would not thwart the enthronement of the Lamb—the heir to the Davidic throne—and his church on Mount Zion (14:1). God's retaliatory judgments against the evil trinity that culminate with this enthronement are simulated and narrated in chapters 15–20. From here, as a son, he is given the nations as his heritage, the ends of the earth as his possession after judging them (chapters 16–20). The overwhelming nature of his victory is described as breaking them with a rod of iron and dashing them to pieces like a potter's vessel (Ps 2:8–9).

¹*And as I watched, and lo, the Lamb stood on Mount Zion, and with him 144,000 having his name and his father's name written on their foreheads.* ²*And I heard a sound from heaven like the roar of rushing waters and like a great thunder. The sound I heard was like that of harpists playing their harps.* ³*And they are singing a new song before the throne and before the four living creatures and the elders. No one was able to learn the song except the 144,000 who had been redeemed from the earth.* ⁴*These are those who were not defiled with women, for they remained virgins. They follow the Lamb wherever he may go. They were purchased from among mankind as firstfruits to God and the Lamb* ⁵*No lie was found in their mouths; they are blameless.*

As John watched the visionary stage, he saw a setting of Mount Zion, the city of David (vv. 1). The Lamb is seen with the symbolic 144,000 sealed saints who have his and his father's names on their foreheads. The seal they had earlier received (7:4) can now be identified as the names of the Lamb and his father—the name by which believers are baptized. Here, the 144,000 are described as the firstfruits for God and the Lamb who had been redeemed from mankind (vv. 4). Just as in chapter 7, they are later joined by the full harvest that is reaped from the earth (vv. 14–16). These two groups, now gathered at Mount Zion, simulate the present standing of the saints (Heb 12:22–24).

John heard harpists singing loudly in heaven before the throne, the four living creatures, and the elders. Revelation 15:2–4 reveals that the song of the harpists in heaven was the victor's song, referred to as the song of Moses, the servant of God, and the song of the Lamb. The song of Moses (Exod 15:1–19) was a victors' song. The 144,000 saints were the only ones who were able to learn the song. This suggests that they, like the Israelites after

God's conquest of the Egyptian army in the Red Sea, had been redeemed and had overcome the evil trinity by the blood of the Lamb and the word of their testimony (12:11). It is only such who could sing a victory song.

The 144,000 saints are described as virgins (vv. 4). Notably, just as many other symbols in Revelation are not literal, so is the description of the 144,000 as virgins. This virginity stands for total fidelity to God. They had not defiled themselves with the sinful and idolatrous ways of the world. As such, they did not bear the mark of the beast—sin. Instead, they follow the Lamb wherever he goes. To follow the Lamb wherever he goes describes their total fidelity to the Lamb. Their other description is that no lie was found in their mouth; they are blameless (vv. 5). They are also described as the redeemed (reaped) from humanity and firstfruits of God and the Lamb. Describing them as firstfruits anticipates a full harvest of the multitudes from every nation, tribe, people, and language (7:9-17). These are later shown being reaped as the fully ripe harvest (14:15-16).

⁶Then I saw an angel flying in midair, and he had the eternal gospel to proclaim to those who live on the earth—to every nation, tribe, language, and people. ⁷He said in a loud voice, "Fear God and give Him glory because the hour of his judgment has come. Worship him who made the heavens, the earth, the sea, and the springs of water." ⁸A second angel followed and said, "Fallen! Fallen is Babylon the Great, which made all the nations drink the maddening wine of her adulteries." ⁹A third angel followed them and said in a loud voice; "If anyone worships the beast and its image and receives its mark on their forehead or on their hand, ¹⁰they too will drink the wine of God's fury which has been poured full strength into the cup of his wrath. They will be tormented with burning sulfur in the presence of the holy angels and of the Lamb. ¹¹And the smoke of their torment will rise forever and ever. There will not be rest day or night for those who worship the beast and its image, or for anyone who receives the mark of its name." ¹²This calls for patient endurance on the part of the people of God who keep his commands and remain faithful to Jesus. ¹³Then I heard a voice from heaven say, write this Blessed are the dead who die in the Lord from now on." "Yes," says the Spirit. "They will rest from their labour, for their deeds will follow them."

A new visionary scene is ushered by the appearance of a new cast of three angels (vv. 6). The first is seen flying directly overhead with an eternal gospel to proclaim to those who dwell on earth: every nation, tribe, language, and people. His gospel is a call to fear God. It was a rapprochement that if slighted would lead to judgment. These last tier judgments are simulated in the visionary revelation narrated in chapter 16. A second angel followed pronouncing the judgment and fall of Babylon the Great, which is later simulated and narrated in chapters 17 and 18. The third angel followed pronouncing torment that was in store for those having the mark of the beast. This torment is later simulated and narrated in 19:11-21.

The message by the three angels is so dire. It calls upon the saints who keep the commandments of God and put their faith in Jesus to patiently endure the tribulations that were simulated and narrated in chapters 12 and 13. A voice from heaven told John to write, "Blessed are the dead who die in the Lord from now on." "Blessed indeed," says the Spirit, "that they may rest from their labours, for their deeds follow them!" (vv. 13). A voice from heaven telling John to write shows that this admonition is gravely important. It exhorts the saints to steadfastly hold on to faith in the Lord even if it results in their martyrdom. It trumpets and ingrains the fact that it is more blessed to die for the cause of Christ than have temporary reprieve from the tribulations inflicted by the evil trinity only to face the wrath of God at the end.

14I looked, and there before me was a white cloud, and seated on the cloud was one like the son of man with a crown of gold on his head and a sharp sickle in his hand. 15Then another angel came out of the temple and called in a loud voice to him who was sitting on a cloud, "Take your sickle and reap because the time to reap has come, for the harvest of the earth is ripe." 16So he who was seated on the cloud swung his sickle over the earth, and the earth was harvested. 17Another angel came out of the temple in heaven, and he, too, had a sickle. 18Still, another angel who had charge over the fire came from the altar and called in a loud voice to him who had a sharp sickle, "Take your sharp sickle and gather the clusters of grapes from the earth's vine, because its grapes are ripe." 19The angel swung his sickle on the earth, gathered its grapes, and threw them into the great winepress of God's wrath. 20They were trampled in the winepress outside the city, and blood flowed out of the press, rising as high as the horse's bridle for a distance of 1600 stadia.

One familiar with Dan 7:13 would identify the one coming seated on the cloud as the Son of Man—the Christ (vv. 14). Echoes from the rock that shattered the kingdoms of the world in Nebuchadnezzar's dream (Dan 2:34-35; 44-45) suggest that it represented the same kingdom as the one established by the one like the son of man who came riding on a cloud in Dan 7:13-14. Collectively, the echoes from Daniel's visions suggest that the scene under review may be simulating the exaltation of the saints in Christ (Eph 2:6, Heb 12:22-24).

The voice of the angel crying from the temple was a visionary audition interpreting the simulated reaping as a conversion and ingathering of the gentile saints to join the 144,000 firstfruits on Mount Zion (Heb 12:22-24).

Jesus used the metaphor of harvest in two ways. In Matt 9:36–38 and John 4:35, he used it as a metaphor for people who are yet to be won to faith through the preaching of the gospel. It is also used as a metaphor for recompensing both the believers and unbelieving after the last judgment (Matt 13:30). In Revelation, the word "harvest" is also used as a metaphor for two functions. It is used as a metaphor for the ingathering of the saints (grain, presumably wheat) who heard and believed the eternal gospel whose pronouncement was simulated by the three angels (vv. 6–9). It is also used as a metaphor of the judgment of sinners (grapes) who did not believe the eternal gospel. This is the same gospel whose proclamation was simulated by the two witnesses in 11:3–7.

After the reaping of the wheat, there appeared another angel with a sickle. Again, the command by the angel in charge of the altar fire to the grape-reaper to commence his work of reaping grapes interprets the action of this reaper. Dennis E. Johnson has aptly argued that the harvest of the grain symbolizes the gathering of the church for salvation and the grapes harvest portrays the gathering of the wicked for destruction.[17] Trampling of the grapes outside the city simulates the looming outpouring of God's wrath upon those who slight God's rapprochements and their exclusion from the commonwealth of the saints. The scene showing the blood of the grapes flowing from the winepress and rising as high as the horse's bridle for a distance of 1,600 stadia demonstrates the severity and extensiveness of the wrath of God against those who slight God's grace rapprochements in the gospel.

Strategic and Communicative Acts in Rev 14

The visionary scene showing the Lamb of God with the 144,000, who alone could learn the song of Moses and the Lamb sitting with the Lamb on Mount Zion, is an apt strategic act. It had the efficacy to evoke desire to be part of the number of the sealed remnants who would be redeemed from the earth, leading to greater fidelity to orthodoxy and orthopraxis. It would also cause the saints to despise the pain of tribulations leading to patient endurance.

The auditions by the three angels are communicative acts that urged John's audience to hearken to God's rapprochements in the gospel and to worship him as a just God, not to be unequally yoked with the evil systems of Rome, and to resist the mark of the beast.

Showing a simulation of the continuous reaping of the saints throughout the unfolding history that culminates with the end-time reaping of the

---

17. Johnson, *Triumph of the Lamb*, 211.

righteous as harvesting wheat and the outpouring of God's wrath upon the obdurate as gathering and trending grapes is a strategic act. It evokes the desire to be counted among the righteous harvest and to spite the final state of the sinful. It was intended to urge repentance, uncompromised lifestyle, and patient endurance among the saints in the seven churches.

Application of Evocations in Rev 14

This visionary revelation simulates the promised bequest of the saints who endure the tribulations of the evil trinity. It also simulates the bitter judgment of those who succumb to tribulations by the evil trinity and are marked with the mark of the beast. It is a call to either choose to live an uncompromised life and reap its eternal rewards or to succumb to the tribulations of the evil trinity and suffer its eternal consequences.

The simulation of the imminent outpouring of God's wrath on sinners must have jolted the primary audience, as it would Christians of all ages, to shun every approach of evil. Similarly, the simulation of the reward of eternal life must have evoked and still evokes deep longing to be counted among the number of the harvested saints. Consequently, it leads to faithfulness to the apostolic doctrine, practice of faith, and patient endurance in tribulations.

Chapter 6

Defeat of the Evil Trinity and the Final Judgment (15:1—20:15)

PRELIMINARY OBSERVATION

THIS SECTION SIMULATES THE last-tier judgments on the evil trinity and the obdurate world that culminates in the last judgment otherwise referred to as the white-throne judgment. These judgments are meted on the evil trinity and the obdurate who, notwithstanding God's rapprochements in the work of Jesus on the cross, represented by the slain Lamb (5:6), the preaching of the gospel (6:1–2; 11:3–6; 14:6; 18:4), and disciplinary judgments (8:2—9:21), snubbed him. It also simulates the takeover of the kingdom of the world by God (19:6), Christ, and the saints (20:4).

REV 15

VICTORIOUS SAINTS SING THE VICTOR'S SONG

[1]*And I saw another great and marvellous sign in heaven; seven angels with seven last plagues, last because with them God's wrath is completed.* [2]*And I saw what looked like a sea of glass glowing with fire and standing on the sea, those who had been victorious over the beast and its image and over the number of its name. They had harps given to them by God.* [3]*They sang the song of God's servant Moses and of the Lamb: Great and Marvelous are your deeds, Lord God Almighty. Just and true are your ways, King of the nations.*

> ⁴*Who will not fear you, Lord, and bring glory to your name? For you alone are holy. All nations will come and worship before you, for your righteous acts have been revealed."* ⁵*After these things, I looked, and I saw the inner sanctum of the tent of the testimony in heaven opened.* ⁶*Out of it came the seven angels with the seven plagues. They were dressed in clean, shining linen and wore golden sashes around their chests.* ⁷*Then, one of the four living creatures gave to the seven angels seven golden bowls filled with the wrath of God, who lives forever and ever.* ⁸*The holy of holies was filled with smoke from the glory of God and from his power, and no one could enter in until the seven plagues were completed.*

This second portent comprises seven angels with seven plagues, which are described as the "last because with them God's wrath is completed (Greek: ἐτελέσθη, *etelesthē*)," that is, fully quenched (vv. 1). Basically, the description of the plagues as the last contrasts them with the judgments that were simulated after breaking the second, third, and fourth seals and blowing of the first four of the seven trumpets. One of the views offered by G. K. Beale and David H. Campbell as the most probable is that "last" (Greek: *eschatos*) more likely indicates the sequential order in which John saw the visions rather than the chronological order of the events depicted in the visions.[1] While this position has some merit, it would not have added any evocative value to the visionary revelation.

Describing the plagues as the last and that "with them, the wrath of God is fully quenched" suggests that they are the last-tier judgments. They are meted throughout the unfolding history on the obdurate who slight God's rapprochements in the preaching of the gospel (6:1–2), the decreed judgments resultant of the fall of Adam (6:3–8), and the disciplinary cum retributive judgments against the sinners and persecutors of the saints (8:2–12). This portrayal and understanding would evoke fear of ever facing such severe plagues leading the churches to greater watchfulness and repentance for those entrapped in heresy and sin.

John also saw another cast of those who had triumphed over the beast and its image and the number of its name. They were standing on (Greek: ἐπί) what looked like a sea of glass glowing with fire. They definitely included the 144,000 firstfruits and the reaped saints from across the earth (14:16). There was also an inconspicuous cast of the reaped grapes—the sinners, victims of the wrath of God, who, though God had shown abundance of grace in the gospel and rapprochements in disciplinary judgments, had slighted it. The judgment of these obdurate sinners had earlier been simulated by throwing the harvested grapes in the great winepress of the

---

1. Beale and Campbell, *Revelation*, 315.

wrath of God (14:17–20). In this visionary simulation, the same winepress is symbolized by a sea of glass mingled with fire.

To further enthuse the saints to unwaveringly follow the Lamb, they are incorporated as the judges who oversee judgment of the obdurate sinners. The winepress of God's wrath, which is now symbolized by a sea of glass mingled with fire, is now represented as a footstool of Jesus and the saints who had conquered the beast and its image and the number of its name. These overcomers had harps given by God. They sang the song of God's servant Moses and the Lamb. The song extols God for his great, marvellous, just, and true deeds. The question in the song, "Who will not fear you Lord and bring glory to your name?" shows that God's exceeding holiness deserves reverence, fear, and glory from all humanity. This scene echoes Ps 110:1–7, which extols the victory and enthronement of the Messiah.

The preposition describing where the triumphant saints were standing in relation to the fiery sea of glass is "upon" (Greek; ἐπί, epi). However, the NIV translates it as "beside." These two translations confer the sentence and scene very different meanings. Translating the preposition as "upon" confers the meaning that the sea of glass is Jesus' and the saints' footstool as they judge the world (Ps 110:1–7; Mal 4:3), whereas "beside" confers the meaning that Jesus and the saints would be joyful bystanders as judgment is executed on the sinful world. However, since Jesus and the saints will judge the world (1 Cor 6:2–5; Rev 20:4), then the most probable translation is "upon."

Semiotically, this sea of glass is different from the one in 4:6. The former, God's magnificent footstool, signifies God's majesty. The latter signifies the judgment of the enemies of Jesus and the saints who have become Jesus' and the saints' footstool (Ps 110:1–7; Luke 20:43). The symbolism also shows that the victorious saints are likewise enlisted as part of the jury in the judgment of Satan and the world (20:4).

The victorious saints were heard singing the song of Moses and the song of the Lamb. This song compares the joyous experience of those who will overcome the tribulations by the evil trinity with the experience of the Israelites after their redemption from Egypt (Exod 15:1–18). Here, the redemption and sustenance of the church throughout the unfolding history is depicted in light of the Exodus experience. The song celebrates her victory over the dragon, beast from the sea, and beast from the land. Viewed this way, the visionary simulation evokes hope to the church as she sojourns in her final exodus to her eternal home—the new heaven and new earth. Finally, the song of Moses and the Lamb worships God for decreeing just and well-deserved judgments that were to be simulated by the great and amazing portent described in vv. 1.

John then saw the inner sanctum of the temple (Greek: ναός, *Naos*) in heaven being opened. It is comparable to the tent of meeting in the wilderness during the Israelites' exodus. The tent of meeting was the courtroom in which Moses judged the children of Israel (Exod 33:7). It was also the place where Moses would intercede for the Israelites before God (Exod 33:1–17). Mirroring the present scene using imagery of the tent of meeting where judgment and intercessory were performed, serves as an interpretive cue. It shows that the ensuing vision was similarly simulating judgments of the obdurate. It also prepares the reader for the audition debarring intercession for the obdurate sinners until the wrath of God is fully poured on earth (vv. 8). The seven angels had seven plagues that would be poured on those who, despite having been shown God's grace in the preaching of the gospel, and the cajoling disciplinary judgments, slight it. The seven angels' priestly garments of pure, bright linen, with golden sashes around their chests, depict them as simulating God's righteous judgments.

The four living creatures then gave the seven angels seven golden bowls full of God's wrath. The seven angels are depicted as having had the plagues before they were given the bowls of God's wrath (vv. 6). It appears that each angel was to simulate the execution of one of the seven judgments that together quench the wrath of God against the obdurate. It also appears that the severity of these judgment plagues increases progressively from the first to the seventh (16:1–21). The disciplinary nature of these judgments, which gives room for repentance, demonstrates God's manifold grace as well as his justice. This scene shows that these plagues are unleashed upon people whose stubbornness has provoked God's wrath. Their stubbornness is highlighted by noting that notwithstanding the severity of the plagues, they did not repent (16:9, 11). They are depraved beyond redemption. This obstinacy is a prelude to the final judgment.

Then, John saw the temple, from where the angels came, filled with smoke from the glory and power of God. He auditions that "no one is allowed to get into the temple before the seven angels pour their bowls" (15:8). Ian Boxall interprets this scene as a barring of the entrance of the tent of meeting until the prayers of the saints, referred to in 5:8, are answered.[2] Thus, he sees the bowl judgments as an answer to the prayers of the saints. However, the worldwide nature of the victims suggests that the audition that "no one is allowed to get into the temple before the seven angels pour their bowls" shows that, once these last-tier judgments have been pronounced, God would not heed any prayer to reverse their execution. An example of such judgments is God's refusal to answer Samuel's prayer for Saul (1 Sam

---

2. Boxall, *Revelation*, 222.

16:1). This suggestion disparages the doctrine of purgatory and shows the futility of praying for dead sinners. Their lot is the second death. Holding this position would elicit evocations of fear and a strong desire to be watchful over the encroachment of sin in the individual and church.

Strategic and Communicative Acts in Rev 15

Showing the portent of seven angels with the last seven plagues is a strategic act. It is complemented by the communicative act in the audition "for with them the wrath of God is completed," in other words, "fully quenched." Furthermore, the audition, "with them, the wrath of God is quenched," highlights the finality of the judgments about to be simulated. The fact that the door for any intercession against execution of the judgment was closed must have evoked shivers among John's audience, leading the wayward to repentance. At the same time, the assurance of vindication comforted the persecuted saints.

Simulating the joy of the victors, in the scene showing those who had conquered the beast and its image and the number of its name, standing upon the sea of glass mingled with fire singing the song of Moses and the Lamb was gratifying to the seven churches. They saw their victory over the beast mirrored in the simulation. Moreover, it encouraged them to endure tribulations visited upon them by the evil trinity.

Showing one of the four living creatures giving seven golden bowls of God's wrath to the seven angels and the sanctuary being filled with smoke so that none could enter to intercede for the victims of God's wrath until the seven plagues were fully poured is a strategic act. It evoked fear that scared the seven churches from their lackluster historical situation that was described in the personalized covering letters (2:1—3:22). This visionary scene could jolt even the dead Sardis to fan her spiritual embers that were about to be extinguished.

Application of Evocations in Rev 15

Simulating the irrevocable nature of the last seven plagues was primarily intended to evoke fear that would lead the wayward in the seven churches to repentance before it was too late. It was also intended to assure the persecuted saints of their vindication thereby evoking patient endurance in their tribulations. It was encouraging to be assured that the saints will judge their tormentors. The scene showing the victorious saints singing the song of

Moses and the Lamb must have evoked zeal, fortitude, and deep satisfaction in following and serving God.

The visionary situation and the needs being addressed by this visionary revelation are common to the church of all ages. As such, the evocations generated by this scene's strategic acts would similarly evoke repentance in the wayward among today's church. Similarly, the strategic acts generated by showing the jubilation of the victorious saints can enthuse today's persecuted church to patiently endure tribulations as she awaits her soon-to-be-revealed vindication in the outworking of the last seven plagues as history unfolds.

REV 16

EXECUTION OF GOD'S LAST TIER JUDGMENTS

¹Then I heard a loud voice from the temple saying to the seven angels. "Go. Pour the seven bowls of God's wrath on the earth." ²The first angel poured his bowl on the land, and ugly, festering sores broke out on the people who had the mark of the beast and worshipped its image.

In this scene, John first hears a loud voice from the inner chamber of the tent of witness. This loud voice can be identified as coming from Jesus. He is the one directing the visionary revelation. The seven angels are part of the visionary cast, while the bowls full of God's wrath and the act of pouring the wrath of God on the world are symbols. They represent the judgment arising out of peoples' obduracy, notwithstanding God's grace rapprochements. Thus, these symbols represent events and theological themes outside of the constituent symbols. This observation suggests that we do not expect a moment in the unfolding history when a bowl full of the wrath of God will be physically or spiritually handed over to an angel to be poured on the earth. Instead, we expect the outworking of God's consequential decrees that are outworked as and when man stubbornly slights God's rapprochements in the work of Jesus on the cross. This visionary scene simulates part of the last-tier judgments that are meted on those who do not respond to God's rapprochements in the gospel message and the disciplinary judgments that were simulated after the blowing of the first four trumpets.

The first angel simulated an ongoing outworking of God's decreed judgments against obdurate sinners by pouring the contents of his bowl on the earth. As a result, harmful and painful sores broke out on the people who had the mark of the beast and who worshiped his image (vv. 2). A recall of a similar judgment in Egypt (Exod 9:8–10) illumines the nature of this woe. This is a discriminative judgment against the world and part of the lukewarm and dead church for their sin that is otherwise described as having the mark of the beast and worshiping its image. Though it is a last-tier judgment, it also serves as a rapprochement to those who witness its devastating effect. Once unleashed, there is no intercession that can persuade God to reverse these last-tier judgments.

³ *The second angel poured out his bowl into the sea, and it turned into blood like that of a dead person, and everything in the sea died.*

This second woe is a buildup of the judgment that is simulated when the first angel poured his bowl of God's wrath. It complements the impact of the simulation of the first plague. It is similar to the judgment meted when the second trumpet blowing angel sounded his trumpet. Whereas a third of the living creatures in the sea died in the former judgment, everything in the sea died in this judgment. It seems to be a heightened form of the former. Again, whereas the former was a disciplinary judgment and a rapprochement, the latter has an element of retribution. It would have a negative impact on international trade and more so transport of food leading to famine and death in many places. The judgment would also be intended to persuade those who witness its grave impact to repent of their idolatries.

⁴ *The third angel poured out his bowl on the rivers and springs of water, and they became blood* ⁵ *Then I heard the angel in charge of the waters say: "You are just in these judgments, Oh Holy One, you who are and who were;* ⁶*for they have shed the blood of your holy people and your prophets, and you have given them blood to drink as they deserve."* ⁷*And I heard the altar respond: "Yes, Lord God Almighty, true and just are your judgments."*

The judgment that is simulated by pouring a bowl full of a plague that turns the rivers and springs of water into blood recalls the judgment in Egypt (Exod 7:17–21). It is similar but a heightened form of the judgment that was simulated when the third trumpet-blowing angel sounded his trumpet (8:19–11). Particularly, this visionary revelation simulated a judgment that would be visited on those who had shed the blood of God's saints. The accompanying audition shows that it was a just recompense on persecutors of the martyrs. It is the answer to the cries of the martyrs whose souls were seen under the altar pleading for vengeance (6:10).

⁸ *The fourth angel poured out his bowl on the sun, and the sun was allowed to scorch people with fire.* ⁹ *They were seared by the intense heat and cursed God's name, who had control over these plagues but did not repent and glorify him.*

The fourth angel simulated a judgment in which God used a heat wave as an instrument of his wrath. Just as the judgment that was simulated when the fourth trumpet-blowing angel sounded his trumpet, this one also affected the sun. Whereas the former dimmed a third of the light giving heavenly bodies, this one unleashed a heat wave that scorched people with fire. Auditioning that they did not repent suggests that this judgment would be aimed at engendering repentance and doxology to God. However, shockingly, even after experiencing such an intensified sentence, the victims did not repent and glorify, but instead they cursed his name. This observation is aimed at justifying God for the succeeding judgments that culminated to the final judgment.

¹⁰The fifth angel poured out his bowl on the throne of the beast, and his kingdom was plunged into darkness. People gnawed their tongues in agony ¹¹and cursed the God of heaven because of their pains and their sores, but they refused to repent of what they had done.

The judgment simulated by the fifth angel is specific on the throne of the beast and his kingdom. It is reminiscent of a similar judgment on Egypt (Exod 10:21-23). However, this judgment appears to be more grievous than the Egyptian plague. It causes pain and sores and gnawing of tongues in pain and anguish on the beast and his kingdom. Disappointingly, the subjects of the beast's kingdom did not repent but instead cursed God. Over and above suggesting that having the mark of the beast is a sin that can be repented, the director of the visionary revelation is also showing how stubborn the kingdom of the beast was despite God's complementary rapprochements in judgments. After all, just like Egypt, it had its emperor who was worshiped as a god. Like Pharaoh in Egypt, they may have been asking, "Who is the Lord, that we should obey his voice?" (Exod 5:2). The stubbornness revealed in this visionary scene is used to justify God's final judgment on the sinful world.

¹²The sixth angel poured out his bowl on the great river Euphrates, and its water was dried up to prepare the way for the kings of the East. ¹³Then I saw three impure spirits that looked like frogs; they came out of the mouths of the dragon, the beast, and the false prophet. ¹⁴They are demonic spirits that perform signs, and they go out to the kings of the whole world to gather them for the battle on the great day of God Almighty. ¹⁵"Look, I come like a thief! Blessed is the one who stays awake and remains clothed so as not to go naked and be shamefully exposed." ¹⁶Then, they gathered the kings together to the place called Armageddon in Hebrew.

This scene simulates prophesied end-time, Satan-instigated apostasy and obduracy that will arouse God's wrath against Satan, the apostate and the obdurate world resulting to execution of the last judgment on a day referred to as the day of the Lord (Ezek 38:14-14, Dan. 12:1-2). Imagery from past acts of deliverance in the drying up of the Red Sea and River Jordan is reused in the reverse in this simulated battle array at a place called Armageddon in Hebrew. Whereas in the Egyptian exodus experience, the waters of the Red Sea and River Jordan were dried up to facilitate safe passage of Israel, this time around, the Euphrates is dried up to allow the kings of the east to cross over and prepare for battle on the great day of God the almighty. The evil trinity's seduction of the kings of the earth shown in verse 14 and the exhortation to the believers in verse 15 suggest that some of the saints would also be seduced to apostatize. The seduction also indicted the beast, false prophet, and the seduced world for their obduracy to God's various rapprochements.

This woe is simulated as a yet-to-be-fought battle. It was, however, simulated in the scene narrated in 9:19–21. It is further compared to a fierce battle against the saints by a confederate of Satan, after he is released from the abyss, and the mythical kings/kingdoms of Gog and Magog (20:7–9). These symbolic kings/kingdoms are similarly used in Ezekiel's oracle to assure Judah that God, her Suzerain King, would jealously protect her against any invaders who would attack her at a time of her peace and favor with God after the exile. This depiction was used to show Judah that as long as she remains faithful to God, he would always vindicate his holiness (Ezek 38:16), show his greatness, and make himself known in the eyes of many nations (Ezek 38:23) by protecting her from her would-be mockers and invaders. This visionary revelation draws its imagery from Ezekiel's oracle to encourage the church that God will be there for them as they face attacks from the evil trinity.

The great day of the Lord God almighty points to the day when God judges the world for apostasy and obduracy (Joel 3:2, 12; Zeph 3:8; Zech 12:3). The events precipitating the great day of the Lord are shown to be the work of evil spirits, hereby simulated by frogs coming out of the mouth of the dragon, beast from the sea, and beast from the land. Coming out of the mouth shows that they will use seductive lies comparable to the devil's deception of Eve in Eden. They usually deceive by performing counterfeit signs (vv. 14). Signs, in the gospels, were used to glorify Jesus and prove that he was indeed the Christ, the son of God (John 20:30). But the signs performed through deceptive spirits glorify the dragon, the beast, and the false prophets. They are aimed at subverting the saints' faith and trust in God.

Through the performance of signs, the frog spirits from the unholy trinity, hopping from one earthly king to another, will entice and gather them at a place that in Hebrew is called Armageddon—the mountain of destruction.[3] Armageddon is not a specific geographical location. To a great degree of probability, it is used to symbolize a Satan-induced worldwide state of hardness of heart and rebellion against God and the gospel, which inevitably kindles God's wrath against the disobedient (Col 3:6) leading to their destruction. Robert H. Mounce rightly argues that this apostasy and God's response are described as warfare to depict the conflict and the victory to follow as vividly as possible.[4]

Whereas the acts shown after pouring the contents of the sixth bowl simulate a worldwide satanic deception and rebellion against God, the events shown after pouring the contents of the seventh bowl reveal God's response to this rebellion by bringing the world to an end. Armageddon, therefore, describes an end-time rebellion against God that is followed by his response of judging the world. Koester argues that Armageddon is a derivative of Mount Megiddo, a place where God fought battles for his people, and as such, it is a "place name that portends the coming destruction of the adversaries of God."[5] His conclusion agrees with this commentary's argument.

Readers would have liked the vision director to identify the events signified in the symbols and metaphors used in these visionary revelations. This was not his intention. Rather, he intended to embed the visionary revelation with strategic acts that would evoke responses that would positively change the historical situations of the primary and the secondary readers. This particular visionary revelation was meant to demonstrate the effect of the wrath of God against ungodliness as well as reveal God's hatred of sin to engender a turnaround to godly living (Rom 1:18).

The exhortation to the seven churches is put in parenthesis in the ESV: "Behold I am coming like a thief! Blessed is the one who stays awake, keeping his garments on, that he may not go about naked and seen exposed" (vv. 15). Here, John, (now a prophet to many peoples, nations, languages. and kings (10:11) is speaking in the name of Jesus Christ. Blessedness is pronounced on those who stay awake and are clothed. The saints are being urged to resist the lies of the unholy alliance of the dragon (Satan), the beast (evil regimes), and the false prophet (compromising religion) that will lead many to apostasy in the unfolding history.

---

3. Caird, *Revelation*, 207.
4. Mounce, *What Are We Waiting For*, 83.
5. Koester, *Revelation*, 153.

> [17] The seventh angel poured his bowl into the air, and out of the temple came a loud voice from the throne saying, "It is done!" [18] Then there came flashes of lightning, rumblings, peals of thunder, and a severe earthquake. No earthquake like it has ever occurred since mankind has been on earth, so tremendous was the quake. [19] The great city split into three parts, and the cities of the nations collapsed. God remembered Babylon the Great and gave her the cup filled with the wine of the fury of his wrath. [20] Every Island fled away, and the mountains could not be found. [21] From the sky, huge hailstones, each weighing about a hundred pounds, fell on the people. And they cursed God on account of the plague of hail because the plague was so terrible.

When the seventh angel poured his bowl, John heard a voice from the throne declaring "it is done!" The thing declared as having been done is the fulfilment of the mystery of God mentioned in 10:7. The event is also simulated in 8:1, 11:19, and 14:14–20. It is the downfall of all the kingdoms of the world (represented by the collapse of the cities of the nations, including the great city of the time—Rome), the judgment of the whole world (20:11–15), and the passing away of the extant heaven and earth (21:1). Auditioning that the islands flew away and that the mountains could not be found shows that there was no hiding place from the horrors of the final judgment. The severity of the plague is compared to huge hailstones, each weighing about a hundred pounds, falling on the people. The efficacy of the embedded strategic act is heightened by the audition that the people cursed God on account of how terrible the plague was (vv. 21). Cursing God is a desperate invitation of death to escape the terrible pain of the plague (Job 2:9).

Strategic and Communicative Acts in Rev 16

A simulation of God's wrath being poured on those who had succumbed and received the mark of the beast constitutes a strategic act. It must have evoked fear in the saints of ever being judged as deserving such painful affliction. These were more grievous than the pain and suffering they would endure in opposing the evil trinity. It is a powerful impression that they would rather endure the present sufferings to later be rewarded with eternal life than enjoy the pleasures of sin in the present and suffer disciplinary judgments in the unfolding history that would culminate to such a severe retributory judgment.

Pouring the second, third, and fourth bowls together with the accompanying auditions pronouncing a death sentence (being given blood to drink, for they shed blood) is a strategic act. It must have evoked great fear in the lukewarm and dead churches and in the saints who were following the teachings of the Nicolaitans and the practices of Balaam. It was also aimed at evoking disdain for Romish debauchery disguised as pleasure.

Finally, showing the deception of the devil and his cahoots, personified as frogs coming out of the mouths of the dragon, the beast, and the false prophet, being peddled all over the world to subtly draw people to rebel against God was a very efficacious strategic act. It warned the saints against being covertly or overtly lured into sin. Further, it evoked watching and prayer for strength and discernment.

Application of Evocations in Rev 16

The church in Smyrna was going through tribulation (2:9); same with Pergamum (2:13) and Philadelphia (3:10). The others were going through trials and temptations of various kinds depending on their social, economic, and religious contexts. All these issues were impacting their response to faith and Christian praxis. The evocations generated by the strategic acts in the visionary revelation narrated in this chapter were intended to arouse an assurance of vindication which in turn emboldened the saints' endurance in tribulations. They were also intended to evoke repentance in those who may have succumbed to sin.

Persecuted secondary readers of all ages would also be assured of eventual vindication. This in turn would birth patient endurance in their tribulations. The saints going through daily trials and temptations would equally be emboldened in their struggles against sin. Readers who are entangled in sin would be urged to repent, watch and pray as they await the coming of their saviour Jesus Christ. Finally, these woes urge readers to always appraise their ways and conform them to the dictates of the word of God.

REV 17–19:4

JUDGMENT OF THE GREAT PROSTITUTE

[1] *Then one of the seven angels having the seven bowls came and said to me, "Come along, I will show you the judgment of the great prostitute who is seated on many waters,* [2] *with whom the kings of the earth have committed adultery, and the inhabitants of the earth have been intoxicated by the wine of her adulteries."* [3] *So he carried me away in the spirit into a wilderness, and I saw a woman sitting on a scarlet beast full of blasphemous names, and it had seven heads and ten horns.* [4] *The woman was clothed in purple and scarlet and adorned with gold, jewels, and pearls. Holding a golden cup full*

of abominations and the impurities of her fornication, ⁵*and on her forehead was written a mystery name: Babylon the great, mother of harlots and earth's abominations.* ⁶*And I saw that the woman was drunk with the blood of the saints and the witnesses to Jesus. When I saw her, I was greatly amazed.*

This chapter narrates a visionary simulation that introduces the nature and judgment of an entity metaphorically described as the great prostitute who is seated on many waters, with whom the kings of the earth have committed adultery, and the inhabitants of the earth have been intoxicated by the wine of her adulteries (vv. 1–2). The prostitute stands in metonymy for the city of Rome (vv. 9, 18), which in turn is used in synecdoche of part for whole to stand for an idolatrous, adulterous, and sin-soaked world that opposes God and kills his saints. The chapter also describes the power structures that work out the prostitute's heinous agenda. Her description and symbolism suggest that they are a visionary foil which magnifies the power and gait of the prostitute and the vileness of the instrumentality with which she intoxicates the inhabitants of the earth. In turn, this foil magnifies God's salvation, glory, power (19:1) and his true and just judgments when he finally avenges the blood of his servants on her (19:2).

The derogatory title "the great prostitute" is a metaphor. The Old Testament uses the metaphor "prostitution" in two ways. When used in reference to Israel, it describes her backslidden state from the worship of the true God, who alone is worthy of worship, to the worship of other gods (Lev 17:7; Isa 1:21; Jer 3:1). When it was used in reference to other nations, it referred to affluent cities that attracted kings and merchants from other nations to visit for diplomacy, trade, tourism, and at times to sample the host's orgies and debauchery. In the process, if the host nation was idolatrous, the visitors would also be sucked into her idolatry (Isa 23:15–18; Nah. 3:4). Adela Yarbro Collins supports this position in her supposition that "the harlot image was applied by the prophets both to the people of God (Hos 4:12–18; Isa 1:21; Jer 3:3–10; Ezek 16:15–58, 23:1–49) and their enemies (Nah 3:4; Isa 23:15–18). When applied to the people of God, the image is related to foreign alliances and cultic practices."⁶ These two images were in view in this visionary simulation.

At the time John saw this visionary revelation, the Roman Empire allowed polytheism. According to Keener, "Official state worship included not only worship of the emperor but also the worship of the goddess Roma."⁷ As such, the tag of a prostitute was apt for Rome. The Old Testament described cities built by the coast as sitting on many waters (Ezek 27:3). Rome,

---

6. Collins, *Crisis and Catharsis*, 121.
7. Keener, *Revelation*, 405.

built beside the Tiber River, could be described as sitting on many waters. However, in this scene, the guiding angel identifies the many waters the prostitute sat on as peoples, multitudes, nations, and languages (vv. 15). Apart from being idolatrous, she was also accused of intoxicating the earth's inhabitants with her adulteries. The word intoxication describes the seduction, entrenchment, and proliferation of sinful Romish ways in the then-known world.

The symbol of the desert (vv. 3a) echoes Israel's exodus through the wilderness for forty years before she entered the promised land. In this visionary scene, the wilderness symbolizes the church's perilous context of tribulations in form of trials, temptations, and persecutions in the unfolding history as she awaits her blessed hope—the glorious appearing of our great God and savior, Jesus Christ (Titus 2:13).

The beast on which the prostitute sat on recalls the beast from the sea in 13:1. It represents the Roman Emperors. The blasphemous names covering the beast may be referring to the deification of the emperors. They also act as a charge sheet of the sins for which she was to be judged. The scarlet color of the beast is a fear-evoking representation of its bloody persecution of the saints. "To sit" stands for "to be enthroned," "to dwell," or "to literally sit on." The prostitute's posture revealed the identity, nature, and extent of her influence. Noting that the seven heads stand for the seven hills identifies the woman as the city of Rome, which was built on seven hills. The entire symbol revealed the vastness—in space and time of power—and influence of her dominion.

The prostitute's royal adornment and sheer opulence represent the city's political power and the seduction of the world into her sinful lifestyle. Outwardly, she appeared admirably adorned, but the cup in her hand unmasks her real character. The cupful of abominations and impurities of her sexual immorality represents Rome's sensuality, idolatry, and unfair business practices.

Noting that her name is mysterious shows that it is embedded with symbolic meaning. The name "Babylon" ascribes attributes of old Babylon to the city of Rome. It echoes the oppression of God's people and the boasting of Nebuchadnezzar (Dan 4:30). However, just as God punished Nebuchadnezzar for his boasting over the splendor of Babylon (Dan 4:30), so would he punish Rome (19:20). Referring to Rome as Babylon also compares her destruction of the Herodian temple and persecution of the church for refusing to worship her emperors and their images with Babylon's destruction of Solomon's temple, exiling the Jews, and forcing them to worship her emperor's image (Dan 3:1-6). The prostitute could also represent future religio-political ideologies and leaders who would work against God's people and the gospel. The adjective "mother" shows that the city of Rome was the inventor and hub of immorality and idolatry.

She was depicted as drunk with the blood of the saints, the blood of those who bore the testimony of Jesus (vv. 6). This description identifies the prostitute as a passionate persecutor of the saints. The parallelism in the depiction highlights the innocence of the saints and the honorable charge for which they were persecuted and killed—they bore the testimony of Jesus. John notes that when he saw the prostitute, he was greatly astonished. He purposely aimed at evoking the same astonishment in his audience (vv. 6b).

The symbolic representation of Rome is an unchallengeable charge sheet against her. It is a gory picture of the sins for which she was to be judged. This portrait is meant to enlist the readers to be part of the jury to condemn Rome and, in so doing, condemn all forms of waywardness in their lives. It also justifies God for judging her. The embarrassingly explicit symbolism evoked abhorrence for her seductive and idolatrous lifestyle.

The portent of this prostitute is contrasted with the bride of the Lamb (21:9), who also stands in metonymy for a contrasting city—the New Jerusalem—which in turn stands in synecdoche of part for whole for the new heaven and earth, which is adorned with the righteous deeds of the saints (19:8) and in which the presence of God pervades as to qualify to adopt Ezekiel's description—Jehovah Shammah (Ezek 48:35). This contrast is aimed at evoking deep abhorrence of the sinful ways of Rome and a yearning for the promised eternity with God in the new heaven and earth.

[7] Then the angel said to me, "Why are you so amazed? I will tell you the mystery of the woman and of the beast with seven heads and ten horns that she rides. [8] The beast you saw, once was, and now is not, and yet will come up out of the abyss and go to its destruction. And the inhabitants of the earth, whose names have not been written in the book of life from the foundation of the world, will be amazed when they see the beast because it was and is not and is to come. [9] This calls for a mind that has wisdom; the seven heads are seven mountains on which the woman is seated; also, they are seven kings, [10] of whom five have fallen, one is living, and the other has not yet come, and when he comes, he must remain only a little while. [11] As for the beast that was and is not, it is an eighth, but it belongs to the seven, and it goes to destruction.

[12] And the ten horns that you saw are the ten kings, who have not yet received a kingdom, but they are to receive authority as kings for one hour together with the beast. [13] These are united in yielding their power and authority to the beast, [14] they will make war on the Lamb, and the lamb will conquer them for he is the Lord of lords and King of kings, and those with him are called and chosen and faithful.

¹⁵And he said to me, "The waters you saw, where the harlot is seated are peoples and multitudes and nations and languages. ¹⁶And the ten horns that you saw, they and the beast will hate the prostitute, make her desolate and naked, devour her flesh, and burn her up with fire. ¹⁷For God has put it into their hearts to carry out his purpose by agreeing to give their kingdom to the beast until the words of God will be fulfilled. ¹⁸The woman you saw is the great city that rules over the kings of the earth."

The guiding angel's question, "Why are you astonished?" (vv. 7), is a rhetorical question. It is meant to prepare John for more astonishment after the angel thoroughly explains the "mystery of the prostitute and the beast she rides which had seven heads and ten horns" (vv. 7). Noting that the prostitute did not only sit on the beast but also rode it, suggests that Rome used the beast and their vassal kings to further her political, economic, and cultic agenda.

The angel described the entity signified by the beast as "once was, now is not, and yet will come up from the abyss and go to its destruction" (vv. 8a). Mounce has postulated that "once was, now is not, and yet will come up from the abyss and go to its destruction" is an obvious parody of the Lamb, who was put to death yet came back to life and now is alive forever (1:18; 2:8).[8] It is doubtful whether a divine director of the vision would use such a caricature of the Lamb to show the attributes of his sinful opposers. Furthermore, it would not have any evocative or rhetorical value to the audience, a necessity in every strategic or communicative act in the visionary revelation.

Other scholars have hypothesized that this description fits Nero, who committed suicide in 68 CE. A legend speculated that Nero would resurrect to wage war against Rome.[9] It is also doubtful that a divinely guided visionary revelation would use such absurdity to advance its course. Even if the vision were John's apocalyptic method of communicating his theology, it would still be doubtful that a minister of John's Hebraic background and monotheistic inclinations would ascribe resurrection power outside the ambit of the only true God, who alone has numinous power to resurrect the dead.

However, it is feasible to envision a personified persecution akin to the one visited upon Christians by Nero being visited upon the believers by future emperors. In this case, the beast would be an ideology and not a person. The phrase can also refer to the devil, who had exercised unbridled power on earth; thus, "he was" (12:7-8) but at the time of showing the vision "was

---

8. Mounce, *Revelation*, 314.
9. Keener, *Revelation*, 338.

not" because he was incapacitated by the work of Jesus Christ on the cross, as one incarcerated in the abyss (20:1). But towards the end of time, he will be allowed to instigate a short-lived apostasy (20:3, 7). Afterward, he will be thrown into a lake of fire to simulate his painful and eternal damnation (20:10).

The certainty expressed in the audition describing the release of the beast from the abyss favours the supposition that the beast also role-plays the devil. He is contrasted with the Lord God who was, is, and is to come (1:4; 8). The devil is the only one who can awe the inhabitants of the earth, whose names are not written in the book of life from the creation of the world when he is loosed from the abyss to make war with the Lamb (20:7-8). Indeed, the empire operated under his influence. Arguably, such an audition is a communicative act that serves to minimize the fear which Satan evokes in the saints, thereby evoking contempt towards him and greater endurance of his instigated tribulations.

What the angel is about to reveal in the next audition requires a mind with wisdom (vv. 9). The referred wisdom was the knowledge of the extant historical situation which included the empire's geography, social, political, and religious affairs. The guiding angel identified the seven heads of the beast as the seven hills on which the woman sits (vv. 9). A mind with the knowledge of the empire's geography would have known that Rome was built on seven hills. This explanation identifies the woman as signifying the idolatrous city of Rome.

Historically, the seven heads may also refer to successive kings who ruled Rome. Five have fallen, one is, the other has not come, but when he does come, he must remain for only a little while (vv. 10). Because of the time distance and lack of a mediating pre-understanding, scholars have tried in vain to match these kings with the historical emperors of Rome. However, this visionary revelation is not aimed at revealing historical or eschatological reality. Instead, it is meant to inspire faith and hope in God and evoke resilience to tribulations. Suffice it to note that Rome was led by emperors assisted by their vassal kings in its provinces.

Over and above the description of the beast as one that "once was, now is not, and yet will come up out of the Abyss and go to destruction" (vv. 8), it is further said that it also references an eighth king who belongs to the seven (represented by the heads) and is going to destruction (vv. 11). Thus, the beast could be signifying more than one referent. Whichever is the referent, the saints can take courage in that these persecuting powers will go to destruction sooner than later (17:14, 19:19–20, and 20:10).

Alongside the kings, signified by the beast's heads, are other kings, (signified by the beast's ten horns) (vv. 12). They will receive authority for just one hour. This audition suggests that these kings could be the end-time kings who would be enlisted by the dragon to wage war against the Lamb and the saints (16:14; 19:19–21; 20:8–9). It also emphasizes the short tenure of their opposition to the saints. This litotic emphasis evoked comfort in the saints who were facing persecution.

The audition "they have one purpose and will give their power and authority to the beast" explains that they perform the same task as the beast (vv. 13), that is, wage war against the Lamb. However, the Lamb will triumph over them because he is the Lord of lords and the King of kings, and with him will be his called, chosen, and faithful followers (vv. 14). Thus, this audition describes an event similar to the one narrated in 16:12–16, 19:19–21, and 20:7–10. The beast role-plays Satan or satanic forces.

Identifying the waters where the prostitute sits as peoples, multitudes, nations, and languages (vv. 15) shows the proliferation of the whore's seduction among the peoples of the earth in both space and time. The angel then auditioned that at a future time, the beast, in alliance with other kings represented by the ten horns, will hate *the* prostitute and bring her to ruin (vv.16). Thus, she will self-destroy herself from within with the connivance of her emperors and vassal kings. However, Rome was used to represent the whoring world then and in the unfolding history. The fate of the whore is explained using imagery borrowed from Judah's fate, as explicated in Jer 4:30–31, where the prophet warns whoring Judah that eventually, her erstwhile suitors would despise and seek her life. The aftermath of the whore's overthrow is simulated in the visions narrated in chapter 18. The prostitute's judgment is hope-inspiring to people facing tribulation at the hands of similar victims of God's future judgment.

The guiding angel identified the whore as signifying the city of Rome (vv. 18). Representing Rome in the symbol of a harlot, whereas a harlot stands for idolatry, shows that in visionary metalepsis, the whore in the vision stands for idolatry and blasphemy that were the characteristics of the empire, its emperors, and provincial kings. Just as Nero, the enigmatic persecutor of the church was used to personify latter-day persecutors and persecution, so is his former seat, the city of Rome, used to represent persecution of the saints, idolatry, and sin in the world in the unfolding history. This harlot city is later contrasted with the virgin, the bride of the Lamb of God, and the longing of the church—the New Jerusalem (21:2). Whereas New Jerusalem represents the habitation of God among the saints in the new heaven and new earth, Rome represents the work of Satan in the present heaven *a*nd *e*arth. Whereas the New Jerusalem is eternal, Rome is temporal—"was, is not and is to rise from the bottomless pit to face eternal damnation" (vv. 8).

Though many studies have tried to identify the referents of the symbolic cast in this visionary scene, it is noteworthy to point out that the primary intention of showing the vision does not envisage identification of the exact personages, dominions, and events represented by the visionary cast. Similar to prehistoric narrative hagiography, divine visions do not necessarily demand authentication of the scientific or historical exactness of the simulated events. Whereas prehistoric narrative hagiography seeks to build faith, divine visions are strategic acts that seek to elicit evocations that would engender urgently needed change.

Strategic and Communicative Acts in Rev 17

Showing the alluring worldly city in the symbol of a woman alluringly arrayed in purple, scarlet, gold, jewels, and pearls constitutes a strategic act. Her real character is revealed in the golden cup she holds in her hand full of the filth of her abominations and the impurities of her sexual immorality. It is further enhanced by the name on her forehead: "Babylon the great, mother of prostitutes and earth's abominations" (vv. 5). This strategic act is meant to cause the saints to cringe from the allure and subtlety of Romish sins.

Auditioning that the woman was drunk with the blood of the saints shows the reason for her punishment. It was aimed at justifying God's wrath and judgment. The gory and explicit symbolic description of her sins and judgment was meant to show how obnoxious sin is to evoke repentance of the lovelessness in Ephesus and sexual immorality in Pergamum and Thyatira. It would also resurrect dead Sardis and revive the spiritual embers of lukewarm Laodicea.

Predicting the demise of Rome by the treachery of her emperors and their vassal kings minimizes the image of invincibility and awe with which she was perceived by her subjects. It is a strategic act that could evoke hope and contentment among the persecuted saints in the knowledge that they will soon be vindicated against their persecutors.

Application of Evocations in Rev 17

Revealing the sins of Rome, and that she would be judged for her atrocities against the church, pacified and vindicated the saints who were suffering persecution at her hands. It not only assured them that God would finally give them justice but was also a strong encouragement against succumbing to compromise with Romish ways. Finally, it called the wayward and those who had received the mark of the beast to repentance.

The contemporary church operates within governments, social systems, and ideologies that are more idolatrous and seductive than the first-century Roman system. Though the human rights movements and other watchdog agencies are constantly blowing the whistle against nations that persecute people for their faith, we still have rogue states which persecute Christians. Other subtle methods used to inculcate evil in the world are the mainline media houses and the world-wide-web. Human rights groups also campaign for unbiblical rights such as abortion, homosexuality, and other immoral and unbiblical practices. These vices are more subtle, intrusive, and pervasive than religious controls and persecutions by rogue governments. The strategic acts in this visionary revelation are efficacious enough to evoke hatred of the sins prevalent in first-century Rome that are also widespread today in very subtle forms.

REV 18

WORLD LAMENTS OVER THE JUDGMENT OF BABYLON THE GREAT

¹After this, I saw another angel coming down from heaven. He had great authority, and the earth was illuminated by his splendor. ²With a mighty voice, he shouted, "Fallen! Fallen is Babylon the Great. She has become a dwelling for demons and a haunt for every impure spirit, a haunt for every unclean bird, a haunt for every unclean and detestable animal. ³For all the nations have drunk the wrath of the wine of her adulteries. The kings of the earth committed adultery with her, and the merchants of the earth grew rich from her excessive luxuries."

This scene is a continuation of the previous visionary simulation. However, it is introduced by a different angel who auditions the aftermath of God's judgment of Rome as aforementioned (17:16-17). His words, "Fallen! Fallen is Babylon the Great!" depict the whoring city as having been already fallen. After this, he described the aftermath of the fall. He compares her changed fortunes from royalty, riches, and glamor to being a place that is only fit to be dwelt by demons, a haunt for every unclean spirit, a haunt for every unclean and detestable bird, and a haunt for every unclean beast (vv. 2). In Middle Eastern and many African cosmologies, places where unclean birds such as owls live are associated with evil spirits, death, and bad omens. The contrast between Babylon's former admirable mien and her abhorrent state after God's judgment demonstrates how fearful it is to face the wrath of God.

The angel then explains the reason why Babylon was so harshly judged. She was the hub of sin, as shown in the statement that "for all the nations have drunk the wrath of the wine of her adulteries. The kings of the earth committed adultery with her, and the merchants of the earth grew rich from her excessive luxuries" (vv. 3). Thus, she seduced the kings of the earth into her sinful ways, and now they share in the wrath occasioned by her sins. Her love for luxury and opulence attracted merchants who supplied her with goods and services to satisfy her insatiable licentious lifestyle. For this, she attracted the punishment being pronounced against her. This sentence evoked fear and warned the seven churches not to succumb to Romish-instigated tribulations and the allure of her licentious lifestyle.

[4] *Then I heard another voice from heaven say, "Come out of her, my people, so that you will not share in her sins so that you will not receive any of her plagues;"* [5] *for her sins are piled up to heaven, and God has remembered her crimes.* [6] *Give back to her as she has given; pay her back double for what she has done. Pour her a double portion from her own cup.* [7] *Give her as much torment as the glory and luxury she gave herself. In her heart, she boasts, 'I sit enthroned as queen. I am not a widow; I will never mourn.* [8] *Therefore, in one day, her plagues will overtake her; death, mourning, and famine. She will be consumed by fire, for mighty is the Lord God who judges her.*

[9] *When the kings of the earth who committed adultery with her and shared her luxury see the smoke of her burning, they will weep and mourn over her.* [10] *Terrified at her torment, they will stand far off and cry, "Woe! Woe to you, great city, you mighty city of Babylon! In one hour, your doom has come!"* [11] *"The merchants of the earth will weep and mourn over her because no one buys their cargoes anymore,* [12] *cargoes of gold, silver, precious stones and pearls, fine linen, purple, silk, and scarlet cloth; every sort of citron wood and articles of every kind, made of ivory. Costly wood, bronze, iron, and marble* [13] *cargoes of cinnamon and spice, incense, myrrh and frankincense, wine and olive oil, fine flour, and wheat; cattle and sheep; horses and carriages, and human beings sold as slaves.* [14] *"They will say. 'The fruit you longed for is gone from you. All your luxury and splendour have vanished, never to be recovered;* [15] *The merchants who sold these things and gained their wealth from her will stand far off, terrified at her torment. They will weep and mourn* [16] *and cry out Woe! Woe to you, great city, dressed in fine linen, purple and scarlet, and glittering with gold, precious stones, and pearls!* [17] *In one hour, such great wealth has been brought to ruin!' Every sea captain, all who travel by ship, the sailors, and all who earn their living from the sea, will stand far*

off. ¹⁸ *When they see the smoke of her burning, they will exclaim., 'Was there ever a city like this great city?'* ¹⁹ *They will throw dust on their heads and cry out with weeping and mourning, "'Woe! Woe to you, great city, where all who had ships on the sea became rich through her wealth! In one hour, she has been brought to ruin'* ²⁰ *"Rejoice over her, you heavens! Rejoice, you people of God! Rejoice, apostles and prophets! For God has judged her with the judgment she imposed on you."*

The great authoritative angel's warning through auditioning Rome's judgment and its awful aftermath is followed by a rapprochement in a plea (vv. 3) by a voice from haven. It is addressed to some in the seven churches, hereto referred as "my people" to "come out of Babylon," lest they share in her sins and consequent judgment. Her sins are said to be piled up to heaven. To be piled up to heaven is an idiomatic expression showing that Rome's sin had preceded her (1 Tim 5:24), a result of which God remembered her iniquities (vv. 4-5). Her judgment is therefore certain. Essentially, this is a call to the seven churches not to be unequally yoked with the sinful ways of doomed Rome.

The voice from heaven prays for a recompense of a double portion of judgment similar to the atrocities she had done against her subjects (vv. 6). The prayer is framed in conformity to Jesus' word in Luke 6:37-38—"Do not judge, and you will not be judged. Do not condemn, and you will not be condemned. Forgive and you will be forgiven. Give, and it will be given to you. A good measure, pressed down, shaken together and running over, will be poured into your lap. For with the measure you use, it will be measured to you." The voice from heaven amplifies the recompense by praying, "Give her as much torment and grief as the glory and luxury she gave herself" (vv. 6-7). What she never imagined could befall her was willed to be visited upon her—death, mourning, and famine. God's fast and furious judgment when provoked by man's stubbornness is shown in the pronouncement that Rome's plagues will come "in a single day, death and mourning and famine and that she will be burned up with fire; for mighty is the Lord God who has judged her" (vv. 8).

The voice from heaven continued to audition the severity of Babylon's judgment (vv. 9-20). It describes the swiftness of God's judgment by enacting a dirge of the kings of the earth bemoaning the fall of Babylon (vv. 9-10). The wailing of the worldly kings on seeing Rome's judgment demonstrates how despicable sin is. It also shows how grave its consequences are. This eerie demonstration was intended to jolt a section of the seven churches, especially the church in Sardis and Laodicea, to repent of their compromise with the sinful world systems and respond fully to the gospel.

It also speaks to the heretics in Pergamum and the sexually immoral in the church of Thyatira to turn away from their waywardness.

The voice from heaven continued to audition the disgraceful downfall of Babylon from wealth and splendor to utter ruin through envisioning a dirge by merchants of the earth who sold their cargoes to Rome at the height of her prosperity (vv. 11–17a). The dirge was sung in the historical present (present indicative mood) to make it more evocative. Such lamentation as "they weep (Greek: κλαίουσιν, klaiousin) and mourn (Greek: πενθοῦσιν, penthousin) because they had lost an important business partner and no one bought their cargo anymore" (vv. 11) highlights the severity of Rome's judgment. It also showed the futility of pursuing worldly glory at the expense of faith and trust in God. It prompted John's audience not to be envious of the arrogant when they saw the prosperity of the wicked (Ps 73:3). Instead, it urged them to trust in God. It also shows that when the judgment of God is finally visited on the sinner, even friends and acquaintances cannot offer help.

The heavenly voice auditioned a third lament by the shipmasters and seafaring men, sailors, and those whose trade relied on the sea (vv. 17b–19). They mourned the great downfall of the unparalleled city that was the lifeline of their businesses. Their dirge is reported in the past tense. Thus, they are portrayed as having witnessed the last embers of the devastation and downfall of Rome. They are said to have stood (Greek: ἔστησαν, estēsan) far off and cried (Greek: ἔκραζον, ekrazon) as they saw (βλέποντες, blepontes) the smoke of her burning. Their lament simulates great anguish more so because the demise of the city was a death blow to their business. This lament was concluded with an encouragement to the heavens, saints, apostles, and prophets, who had faced persecution and martyrdom while on earth to rejoice because God had avenged them against Rome by judging her with the same judgment that she had imposed on them (vv. 20). The encouragement shows that Rome's judgment was an answer to the martyrs' prayers for vindication (6:9–11).

²¹ Then a mighty angel picked up a boulder the size of a large millstone, threw it into the sea, and said, "With such, the great city of Babylon will be thrown down, never to be found again. ²² The music of harpists and musicians, pipers and trumpeters, will never be heard in you again. No worker of any trade will ever be found in you again. The stone of a millstone will never be heard in you again. ²³ The light of a lamp will never shine in you again. The voice of bridegrooms and brides will never be heard in you again. Your merchants were the world's most important people. By your magic spell, all the nations were led astray. ²⁴*In her was found the blood of prophets, God's holy people, and all who have been slaughtered on the earth."*

Finally, John saw a simulation summarizing Rome's judgment. It was simulated by a mighty angel who picked up a giant boulder, the size of a millstone and threw it into the sea. This demonstrative act was followed with the audition "with such violence, the great city of Babylon will be thrown down, never to be found again. The music of harpists and musicians, pipers, and trumpeters, will never be heard in you again. No worker of any trade will ever be found in you again. The sound of the millstone will never be heard in you again. The light of a lamb will never shine in you again. The voice of the bridegroom and bride will never be heard in you again. Your merchants were the world's important people. By your magic spell all the nations were led astray. In her was found the blood of the prophets and of God's holy people, of all who have been slaughtered on the earth" (vv. 21–24). In some African cultures, the pronouncement of a curse is accompanied by breaking a cooking pot with the words "may the one who has done such a thing break to smithereens like this pot." Such curses cause shivers in the ones who witness their pronouncement. Likewise, the narration of this visionary revelation must have sent shivers among the audience. It echoes Matt 18:6—"But whoever causes one of these little ones who believe in me to sin, it would have been better for him to have a great millstone fastened around his neck and drowned into the depth of the sea." Rome had caused the kings, merchants, seafarers, and some believers to sin against God. She had to face the full wrath of God.

REV 19:1–4

¹*After this, I heard what sounded like the roar of a great multitude in heaven shouting, "Hallelujah! Salvation, glory, and power belong to our God, ²for true and just are his judgments. He has condemned the great prostitute who corrupted the earth by her adultery. He has avenged on her the blood of his servants." ³And again they shouted, Hallelujah! The smoke from her goes up forever and ever." ⁴The twenty-four elders and the four living creatures fell and worshipped God, who was seated on the throne. And they cried, Amen, Hallelujah!"*

After the visionary scene enacting the gruesome aftermath of Babylon's judgment, John heard a heavenly throng praising God for her judgment. The praising multitude can be identified as the people of God, apostles, and prophets (18:20). They were called upon to rejoice, for God had judged the great prostitute with a judgment of equal measure to the tribulation she had imposed on them (18:20). The phrase "salvation, glory and power belong to our God, for true and just are his judgments" suggest that much as God's true judgments show God's glory and power, they are also salvific in nature.

"Hallelujah!" is a call to praise God. It is also an expression of praise. John is made to hear the praise in heaven over the judgment on Babylon to highlight its centrality. By it, God avenged on Babylon the blood (death) of his servants. It is also the commencement of the judgments that dethrones the dragon and his minions after which the everlasting kingdom of God in the new heaven and earth is established. In contrast to the earth's lament over the severe judgment of Babylon, heaven praises God for his true and just judgments over her. The contrast shows that the things that are seen by the lamenting world as enviable, great, and mighty (18:9), delicacies and splendors (18:14), riches and wealth (18:19) are seen by heaven as corruption and immorality (19:2).

The further call to praise, "Hallelujah! The smoke from her goes up forever and ever" (vv. 3), praises God for the severe and eternal judgments meted on Babylon—the great prostitute. Finally, the twenty-four elders and the four living creatures joined in the worship of God for avenging the saints by falling down in worship to God, saying, "Amen. Hallelujah!" (vv. 4). As representatives of the heavenly host, the twenty-four elders and the four living creatures agree with the once-persecuted servants of God, the prophets, and the apostles in their worship and rejoicing with an "Amen Hallelujah" (vv. 4).

Strategic and Communicative Acts in Rev 18:1—19:4

The strategic act embedded in throwing a bounder into the sea must have greatly shocked John and his audience. The audience must have experienced a shock therapy that would evoke 1) assurance of total vindication for their persecution by Rome, and 2) fear of acting in ways that would lead to being judged as Rome was. Assurance of total vindication would further evoke perseverance in tribulation. Fear would also evoke repentance.

Simulation of the joy in heaven over God's severe but just judgment of Mystery Babylon is an apt strategic act. First, it exposed God's loathing and disgust for sin and desire for man's undivided loyalty. Being unequally yoked with Babylon is referred to as prostitution and corruption of the earth (vv. 2). Auditioning that the "smoke of the judgment of God rises forever" shows the severe and eternal effects of rousing the wrath of God through slight of the great salvation that he has wrought in the death of Jesus. Thus, the simulation served as a serious warning to the seven churches not to entertain sin of any kind.

Application of Evocations in Rev 18:1—19:4

This vision explicitly exhorts John's audience not to be unequally yoked with sinful worldly systems. The message "Come out of her, my people, so that you will not share in her sins so that you will not receive any of her plagues" is communicated very powerfully. It is heaven's call to every believer to shun the world's sinful ways and pursue holiness.

The church in Thyatira must have been shaken by the simulation of the judgment against the great prostitute. Rome's sins were similar to the sins of some of her members. Similarly, the fall of Rome must have served as a warning and rebuke to the pride of the churches in Sardis and Laodicea, which like her, prided in lacking nothing but godliness.

The vices identified in the churches in Sardis and Laodicea are common vices that have stalked the church throughout history. Countries and individuals in the present world are in a mad race for riches, glamor, and honor. World business is carried out through deceit. Trade deals are negotiated through arm-twisting tactics as countries and individuals seek undue advantage over one another. Seductive advertisements, corruption, and all manner of sin are served together with trade.

The sins of idolatry and adultery are very prevalent in our days. Hedonism and materialism are the main goddesses and gods of our time. If Rome's idolatry and immorality attracted God's judgment, ours would attract the same. The strategic acts in this visionary revelation should equally jolt us to forsake these gods and goddesses to follow the living God who alone is worthy to be praised.

REV 19:5-10

TAKEOVER OF THE KINGDOM OF BABYLON THE GREAT BY THE ALMIGHTY GOD

⁵And a voice came from the throne, saying, "Praise our God, all you his servants, you who fear him, both great and small!" ⁶Then I heard what sounded like a great multitude, like the roar of rushing waters and like loud peals of thunder, shouting: Hallelujah! For our Lord God Almighty reigns. ⁷Let us rejoice and be glad and give him glory! For the wedding of the Lamb has come, and his bride has made herself ready. ⁸And it was given to her that she should be clothed in fine, bright and clean linen." (Fine linen stands for the righteous acts of the saints). ⁹*Then the angel said to me, "Write this, "Blessed are those who are invited to the wedding supper of the Lamb!" And he added, "These are the true words of God."* ¹⁰*At this, I fell at his feet to worship him. But he said to me, "Don't do that! I am a fellow servant with you and with your brothers and sisters who hold the testimony of Jesus. Worship God! For it is the Spirit of prophecy who bears the testimony of Jesus."*

After John saw the simulation of the heavenly praise of God for overthrowing the harlot city, he saw the simulation of the consequential takeover of her kingdoms by God. John heard a voice from the throne calling all God's servants, those who fear him, both great and small to praise God (vv. 5). Here, the throne is used in synechdoche for the entire host in the heavenly court room except God. God's servants could be the same persons who had been called to rejoice over the severe judgment of the great prostitute (18:20). They could also include the readers of the text who, this far, are immersed into the narration of the visionary revelation. The response "Hallelujah! For our Lord God Almighty reigns" is an exclamation of joyful doxology. It suggests that the consequential outcome of the overthrow of the harlot city is the complete takeover of the kingdoms of the world by the almighty God (vv. 6). The succeeding phrase "Let us rejoice and be glad and give him glory! For the wedding of the Lamb has come and his bride has made herself ready" (vv. 7) puts the reign of God in progressive parallelism with the wedding of the Lamb. The parallelism shows that the two are synonymous. Ian Paul rightly opines, "The reign of God here is expressed precisely in the unhindered union of Jesus with his people as the wedding of the Lamb for which his bride has made herself ready."[10]

The bride, wedding, marriage, and wife motifs have been used in the Christian Scripture to describe various aspects of the relationship between YHWH and Israel (Jer 31:32; Hos 2:19–21), as well as aspects of the relationship between Christ and the church. In the Israelite culture of John's time, after the betrothal and payment of the dowry, the groom would leave the bride in her father's home. Meanwhile, he would return to his father's home to prepare a matrimonial house for his new bride, plan and prepare for a wedding banquet after which, on a day unbeknown to her, he would return to take her to the wedding ceremony and a celebratory banquet in their future matrimonial home.[11] In the New Testament, these motifs have been used to describe aspects of gospel proclamation, soteriology, the relationship between Jesus and the church, the second advent of Christ and the

---

10. Paul, *Revelation*, 129.
11. Paul, *Revelation*, 129.

transition of the saints from the extant heaven and earth to the new heaven and earth.

Apostle Paul drew heavily from these motifs. He likened his preaching to an espousal of the church to Christ to underscore the faithful stance that the church ought to cultivate towards Christ (2 Cor 11:2). He also likened the atoning death of Jesus Christ to a bride price (1 Cor 6:20; Gal 3:13–15). This was to elicit the believer's reciprocal love and undivided loyalty to Jesus Christ. He again likened the continuous nourishment of the church in the unfolding history and the expected reciprocal submission of the church to Christ to the relationship between a husband and a wife (Eph 5:22–33). This was to elicit spousal obligations and commitment to one another and to also teach the readers of the text on the obligations of the church to Christ. Likewise, Jesus likened his ascension to the bridegroom's return to his father's home to build a matrimonial house (John 14:1–3). He did this to comfort the church and to elicit hope as she sojourns throughout the unfolding history. He also likened the expected faithful life of the church in the unfolding history to the bride's faithfulness as she awaits the groom to return and take her to the wedding and marriage supper (Matt 25:1–13) at a date unbeknown to her. He did this to engender the church's vigilance against the devil's schemes. Finally, he likened his second advent to the return of the bridegroom to take his bride to his newly prepared matrimonial home (Matt 25:1–13).[12] This was to elicit hope and engender patient endurance in trials and persecutions for her faith.

Verse 8 follows up and explains how the bride has made herself ready: fine linen, bright and clean, was given her to wear. For the fine linen is the righteous acts of the saints. The middle passive εδοθη of the verb διδωμι "give" suggests that, contrary to the luxurious sin-tainted garment that adorned the great harlot city that was complemented by the cup full of the filth of her adulteries in her hand, the righteous deeds of the saints are the garment that adorn the bride of the Lamb—the New Jerusalem. Here, the New Jerusalem stands in synecdoche for those who would dwell in it—the almighty God, Jesus, and the saints. Thus, the New Jerusalem is not a celestial city. It represents the humongous ark of God's full presence. Unlike the ark in the earthly temple, which represented a limited presence of God, the New Jerusalem is an ark that fills the entire temple, which in turn fills the entire celestial city and finally the whole of the new heaven and earth. So, the peopled New Jerusalem, which is also the new heaven and earth, can be metaphorically described as the bride/wife of the lamb. In their earthly

---

12. Kings and Stager, *Biblical Israel*, 54–55.

sojourn in the unfolding history, the saints, who are already bought by the blood of the lamb can be regarded as the betrothed bride of the Lamb.

There is a difference between the conception of the covenantal relationship between Christ and the church and the visionary revelation's conception of the church as an invitee to the wedding supper (vv. 9), Jesus as the bridegroom, and the New Jerusalem as the bride (21:9-26). The former symbolizes and describes the church's covenantal relationship with Jesus Christ that defines the obligations that should obtain and direct the life of the church on earth in order to please Christ. The latter concept of the church as an invitee is a metaphor that highlights the importance of God's rapprochements in the gospel and disciplinary judgments, which are construed to be an invitation to the wedding supper of the Lamb.

The portrayal of Jesus as the bridegroom and New Jerusalem as the bride (21:9-26) portrays Jesus as the king who has dethroned the great harlot (vv. 1-2), the beast from the sea and the false prophet (vv. 11-21), and Satan (20:1-3, 9-10) and taken over their worldly kingdoms which have now become the kingdom of YHWH and his Messiah (11:15-17; 19:11-21). The full presence of God in the new redeemed kingdom is symbolized by the Ark City (New Jerusalem). This Ark City is conceptualized as the bride of the Lamb to contrast it with her former status as the prostitute who was patronized by Satan, kings of the earth, merchants, and seafarers (17:3–18:24). The contrast was aimed at generating evocations of a strong loathing of the worldly and a deep longing for the heavenly. These evocations were intended to urge the seven churches to resist the allures of the prostituting powers, to endure tribulations, and to uphold orthodoxy and orthopraxy—the righteous deeds of the saints. This time around, being clothed with the righteous deeds of the saints, she attracts Jesus and the full presence of God.

The angel told John to write, "Blessed are those who are invited to the wedding supper of the Lamb" (vv. 9a). The word "blessed," also translated as "happy," is meant to enthuse the audience to respond to the gospel's invitation. The word "invited" (Greek: κεκλημένοι, keklēmenoi), a perfect participle of καλέω, kaleō, shows that the invitation is living to the church and open to the rest of humankind throughout the unfolding history (Matt 22:1-14). This observation does not pose any ambiguity in view of the other concept of the church as the bride of Christ. Both are metaphors for different realities which are intended to engender different responses. Invitees to a wedding were expected to buy new clothes for the wedding ceremony (Matt 22:11). Thus, the expected response in projecting the church as an invitee to a wedding is to awaken her to the grave need to wear wedding clothes—righteous deeds of the saints that would ensure that she is allowed into the wedding supper. On the other hand, the evocation intended in the conception of the church as the bride/wife of Christ is to urge her to keep her covenant obligations as a wife would to her husband (Eph 5:22-32).

The angel added, "These are the true words of God" (vv. 9). The gospel's invitation to the church and the world to the wedding supper of the Lamb is too important to be entrusted to John's finite power of recollection. The angel insisted that it be written. The insistence is intended to highlight the gravity of the invitation so as to elicit a favorable response in faith and trust in the work of Jesus Christ on the cross, which, together with the divine disciplinary judgments, constitute God's invitation. Indeed, elicitation of a positive response to this invitation is the ultimate purpose of showing and narrating the whole of the visionary revelation.

The angel's assertion "these are the true words of God" was so believably overwhelming that John fell in obeisance as a gesture of his agreement. However, the angel stopped him. The angel's reaction to John's obeisance shows that, however lofty a word or deed by servants of God, they do not deserve an iota of praise. Praise and worship belong to God alone. Like the mediating angel, they should realize that "it is the Spirit of prophecy who bears testimony to Jesus" (vv. 10). God's servants are mare mouth pieces, nothing more.

11I saw heaven standing open, and there before me was a white horse, whose rider is called Faithful and True. With justice, he judges and makes war. 12His eyes are like blazing fire, and on his head are many crowns. He has a name written on him that no one knows but himself. 13He is dressed in a robe dipped in blood, and his name is the word of God. 14The armies of heaven were following him, riding on white horses and dressed in fine linen, white and clean. 15Coming out of his mouth is a sharp sword to strike down the nations. "He will rule them with an iron sceptre." He treads the winepress of the fury of the wrath of God Almighty. 16On his robe and his thigh, he has this name written: King of Kings and Lord of Lords.

This and the following visionary revelation (19:11—20:15) simulate Jesus' final work of preparing a place for his bride (John 14:1-3) before he finally takes her to her eternal home—the new heaven and earth. John is still in the wilderness vision stage. In the previous heavenly stage, he had seen another white cavalry horse which had come from a conquest, was given an interim crown, and went out for more conquest (6:1-2). The rider of the white cavalry horse and his armies, in the present scene, may be simulating the tail end of the conquest of the rider of the first white cavalry horse seen in the earlier scene (6:1-2).

The title of the lead rider of the white cavalry horses, "Faithful and True," is the same name given to Jesus in 3:14. The title is affirmed by the parallel phrase, "with justice, he judges and makes war." This description suggests that, he prepares the bride's future abode by overcoming the last tentacles of the power of the great prostitute—the kingdom of the beast, the false prophets, and the kings of the earth who remained on the scene after they destroyed the great harlot (17:16–17). His judgment of the beast and the false prophet is complemented by God's judgment of the devil and the rest of sinful humanity on the white-throne judgment (20:7–15).

The rider is further described as having eyes like blazing fire. This description's similarity with the personality described in 1:14 further confirms that he is role-playing Jesus Christ. The many royal crowns on his head suggest that Jesus is the King over the kings of the earth. On him is written a name which no one knows but himself. This name could be the name of God which in the Jewish religion was not verbalized. He was seen dressed in a robe dipped in blood. This symbolism appears to have been borrowed from Isa 62:1–63:6.[13] Isaiah was depicting a judgment against nations and kings who had mistreated Israel during the time of her disfavor with the Lord. In this scene, John is seeing a visionary simulation of the eschatological judgment of the saints' erstwhile tormentors, Satan, beast, false prophet, and their minions.

His white-apparelled heavenly army riding on white horses is a symbolic emphasis that he judges his enemies efficiently and righteously. This symbolism must have evoked both fear and great assurance of the justice of God. Fear of God's severe judgments would lead to repentance. Assurance of the justice of God would lead to hope for vindication. It would also engender patient endurance in the persecuted saints.

In auditioning that "his name is the word of God," John explicitly identified the lead rider of this white cavalry horse as Jesus the Christ (John 1:1). The sword proceeding from his mouth recalls the admonition to the unrepentant in the church in Pergamum (2:16). It demonstrates that he judges the obdurate by his word. Judging by the word of mouth happens in two ways: 1) proclamation of the gospel (John 3:18, 15:22), and 2) believers' testimony (12:11) and pronouncement and execution of the rapprochement judgments against the devil and fallen humanity (Gen 2:17; 3:14–19; Rev 6:1–8; 8:1–9:21; 16:1–21; 18:1–24; 19:11–21; 20:1–3; 20:8–15).

To rule with a rod of iron (vv. 15) does not signify tyrannical rule. Instead, it shows that nobody can deliver the victims of God's wrath which is provoked by obduracy notwithstanding the offer of his grace. The title "King of kings and Lord of lords" on his robe and thigh shows that Jesus will

---

13. Goldingay, *Isaiah*, 354.

conquer the kings and lords of the earth, and he will be enthroned as the King of kings and the Lord of lords (vv. 16).

¹⁷And I saw an angel sitting in the sun, who cried in a loud voice to all the birds flying in midair, "Come, gather together for the great supper of God, ¹⁸so that you may eat the flesh of kings, generals, and the mighty, of horses and their riders, and the flesh of all people, free and slave, great and small."

Leon Morris opines that the angel in this scene was positioned in the sun to give him a vantage position to call the birds of the air.[14] This commentary suggests that positioning the simulating angel in the sun serves to highlight his very prominent and significant role of announcing the judgment that accomplishes the mystery of God, as had been announced by his servants the prophets (10:7).

Describing the routing and overthrow of the beast, the kings of the earth, and their armies as a great supper of God is a grisly irony. It describes the severity, great extent, and shameful rout of these enemies of God and his saints. To be killed and fed to the birds demonstrated utmost contempt over the victim (1 Sam 17:44-46). This visionary imagery is derived from Ezek 39:4 where God avows that he would vindicate Israel against those who rejoiced over her exile and those who would attack her during her time of favor with the Lord. This visionary scene simulates a similar occurrence, the routing of the beast and false prophet for deluding those who had received the mark of the beast and worshiped his image. It also describes the judgment of those who, notwithstanding the abundance of the grace of God, are obdurate and apostate to a level whereby they can be described as living at a time when Satan is set loose on the world (20:7-9).

¹⁹Then I saw the beast and the kings of the earth and their armies gathered together to wage war against the rider of the horse and his army. ²⁰But the beast was captured, and the false prophet who had performed the signs on its behalf. With these signs, he had deluded those who had received the mark of the beast and worshipped its image. The two of them were thrown alive into the fiery lake of burning sulfur. ²¹The rest were killed with the sword coming out of the mouth of the rider on the horse, and all the birds gorged themselves on their flesh.

The judgment of the prostitute was simulated in chapters 17–18. Simulation of the judgment of the beast, false prophet, and their accomplices completes the judgment of the prostitute and the entire system she had put together to persecute God's people (vv. 11–21). Echoes from Ezek 39:1-8

---

14. Morris, *Revelation*, 232.

suggests that this scene simulates an end-time judgment of the tormenters of the church—the beast and his accomplices the kings of the earth and their armies. Informed by their interpretation of Ezekiel's prophecy in Ezek 38:29; 39:1–8, Beale and Campbell opine that the referenced battle will be a real end time battle between the armies of Christ and the beast and his alliances.[15] However, whereas Ezekiel's prophecy looked forward to an envisaged battle, this scene simulated the end time apostasy that was earlier simulated as the battle of Armageddon in 16:14–16 but in the context of God's judgment against an idolatrous saint persecuting and obdurate world system—the great prostitute (17:1).

The charge sheet against them read "they had deluded those who had received the mark of the beast and worshipped its image" (vv. 20). Jesus had taught that those who cause those who believe in him to stumble, it would be better for them if a large millstone were hung around their neck and they were thrown into the sea (Mark 9:42). The beast and the false prophet were thrown alive into a fiery lake of burning sulfur. The symbol of a lake of fire burning with sulfur demonstrates the terrible gloom and pain that will be the lot of the beast and the false prophet. The banishing of the beast and the false prophet into the lake of fire suggests that this scene simulates an end-time judgment.

The kings of the earth and their armies were killed, with the sword coming out of the mouth of the rider on the white horse. Being killed with the sword coming out the mouth of the rider of the white horse and being fed on the birds of prey who gorge their flesh demonstrates the everlasting shame and contempt that will be the lot of the sinful world (Dan 12:2).

Strategic and Communicative Acts in Rev 19:5–10

The simulation of the praise accorded to God for the inauguration of his kingdom is a strategic act that is meant to evoke the desire to pursue righteous living. It would nudge the saints in Ephesus to revert to their first love, the saints of Smyrna and Philadelphia to be all the more vigilant, the saints in Pergamum to resist the teachings of the Nicolaitans, and the saints in Thyatira to resist the teachings of Jezebel, the false prophetess. It would also resuscitate the dying Sardis from their spiritual comatose and revive lukewarm Laodicea.

The vision showing the rider of the white horse whose name is faithful and true and whose garment is drenched in blood constitutes a strategic act. The blood-drenched garment shows that the rider role-plays the

---

15. Beale and Campbell, *Revelation*, 418.

personality who in an earlier scene was shown trending the grapes of God's wrath (14:19–29). With his word, which is sharper than a two-edged sword, he executes the judgments of God. This strategic act evoked fear of attracting God's wrath through sin. It also engendered comfort in the suffering saints in the assurance of being avenged.

The call to the birds of the air to come and eat the carrion of the kings, captains, horses, and their riders, was a strategic act. It showed that their exalted status could not deliver anybody from the wrath of God. It was aimed at scaring the saints out of any slumber and deadness in sin. Showing the defeat of the beast and his cahoots by Jesus and his armies evoked hopelessness for those who had a modicum of trust in worldly power. Such hopelessness was meant to cajole the audience to place their faith in none other but God.

Application of Evocations in Rev 19:5–10

As the seven churches in Asia Minor heard the narration of this visionary scene, they were encouraged that they had chosen the right path. At the same time, they were enthused to preach the gospel. They were more than encouraged in faith to hear that they were blessed to have been invited to the wedding supper of the Lamb.

The depiction of the judgment of sinners as being feasted on by birds of prey was meant to scare the churches in Ephesus, Pergamum Thyatira, Sardis, and Laodicea from their spiritual shortcomings. The assurance of vengeance also engendered patient endurance in the persecuted saints.

The dragon, the beasts, and the false prophets of our time act in more subtle ways than then. Worship of the dragon is peddled subtly through the electronic media. The entertainment industry has taken minds and hearts captive to the devil. The word of God is no longer preached to convict the world of sin and judgment but to entertain and sustain congregations for financial gain.

The visionary revelation in this chapter can evoke resistance to the world's subtle seduction. The simulation of the defeat of Satan and the joy it elicits in heaven are strategic acts that urge and nudge us to forsake the world, with its allures of fleeting happiness in entertainment, wealth, and other forms of satanic seductions, to follow the Lord.

REV 20

JUDGMENT OF SATAN

¹Then I saw an angel coming down from heaven, holding the key to the bottomless pit and a great chain in his hand. ²And he seized the dragon, that ancient serpent, who is the devil and Satan, and bound him for a thousand years, ³and threw him into the bottomless pit, and shut it and sealed it over him so that he might not deceive the nations any longer until a thousand years were ended. After that, he must be released for a little while.

The majority of the sampled commentaries base their interpretations of this text and indeed the entire chapter on the presupposition that it primarily narrates a visionary simulation of a millennial reign of Christ on the present earth. They only differ on the time it is inaugurated. However, out of the chapter's fifteen verses, only two mention the reign of Jesus, martyrs, and the saints (vv. 4 and 6). Seven verses narrate the binding of Satan for a thousand years, his release and judgment at the end of time (vv. 1–3, 7–10). Five verses narrate the final judgment of sinners (vv. 11–15). Thus, the primary and overriding theme is the binding of Satan by the work of Christ on the cross and the saints' testimonies (12:11). The binding of Satan incidentally but significantly results in the reign of Christ and his saints for a corresponding period. Thus, however significant, exegetically, the reign of Christ is a secondary theme in this visionary scene.

The history of interpretation of the book of Revelation reveals divergent views of the nature, timing, and result of the actual event simulated by the binding and imprisonment of Satan for a thousand years.[16] The bulk of these views are premised on the supposition that there will be a distinct end-time tribulation.[17] The pre-millennial school of thought opines that a great tribulation will precede a literal earthly rule of Christ that will last for a literal thousand years. Others within the same school of thought posit that the one thousand years stand for an indefinite time.[18] The primary and compelling argument against this school of thought is that there is no other collaborating text in the rest of the Christian canon of Scripture supporting this position. Even the programmatic teachings by Jesus Christ in Matt 24, Mark 13, and Luke 21 do not even allude to a literal one-thousand-year rule

---

16. Mounce, *Revelation*, 368.
17. The tribulations are simulated in chapters 12–13.
18. Beckwith, *Apocalypse*, 736.

of Christ. G. K. Beale has advanced a solid argument against this school of thought.[19]

The post-millennial school of thought posits that the so-called great tribulation will happen after the millennial rule of Christ. It suggests that the one-thousand-year rule of Christ is a distinct period when good will triumph over evil, most probably through the preaching of the gospel. Lastly, the amillennial school of thought opines that the thousand-year rule is symbolic of the unfolding history from the ascension of Jesus to his second coming.[20]

Notably, the tendency of many interpreters at this point is to become apologists for a particular view of the millennium.[21] When interpreting this scene, John Sweet's advice that "the first principle of good interpretation, as of good exploring, is to accept the strangeness of the terrain and try to see it on its terms, not blinkered by inherited assumptions"[22] is very apt.

This commentary supposes that the great tribulation consists of the trials and persecutions orchestrated by the dragon, beast, and false prophet. It is spread throughout the unfolding history as shown in the simulations narrated in chapters 12 and 13. It also interprets the events simulated in the opening of the seals, blowing of the trumpets, and pouring of the bowls of God's wrath as God's retributive-cum-rapprochement judgments. Interpretation of this portion has incorporated insights from an analysis of the visionary simulations, an analysis of the evocations generated by the strategic acts embedded in the visionary simulation, insights from intertextuality, an analysis of the sayings of Jesus on his second coming, and insights from cinematography.

Analysis of strategic acts is deemed critical because, as has been observed in the introduction of this commentary, this visionary revelation is embedded more with strategic acts than communicative acts. Intertextuality expands the hermeneutical horizons from a quarantined interpretation of the text. Insights from cinematography have been roped in because Revelation is a narration of a visionary revelation similar to the present-day 3-D cinema.

John has already been shown the simulation of the heinous works of the dragon (12:1-17), Rome and future Romish ideals operating in the world (13:1-18), God's judgments against Rome (17:16-17), her emperor—the beast from the sea, also standing in metalepsis for future antichrists and

19. Beale, *Revelation*, 420–51
20. Beale, *Revelation*, 420.
21. Mounce, *Revelation*, 360.
22. Sweet, *Revelation*, 1.

their ideologies (19:19-20), and the provincial governor of Asia Minor—beast from the land also representing supporters of future antichrists and their ideologies (19:19-20). The question that he would be asking is, "How about the outworking of God's curse on the devil (Gen 3:14-15), who is the instigator of all evil"? The use of the Greek perfect tense κέκριται, *kekritai* (to judge) in John 16:11 shows that in John's theological view, Satan stands judged throughout the unfolding history. Not simulating the outworking of God's curse on him in the unfolding history and his final judgment would deny the saints a vital strategic act that would evoke hope and a foretaste of their eventual vindication.

The other corollary question is, What is the nature of Satan's judgment in the unfolding history and at the end of time? The answer lies in this visionary simulation that is overbearingly interpreted to have simulated a millennial rule of Christ. The supposition that the visionary revelation simulated the millennial rule of Christ obscures the overarching plot: the outworking of God's judgment on his chief adversary in the unfolding history and at the end of time. However, it is undeniable that the defeat of Satan by the death and resurrection of Christ resulted to a reign of Christ and his saints for the corresponding period of Satan's defeat. During this time, the church assumes power over every power of the devil (Luke 10:18-19).[23]

As this scene commences, John saw an angel coming down from heaven, having the keys to the abyss and a great chain. Having keys to the abyss and a great chain symbolizes authority and power over the devils and demons who are deemed to be bound there (Matt 28:18).[24] Notably, he resembles the personality of 1:18, who identified himself as the living one, the one who was dead and who was now alive forever more. He also said that he holds the keys of death and Hades (1:18b). In this scene, the angel hails from heaven, and like the personality of 1:18, he holds the key to the abyss. As such, the angel was definitely role-playing Jesus' conquest of Satan by his work on the cross.

John then saw the angel seize the dragon, the ancient serpent, who is the devil or Satan, and bound him for a thousand years. To bind is to render powerless. Stating the time Satan remains bound as a thousand years is a hyperbole expressed in a time scale. It demonstrates that the work of Jesus on the cross has decisively destroyed the works of the devil (1 John 3:8).

The angel then threw Satan into the abyss, locked and sealed it to keep him from deceiving the nations anymore until the thousand years were ended. The simulation showing Satan being thrown into the bottomless pit,

23. See commentary on 6:1-2.
24. See commentary on 1:18.

from where he cannot deceive the nations anymore, is a symbolic parallelism that demonstrates the decisive victory of the saints over the devil that was won by Christ's death. The sealed lock is a further symbolic parallelism to throwing Satan into a bottomless pit, into which he continues to fall (a symbol for his utter defeat). This parallelism underscores Satan's utter defeat before those who have put their trust in the finished work of Jesus.

John auditions that the devil's incarceration in the bottomless pit will last for a thousand years (vv. 3a). The hyperbole "bottomless" (using depth as a unit of measuring the intensity of Satan's defeat) parallels the hyperbole "one thousand years" (using time as a unit of measuring the completeness of the devil's judgment and the saints' vindication). The visionary imagery is borrowed from the then-extant angelology. Jude 1:6 mentions a similar scenario: "And the angels who did not stay within their position of authority, but left their proper dwelling, he has kept in eternal chains under gloomy darkness until the judgment of the great day."

The simulated one-thousand-year period in which the devil is bound and imprisoned in the abyss represents the duration of the redemption-working, sin-defeating, and therefore Satan-conquering Christ event that runs from Christ's incarnation to his second coming to judge the living and the dead. The simulation of binding and imprisoning the devil in a dungeon and sealing it for a thousand years is undoubtedly a visionary strategic act. It derives evocative efficacy in demonstrating that the Christ event has destroyed the devil's work, thereby giving believers unassailable victory. They conquer Satan by the blood of the Lamb, the word of their testimony, and by not loving their lives, even when threatened by martyrdom (12:11).

Calling Satan "that old serpent" recalls Eve's deceiver in Eden. This description of Satan, followed by the visionary revelation showing an angel binding Satan and throwing him into a bottomless pit simulates the outworking of God's decreed curse upon him (Gen 3:14–15) by the efficacious sin and death-defeating work of Jesus—the seed of the woman.

Jesus continues to crush the head of the serpent, by destroying his nefarious work, until he is eternally vanquished (vv. 10). The death of Jesus delivered the believers from the bondage of sin and death, thus enabling them to overcome Satan's deception for as long as earthly history endures. Indeed, Jesus was manifested to destroy the works of the devil (1 John 3:8b). Stephen S. Smalley notes, "Ὁ Σατανάς (*Ho Satanas*, 'the Satan') occurs in the apocalypse eight times, always with the article; and this suggests that John is referring to the devil's representative office as the figurative agent of wickedness, more than to his person."[25] Thus, he rightly supports the notion that

---

25. Smalley, *Revelation*, 501–2.

Satan's work is shown in this vision as being curtailed instead of the actual imprisonment of the person of Satan.

As was argued in the commentary of 7:1, the sealing of the 144,000 fulfils a similar function as the binding of Satan for a thousand years. The former protects the saints from divinely instigated disciplinary judgments (8:7-12) and the latter protects them from satanic deception throughout the unfolding history (John 17:15; Rev 20:1-3). No wonder the simulation of the sealing of the 144,000 happens on a heavenly visionary stage where John had been ushered in to be shown "what must take place after this" (4:1), whereas the simulation of binding Satan for a thousand years happens on a wilderness visionary stage where John had been called to be shown the punishment of the great harlot (17:1). Again, the outcome of sealing the 144,000 and those who are reaped from the earth is a life with Jesus on Mount Zion (14:1-16) and the result of binding Satan is a reign of the saints for a thousand years (vv. 4-6). Moreover, the simulation of sealing the 144,000 and the great throng from every nation, tribe, people and language generates similar evocations as the simulation of binding Satan for a thousand years.

In the real sense, it does not require an angel to curtail Satan's work. God's self-actualizing decrees are embedded with efficacy to activate actions that accomplish his intentions in their appointed times without the agency of angels, chains, and dungeons (abyss) to imprison the devil. In this scene, the angel is part of a visionary cast simulating the outworking of God's decreed curse on Satan in the redeeming act of Christ's birth, life, passion and resurrection.

The devil's power is curtailed by the efficacious blood (death) of the Lamb and by the saints' testimony and their total surrender to Jesus to the point of martyrdom (12:11). The period when the devil's power is curtailed leading to a reign of Jesus and the saints for a corresponding period is compared to the period envisaged by Isaiah after God delivered his people from the Babylonian exile (Isa 61:1-11). When auditioning the severity of Satan's judgment, it is expressed hyperbolically in terms of the period of his incarceration as a thousand years. This hyperbole engenders two evocations: 1) deep satisfaction in the assurance that the saints are living in the acceptable year of the Lord's favor (Isa 61:2), 2) assurance of Satan's deservedly long judgment. Conversely, simulation of the period of time when the beast is allowed to blaspheme the name of God, make war against the saints, and exercise authority over humanity is litotically minimized to merely a short time. This litotical minimization inspires hope and encourages the saints to patiently endure tribulations.

Graeme Goldsworthy avers that "the millennium is the day of the Lord, the day on which Satan is bound."[26] He further argues that "the thousand years is, as to the quantity, an unknown but perfect period of time. But as to the quality, it is the exaltation of Christ in his glorious rule."[27] Goldsworthy's observation has merit. However, in identifying the one thousand years with the day of the Lord, he places it as a future event. He overcomes this futurist placement by applying it to everyday Christian who he says can transfer their everyday into the day of the Lord and thus can reckon themselves as reigning with Christ.[28]

An intertextual analysis supports the supposition that this scene simulates the outworking of Satan's judgment in the unfolding history (John 16:11). The chain in the hands of the angel supports the notion that he is role-playing Jesus, the strong man who, by his redeeming death and resurrection, binds Satan and vandalizes his kingdom (Matt 12:29; Mark 3:27; Luke 11:21) and takes captivity in sin to be captives to righteousness (Eph 4:8). In Jesus' earthly ministry, devils were heard crying out, "What do you want with us, Son of God"? "Have you come here to torture us before the appointed time"? (Matt 8:29; Mark 5:7). Of course, the answer was yes.

After narrating the simulation of Satan's incarceration for a thousand years, John auditions that after this period, Satan must be released for a little while (vv. 3). Satan's thousand-year imprisonment is contrasted with the "little while" that he is allowed to deceive the nations (16:12–16; 20:3; 8). This "allowance" should not be interpreted as Satan's God-given opportunity to tempt the saints and the world. Instead, it is a simulation of an end-time apostasy that results when people stubbornly slight God's gracious rapprochements (Isa 6:9–10; Mark 4:10–12). It was necessary to simulate his release for a little while to engage him in simulating his instigation of the envisioned end-time obduracy and apostasy (2 Thess 2:3–12), whose intensity can be described as "a time when Satan is let loose."

⁴Then I saw thrones and those who sat on them. Judgment was given to them. Also, I saw the souls of those who had been beheaded for the testimony of Jesus and for the word of God and those who had not worshipped the beast or its image and had not received its mark on their foreheads or their hands. They lived and reigned with Christ for a thousand years. ⁵The rest of the dead did not live until the thousand years are ended. This is the first resurrection. ⁶Blessed and holy is the one who shares in the first resurrection! Over such,

---

26. Goldsworthy, *Gospel in Revelation*, 130.
27. Goldsworthy, *Gospel in Revelation*, 130.
28. Goldsworthy, *Gospel in Revelation*, 130.

the second death has no power, but they will be priests of God and Christ and reign with him for a thousand years.

In the preceding scene, John has just been shown a simulation of the full panorama of Satan's utter defeat by Christ, and by extension the church, in the unfolding history. In this scene, he is shown the resultant reign of Jesus and his saints for the corresponding period of Satan's defeat. Notably, the setting is still on the wilderness stage, where John had first been ushered (17:1) to be shown the judgment of the great prostitute. This setting suggests that this reign happens on the extant heaven and earth. This suggestion is supported in Jesus' saying, "The time is fulfilled. The kingdom of God has come near" (Matt 4:17; Mark 1:15). In Luke 17:21, he says, "The kingdom of God is in your midst."

John saw thrones and those who sat on them. He then saw judgment being vested on those who sat on the thrones. Noting that judgment was given on those who sat on the thrones suggests that a higher power bestowed judgment on those who sat on the thrones. Beckwith suggests that the most probable identification of those given authority to judge are the martyrs who were beheaded for the gospel's sake.[29] However, Daniel unambiguously says that "judgment was given to the saints of the Most High" (Dan 7:22), and the rest of the saints are part of the saints of the Most High. A reading through the narration shows that Jesus' death vested judgment of the devil on both the saints and the martyrs.

John then saw the disembodied souls of the martyrs, and those who had not worshiped the beast or its image and had not received its mark on their foreheads or their hands, living and reigning with Christ for a thousand years. The phrase "those who had not worshiped the beast or its image and had not received its mark on their foreheads or their hands" appears to be a further description of the martyrs. It offers the reason for their martyrdom and eventual exaltation. This scene simulated the martyr's victory over the devil, which was won by Jesus' death, their testimony, and their martyrdom for refusing to worship the beast and its image and refusing to receive its mark on their foreheads and hands (12:11). Carey C. Newman rightly describes such victory as initial or proleptic victory of God.[30] They can be reckoned as having joined Christ's reign over sin and the devil.

The scene echoes Paul's teaching that "If we suffer with him, we shall reign with him" (2 Tim 2:12). This reign should not be understood as an earthly Christocracy. Pentecost has argued that the saints will be resurrected in their physical bodies and will come with Christ to rule physically in the

---

29. Beckwith, *Apocalypse*, 739.
30. Newman, *Jesus and the Restoration of Israel*, 141.

world.³¹ Such a scenario could clash with Jesus' saying in John 14:1-6. Here, Jesus unequivocally says he will take the believers to the place where he has been since ascension. The scenario would also warrant a resurrection of the martyrs and other saints in earthly corruptible bodies that they had put off in death (1 Cor 15:53). It would also denigrate Christ's and apostle Paul's teachings. Christ taught that "when the dead rise, they will be like angels in heaven" (Mark 12:25). Furthermore, Paul says, "flesh and blood cannot inherit the kingdom of God, nor does the perishable inherit the imperishable" (1 Cor 15:50). As such, an earthly Christocracy is not envisaged anywhere in the extant Scripture. The obtaining scenario can only be interpreted as the believers' spiritual reign with Christ which commenced upon Christ's ascension and will run throughout the unfolding history (Eph 1:20).

Nebuchadnezzar's dream (Dan 2:44–45) and Daniel's vision (Dan 7:13–14) show that the kingdom of the Son of Man would commence during the rule of the fourth empire described as iron mixed with clay and the fourth beast-kingdom, both identified as the Roman Empire. This visionary prediction was fulfilled in the Christ event. It supports the suggestion that the thousand years symbolize the unfolding history from the incarnation of Christ to the consummation of the kingdom of God in the new heaven and earth. In earlier visionary scenes, the unfolding history is depicted as 3½ years, 42 months, and 1260 days. By comparing the depiction of the duration of the unfolding history in four visionary scenes, i.e., the time the gentiles trample on the holy city (11:2), the time the two witnesses will prophesy (11:3), the time the woman clothed with the sun will be taken care of in the wilderness (12:14), and the time Satan is bound and incarcerated in the abyss (20:2–3), Dennis E. Johnson rightly concludes that these symbolic periods represent an age in which the faithful church is both suffering and spiritually safe.³²

John auditions that the unsaved dead are not raised together with the saved saints until the thousand years are ended (vv. 5). However, they will be resurrected to face the final judgment (John 5:28, 29; Acts 24:15; Rev 20:11–15). The resurrection of the saints (those who were given judgment) and the martyrs which John calls the first resurrection refers to the believers' conversion. It is referred to as rising from death in sin to righteousness or from death to life (John 5:24; Eph 2:1–5; 5:14; 1 John 3:14). However, Craig R. Koester considers it to be the resurrection of the martyrs and the dead saints before the thousand-year rule.³³ His supposition is premised on

---

31. Pentecost, *Things to Come*, 370–426.
32. Johnson, *Triumph of the Lamb*, 287.
33. Koester, *Revelation*, 741–860.

yet another supposition that there will be a future literal millennial reign of Christ and the saints. However, as has been argued in this commentary, the millennial incarceration of Satan refers to the defeat of Satan in the work of Jesus Christ on the cross throughout the unfolding history. This commentary has also argued that the theme of the reign of the saints was not the primary intention of showing this visionary scene. It was incidental to the theme of Christ's victory over Satan. Moreover, Scripture variously refers to unbelievers as dead in sin and trespasses (Eph 2:1; Col 2:13) or dead even though physically alive (1 Tim 5:6; Rev 3:1). These observations suggest that, as used in this visionary scene, the first resurrection refers to the conversion experience, which gives the believer a right to spiritually sit with Jesus in heavenly places (Eph 2:6). The second death (the physical death) has no power over such. After their physical death, they reign with Christ awaiting the full consummation of the kingdom in the new heaven and earth. However, the sinners' physical death is momentous. It consigns them to hopeless gloom awaiting the final judgment (14:17–20 and 20:11–15).

In Jesus' conversation with Mary after the physical death of Lazarus, Mary told Jesus, "I know he will rise again in the resurrection on the last day" (John 11:23–26). Mary espoused a common view then of a resurrection at the eschaton. However, Jesus had a fuller view. He replied, "I am the resurrection and the life. The one who believes in me will live, even though he be dead, and whoever lives and believes in me will never die. Do you believe this?" Mary said, "Yes, Lord, I believe that you are the Messiah, the son of God, who is to come into the world." In this discourse, we learn John's theological view concerning death and resurrection as taught by Jesus.

Upon faith in the Lord Jesus Christ, the dead in sin are spiritually translated from death to life (John 5:24). This translation is expressed in this visionary scene as a kind of resurrection. For them, even if they die in the body, they live. Thomas R. Schreiner rightly notes, "The life that belongs to believers in this present evil age guarantees that death will never triumph, and so we can say there is an indissoluble connection between the life that believers now possess and the future realization of life forever."[34] But unbelievers are dead in their sins and trespasses. They are reckoned dead, whether physically alive, until the final judgment day when they will be eternally damned. In their detailed discussion of vv. 4–6 that compares the extant views, G. K. Beale and Sean M. McDonough rightly conclude that "the understanding of 20:4–6 as a spiritual reality is consistent with the view reflected elsewhere in both the OT and NT that there will only be one physical resurrection, which occurs at the conclusion of history . . . Thus, the

---

34. Schreiner, *New Testament Theology*, 88.

"first" resurrection of 20:3–6 apparently refers to a spiritual resurrection of saints, followed later by their final physical resurrection.[35]

Thus, chapter 20 narrates a simulation of Christ's unassailable victory over Satan throughout the unfolding history. It also simulates the resultant reign of the saints which was engendered by Christ's redeeming death and by their witness and total surrender to him to the point of martyrdom (12:11). The earlier observation that the events simulated in the visions shown after opening of the seventh seal and before the vision simulating the ushering in of the new heaven and the new earth (21:1) were to happen concurrently with the events simulated in the visions shown after the opening of each of the six seals lends credence to the supposition that the judgment of Satan that was simulated in binding and incarcerating him in the abyss for a thousand years (vv. 1–3) is a continuing phenomenon throughout the unfolding history.[36]

> [7] *And when the thousand years are ended, Satan will be released from his prison* [8] *and will come out to deceive the nations that are at the four corners of the earth, Gog and Magog, to gather them for battle; their number is like the sand of the sea.* [9] *And they marched up over the broad plain of the earth and surrounded the camp of the saints and the beloved city, but fire came down from heaven and consumed them,* [10] *and the devil who had deceived them was thrown into the lake of fire and sulfur where the beast and the false prophets were, and they will be tormented day and night forever and ever.*

As history draws to a close, Scripture predicts that there will be a period of great apostasy (1 Thess 5:1–3; 2 Thess 2:3–12; 1 Tim 4:1). It will be engendered by a Satan-instigated rebellion against Jesus and the saints. He will use agents from all the nations of the earth, hereby likened to Gog and Magog of Ezek 38–39. This short-time rebellion, notwithstanding God's rapprochements, will kindle God's wrath, prompting him to mete the final judgment. It is simulated in the release of Satan from the bottomless pit, who goes out to deceive the nations that are at the four corners of the earth, herein envisioned in the imagery of Ezekiel's prophecy of Judah's invasion by Gog and Magog (Ezek 38–39), to gather them for battle against God's people (vv. 10).

Gog, the chief prince of Meshech and Tubal, was used proverbially by prophet Ezekiel to exemplify the enemy of God's people who would mock them in their time of disfavor with God. He also used the same imagery to exemplify those who would plot to attack them during their time of favor

---

35. Beale and McDonough, "Revelation," 1081–1161.
36. See commentary on 8:1.

after their restoration from exile (Ezek 38:1–39:29). Ezekiel describes how this proverbial Gog would invade from the north with his hordes to despoil the land of Judah and destroy the covenant people who would be peacefully resettled in their land. Comfortingly he also foresaw that the Lord will vindicate his holiness by massacring these invaders.[37] In Ezekiel's vision, God intended to show his people that as long as they keep his covenant, he will vindicate them against those who mock them and defend them from the attacks of their enemies to affirm his holiness and to show that he is the Lord (Ezek.38:23).

The end-time, Satan-led worldwide opposition to Jesus and the church is simulated in the imagery of Ezekiel's image of the opposers of God's people—the proverbial Gog, the prince of Magog (Ezek 38–39). It is highly probable that, in both Ezekiel and Revelation, Gog and Magog are used as an evocative figure of speech, a synecdoche, perhaps because of their northern geographical location in relation to Israel, from which direction the enemies of God's people usually attacked.[38] This fear-evoking imagery highlights Satan's subtility and propensity to beguile and harm the saints (1 Pet 5:8). Highlighting the envisaged fearful works of the enemy of God's people in parallel to the protective care of God is a foil to underscore God's unmatched fidelity in protecting his own. Purposely, it is intended to arouse utmost vigilance and comfort in the seven churches.

The large number of the enemy forces and the broad reach of their devastation suggest that this rebellion and apostasy will be a worldwide phenomenon. Auditioning that this onslaught will be against the camp of the saints, also called the beloved city suggests that it will be aimed at engendering apostasy at a grand scale. In attacking the saints, they would be attacking God, their suzerain king. But then, just as in Ezekiel's oracle, a simulated fire comes down from heaven and devours them (vv. 9). This scene demonstrates that God will jealously protect his people. After this, John saw a simulation of Satan, the instigator of all evil, being thrown into the lake of fire and sulfur where the beast and the false prophet had also been thrown (vv. 10).

This end-time, Satan-instigated, apostasy-engendering rebellion is identical to the woes simulated upon pouring the sixth and seventh bowls of God's wrath in 16:12–21. Its placement at the tail end of the events simulated when the bowls of God's wrath are poured suggests that they simulate the end time events. It is also similar to the event simulated in 19:17–21. This similarity suggests that the rebellion and apostasy referred to as the

---

37. Taylor, "Ezekiel," 242–43.
38. Bullinger, *Figures of Speech*, 639.

battle of Armageddon is the same phenomenon simulated by the battle waged by Satan, Gog, and Magog against Christ and his saints. These three portrayals of the end-time apostasy show that up to and including the time of the apostasy, the earth will be under the physical rulership of the beastly rulers and other earthly kings.

The above observation suggests that the rulership of Jesus, the martyrs, and the saints for a thousand years is a spiritual rule. It runs concurrently with the earthly rule of beastly rulers. This observation further supports the suggestion that the events simulated by the binding and imprisonment of the devil and the resultant rule of Christ and the saints for a thousand years run concurrently with the events simulated after the seven seals are opened, the seven angels blow the seven trumpets, and the seven angels pour the seven bowls of God's wrath on the earth. Thus, the events simulated by the thousand-year incarceration of Satan and the resultant reign of Christ and the saints cover the entire period of the Christ event, wherein his atoning power and the saints' fearless witness have rendered Satan's work against the believing humanity impotent (12:11).

Is the lake of fire literal? I bet not. It is a symbolic metonymy derived from Gehenna, a dump site in Jerusalem. In the days of Jesus, the trash fire in this dump site never stopped burning.[39] This metonymy was used to exemplify the painful and everlasting nature of God's judgment against the evil trinity and the obdurate sinners. Jesus described the place of this judgment as "where the fire never goes out" (Mark 9:43) and "where their worms do not die, and the fire is not quenched" (Mark 9:48), a quotation from Isa 66:24 describing the eternal fate of those who rebel against God. Revelation intensifies the pain and torment that was previously exemplified by the Gehenna fire by using the example of a lake of fire burning with sulfur/brimstone. This progressive exemplification suggests that there is yet to be found a befitting example to compare the extreme pain and torment that will be the lot of the evil trinity and the obdurate sinners. The actual suffering will be more severe than can be presently imagined and symbolized by a lake of natural fire.

In summary, Satan's judgment is meted in three stages: one, his overthrow from heaven (12:7–8). Two, his defeat by the death of Jesus Christ and the believers' testimony to the point of martyrdom (12:11). Three, when God finally banishes him into everlasting torment (vv. 10).

[11] Then I saw a great white throne and him who was seated on it. From his presence, earth and sky fled away, and no place was found for them. [12] And I saw the dead, great and small, standing before the throne, and books were

---

39. Osborn, *Revelation*, 690.

opened. Then another book was opened, which is the book of life. And the dead were judged by what was written in the books, according to what they had done. ¹³*And the sea gave up the dead who were in it, Death and Hades gave up the dead who were in them, and they were judged, each one of them, according to what they had done.* ¹⁴*Then Death and Hades were thrown into the lake of fire. This is the second death, the lake of fire.* ¹⁵*And if anyone's name was not found written in the book of life, he was thrown into the lake of fire.*

After the simulation of Satan's judgment, John was shown a simulation of the final judgment of all humanity. The words describing its setting are similar to the words describing the setting of the simulation of the judgment of Satan (vv. 4). The notable difference is that the judge is seen sitting on a white throne. The throne is portrayed as great and white, to emphasize the finality and justice of the judgment and the impeccability of the judge. The audition that no place was found for the former earth and sky in the presence of the one who sat on the throne shows the incompatibility of sin and God's holiness (vv. 11).

The final judgment was simulated by a visionary cast of one seated on the great white throne, representing God, and others representing all the dead, both great and small. The phrase "great and small" emphasizes the indiscriminate nature of God's judgment. Books are used in the vision to symbolize the unforgetting nature of God. He sees the past, present, and future as a present reality. The first batch of books symbolizes God's knowledge of each person's work. The book of life symbolizes God's knowledge of those sealed as his own and who would inherit eternal life. People's deeds go ahead of them to either condemn or commend them before God (1 Tim 5:24). Thus, the final judgment is meted in righteousness by a God who knows and remembers every human deed (vv. 12).

Regardless of the type of death, every person will be resurrected (vv. 13). According to apostle Paul, "the dead will be raised imperishable, and those who will be alive will be changed. For the perishable must clothe itself with the imperishable and the mortal with immortality" (1 Cor 15:52–53).

The omniscience of God knows those who have the mark of the beast—the sinful. These will be judged as unworthy of the kingdom of God and will be consigned to shame and everlasting contempt (Dan 12:2). After the white-throne judgment of the sinners, there will be no more death. Its sting—sin—will no longer be a factor in the new existence. The eradication of death and Hades is simulated in the scene showing the two being thrown into the lake of fire (vv. 14). Anyone whose name was not found in the book of life was also thrown into the lake of fire (vv. 15). The Greek word γεγραμμένος, gegrammenos, a perfect passive participle of γράφω, graphō (English: "I write"), suggests that those who are spared the lake of fire are those whose names are written and sustained without being erased.

After sin is fully purged, first by the sacrifice of Jesus and finally by the final judgment, the glory and power of God can be fully experienced and enjoyed. The fullness of life is actualized when sin is forever judged and when full recompense is meted on the sinner, either directly in the final judgment or through the vicarious death of Jesus Christ.

Whereas the death of the Lamb quenches the wrath of God against the sinner because of its atoning and vicarious nature, the retributive death of the sinner quenches the wrath of God by purging both the sinner and his sin. The final judgment of Satan, the sinner, and the annihilation of death and Hades that is enacted by throwing them into the lake of fire will usher in an unfettered state of holiness. The saints can then enjoy eternal bliss with God in the new heaven and earth.

Strategic and Communicative Acts in Rev 20

Showing an angel role-playing Jesus binding, chaining, and throwing Satan into the bottomless pit and shutting it is a strategic act. The hyperbolic time symbol "one thousand years" expresses the utter defeat of Satan by the death of Jesus throughout the unfolding history. The expression served to assure the saints of their eternal security and to enthuse them in their faith and witness. The seal placed over the bottomless pit assures the church that no matter the tribulations, the gates of hell cannot prevail against her (Matt 16:18).

The scene showing the resultant reign of Jesus and the saints who included the martyrs, that is, those who had not worshiped the beast or its image, and those who had not received its mark revealed a latent coup d'état, a dethroning of Satan and enthroning of Jesus and the saints. Similarly, the simulation of the resurrection of the dead must have evoked hope and comfort in those facing tribulation to the point of martyrdom. These are very efficacious strategic acts.

The scene showing fire coming down from heaven that consumed the enemies of Jesus and the saints is a strategic act that simulated the severe wages of sin. Similarly, the vision showing Satan being thrown into the lake of fire is a strategic act that would evoke joy in knowing that the chief instigator of sin and rebellion against God is completely and eternally vanquished. It also assured the saints that all their sufferings that were the result of Adam's fall have come to an end.

Finally, the simulation of the final judgment and heaven and earth fleeing from the presence of God (vv. 11) is a strategic act. Noting that no place was found for them suggests that the fleeing of the present heaven and earth will be a complete overthrow of the present sinful world and its support systems. It reveals the fleeting nature of worldly pursuits. One can imagine the regret and shame on the audience who had admired the alluring pleasures of the world.

Seeing the simulation of the dead being resurrected to stand before the throne for the final judgment constituted a powerful strategic act that was complemented by showing the books of works and the book of life. This scene must have evoked questions like, Is my name written in the book of life? How about my works? Would they be commendable before God? These were healthy reflective questions that would jolt the saints in Ephesus to revert to their first love, the saints in Smyrna and Philadelphia to greater fidelity, the church in Pergamum and Thyatira to repent from following the teachings of the Nicolaitans and Baalam, and the churches in Sardis and Laodicea to revival.

Finally, showing death, Hades, and anyone whose name was not found written in the book of life thrown into the lake of fire was a strategic act that evoked both joy and fear. Joy was evoked in the knowledge that death and Hades are forever vanquished. Man can now live forever. Fear was evoked in seeing the dreadful end of the sinner.

Application of Evocations in Rev 20

The simulation of these end-time events was meant to cause the hearers to reflectively visualize the final fate of the world, Satan, and the sinners. Furthermore, the simulation of Satan's defeat by Jesus served to show that Satan and his cronies have no power over the saints. As such, falling into sin is a personal choice. No wonder the angels hailed God as just in his judgments against the devil and his cahoots.

The evocations generated by the strategic acts in this visionary revelation are a morale booster to the present-day Christian communities where alternative cults, occult practices, magic, and witchcraft are practiced. These evocations are also applicable in communities where Christianity competes with other religions. Seeing the demonstration of the power of Jesus over the devil would give them the confidence to anchor their faith solely on Jesus. It diminishes the fear of Satan and his wiles. It also emboldens Christians to proclaim Jesus as the only way (John 14:6).

The symbolism in books that were seen in heaven frighteningly warns the readers to live their lives as people under God's watchful eye and unforgetting nature. There is nothing that is hidden from him. Our good deeds go before us to commend us before him. Equally, our evil deeds go before us to accuse us and to activate the outworking of God's decreed judgments.

Chapter 7

Eternal Dwelling of The Saints (21:1—22:21)

PRELIMINARY OBSERVATION

THESE LAST TWO CHAPTERS narrate the simulation of the unhindered irruption of God into his new dwelling place—New Ark-Temple City in the new heaven and earth, after the first heaven and earth that were marred by sin pass away. Interpreters espouse two models of the new heaven and earth: renewal of the former and replacement.[1] Keener rightly observes that "given such factors as the lack of sea, Revelation seems to use at least the image of replacement."[2] The geographical location of the new heaven and earth in relation to the former heaven and earth is not described. Similarly, very scanty details of the nature of life in the new heaven and earth have been provided. The question that would shed light on this issue is, Which kind of resurrection does the visionary revelation envisage?

While the Old Testament does not explicitly[3] express the idea of resurrection, its narratives and prophetic oracles allude to a life after death (1 Sam 28:1–25; Ps 49:15; Isa 25:8; 26:19: Dan 12:1–3, 13). On the other hand, the New Testament is very explicit on the subject of resurrection. Jesus taught it (Matt 19:29, 22:23–33; Mark 10:10:30; 12:18–27; Luke 18;30, 20:27–38, John 5:28–29, and John 11:24–26). Apostle Paul also taught that there will

---

1. Keener, *Revelation*, 485.
2. Keener, *Revelation*, 485.
3. Travis, "Resurrection," 896–924.

be a resurrection. His most explicit writing on the subject is his disputation with some in Corinth, who said that there was no resurrection of the dead (1 Cor 15:12–58). He described the resurrection body as a spiritual body (1 Cor 15:44) and a heavenly being (1 Cor 15:48–54). He further said that the abode of the resurrected spiritual bodies is heaven (1 Cor 15:47).

The New Testament supports a spiritual resurrection in spiritual bodies. As such, a refurbished earth that supports biological life is not envisaged in Scripture. So, heaven describes a yet to be experienced phenomenon. As such, it is not describable with the extant human thought and language conceptions. This notion was espoused by Paul in his postulation "what no eye has seen, nor ear heard, nor the human heart conceived, what God has prepared for those who love him" (1 Cor 2:9). So, Revelation describes the abode of the saints using lofty but still limited imagery and words within experienced history. However, these imageries and words are used for their efficacy to generate evocations to engender audience actions that would correct the shortcomings in their historical situations.

REV 21

INAUGURATION OF THE NEW HEAVEN AND EARTH

¹*Then I saw a new heaven and a new earth, for the first heaven and the first earth had passed away, and the sea was no more.* ²*And I saw the holy city, New Jerusalem, coming down out of heaven from God, prepared as a bride adorned for her husband.* ³*And I heard a loud voice from the throne saying, "Behold, the dwelling place of God is with man. He will dwell with them, and they will be his people, and God himself will be with them as their God.* ⁴*He will wipe away every tear from their eyes, and death shall be no more, neither shall there be mourning, nor crying, nor pain anymore, for the former things have passed away."*

The visionary revelation narrated in the next two chapters simulates the new abode and mode of existence of the saints. John saw a new heaven and earth replace the old, which had passed away (vv. 1). This passing away is described as fleeing away from the presence of the one sitting on the white throne (6:14, 20:11). Anything marred by sin is incompatible with the presence of God; it flees. The adjective "new" modifying the incoming heaven and earth contrasts their unmarred, eternal, and wholesome nature with the old heaven and earth, which are marred by sin, pain, tears, death, and mourning. The absence of a sea in the new heaven and earth is in line with the Hebrew worldview in which the sea was believed to be the abode of the dreaded Leviathan, the monster of the deep (Isa 27:1). Such a sea could not be envisaged as part of the new heaven and earth, where evil has been fully purged.

Some have postulated that the new heaven and earth are a refurbished old world.[4] However, John saw the old heaven and old earth passing away (Greek; απήλθαν, *apelthan*) to literally move from one place to another (20:11). This audition suggests that the old heaven and earth will move away from the presence of God into the outside (the place of torment). Thus, it is probable that it will consign itself into the lake of fire. Subsistence in the new heaven and earth does not require the body-nourishing nutrients that were necessary for biological life in the old heaven and earth. Life in the new heaven and earth is contingent on a new life-enabling power that is simulated flowing from the throne of God in the symbol of a river of life beside which grows the tree of life that is ever fruitful and whose leaves are for the healing of the nations. Lack of hunger, thirst, death, and anything that offends means that the old heaven and earth and their life-support systems will not be necessary. This suggestion agrees with Jesus' teaching that the resurrected saints will subsist as angels (Matt 22:28).

The presence of God in the new heaven and earth is represented in the symbol of a humongous jewel-bedecked ark of his presence—the New Jerusalem (vv. 2). The old Jerusalem was the seat of the earthly temple where the Ark of God's presence was kept (Exod 25:22). Now that sin, which separated man and God, is eternally purged through the redeeming death of Jesus and finally by the final judgment against Satan and the sinners, God's presence can henceforth fully and perpetually coexist with his saints. The inauguration of this coexistence is simulated by showing the ark representing his presence—New Jerusalem coming down out of heaven from God, prepared as a bride beautifully dressed for her husband. The simile "as a bride adorned for her husband" (vv. 2) contrasts the New Jerusalem with Babylon—the city on the present earth, which was described as a detestable harlot (17:1–6). Whereas the New Jerusalem represents holiness (golden streets), immortality (river of life), and wholeness and wellness (tree of life whose leaves are for the healing of nations), Babylon represents spiritual bondage, tribulation of the saints, immorality, blasphemy, and idolatry. These were the infamous traits of Rome and its metonym Babylon.

---

4. Newton, *Revelation*, 293.

A voice auditioning the spectacle clarifies, "Behold, the dwelling place of God is with man." This clarification suggests that the ark of his presence, the temple, and the city are merged into one entity—New Jerusalem—which is also enlarged, by God's unlimited presence, to encompass the whole of the new heaven and earth. This ark-temple-city, which in synecdoche of part to whole also stands for the new heaven and earth, is referred to as the dwelling place of God. The term "dwelling" denotes perpetual abiding. The eternal and unmarred relationship between God and man is described with the audition "he will dwell with them, and they will be his people, and God himself will be with them as their God" (vv. 3). The consummate relationship that will subsist in the new heaven and earth is expressed using the genitives "his people" and "their God." Man will be the worshiper and God the worshiped and source of eternal life.

Will the earthly adjectives with which God is now described be part of the heavenly worship? By no means! New expressions that describe the eternal God in a realm in which the language and perception limitations in the present world are non-existent will be used. The comparative and superlative expressions in the present heaven and earth will be too limiting to describe the glory and majesty of the ever-present God. The former things contingent on the curse of sin and which were a source of tears (death, pain, sorrow and grief) will have passed away (vv. 4).

⁵And he who was seated on the throne said, "Behold, I am making all things new." Also, he said, "Write this down, for these words are trustworthy and true." ⁶And he said to me, "It is done! I am Alpha and the Omega, the beginning and the end. To the thirsty, I will give from the spring of the waters of life without payment. ⁷The one who conquers will have this heritage, and I will be his God, and he will be my son. ⁸But as for the cowardly, the faithless, the detestable, as for murderers, the sexually immoral, sorcerers, idolaters, and all liars, their portion will be the lake that burns with fire and sulfur, which is the second death."

The description "he who was seated on the throne" is a reverential reference of God. Jews would not designate him with his revealed name "Yahweh" (I AM [the living one]), contrasting him with none living idols in Egypt and Canaan). The word "behold" calls the readers' attention to the importance of the succeeding phrase, "I am making all things new." In this phrase, God stamps the certainty of the changeover from the old heaven and earth to the new. This statement is an assurance to the church that their present suffering will soon be eternally over. The next and very important statement is introduced by the phrase "write this down, for these words are trustworthy and true." The phrase "it is done!" is an assertive phrase showing the definiteness of the soon-coming changeover from the old heaven and earth to the new. By addressing himself as the Alpha and Omega, God is swearing by himself that what he has decreed, in this assertive clause, will surely come to pass. This same statement was expressed in the Old Testament as "I am God, and beside me, there is no other" (Isa 45:5). The rest of the exhortation is meant to urge and nudge the seven churches to focus their hope on the blessedness of hunger and thirst for this wonderful inheritance of the new heaven and earth (Matt 5:3-6). The thirsty are promised the water of life—eternal life that is a product of the grace of God (vv. 6).

The one who overcomes is promised an inheritance of the things that have been shown John in this scene. They will be made God's sons (vv. 7). Calling the victors "sons" highlights their right to be heirs of their father's kingdom. The victors are contrasted with the cowardly, faithless, detestable, murderous, sexually immoral, sorcerers, idolaters, and liars whose place will be in the lake of fire that burns with fire and sulfur, which is the second death (vv. 8). The cowards are those who recanted their faith in Christ when threatened with persecution. The faithless are those who could not trust God and the gospel message but gave in to the mark of the beast to earn worldly favors. As has been postulated before, the saints have all along been reigning with Jesus. They live even if they are physically dead (John 11:26). But the sinners have all along been dead, whether physically alive or dead. For them, being thrown into the lake of fire constitutes a second death which kills both body and soul (Matt 10:28b).

⁹Then came one of the angels who had the seven bowls full of the seven last plagues and spoke to me, saying, "Come, I will show you the bride, the wife of the Lamb." ¹⁰And he carried me away in the spirit to a great mountain, and showed me the holy city, Jerusalem, coming down out of heaven from God, ¹¹having the glory of God, its radiance like a rarest jewel, like a jasper, clear as crystal. ¹²It had a great high wall, with twelve gates, and at the gates, twelve angels, and on the gates, the names of the twelve tribes of the sons of Israel were inscribed. ¹³On the east were three gates, on the north three gates, on the south three gates, and on the west three gates. ¹⁴The wall of the city had twelve foundations, and on them were the twelve names of the twelve apostles of the Lamb.

John is guided by an angel chosen from the same guild as the angel who guided him into the wilderness scene to show him the judgment of Mystery Babylon in chapter 17. In this scene, he guided John to a new visionary stage on a great mountain (vv. 10) to be shown the bride, the wife of the Lamb—the New Jerusalem. Using an angel from the same guild as the angels who showed the great harlot of chapter 17 and a change of setting from the wilderness to a high mountain prepares the audience to expect to be shown a contrasting entity to the great harlot. Gordon D. Fee opines that the New Jerusalem "is imagery for the final glory of God's people themselves."[5] However, using an angel from the same guild as the angel in chapter 17 to take John to the top of a mountain top setting highlights the contrast between the sinful harlot city and the holy bride city. The former is overthrown and, in her place, the latter is installed.

The antithetical juxtaposition of the wilderness visionary stage (17:3) with the high mountain visionary stage (vv. 9–10), former heaven and earth with new heaven and earth, and Rome with New Jerusalem is an evocative picture contrasting dalliance with Satan in sin in the extant heaven and earth with coexistence with God as Jehovah Shammah in the new heaven and earth. As used here, the "bride" and her emphatic parallel "wife" are figurative symbols. They are not used to denote a "mystery union" between Jesus, his saints, and God as has commonly been postulated.[6] As shown earlier, Mystery Babylon—the city of Rome—stands in synecdoche of part for whole, for the extant heaven and earth and in metonymy for its leaders and citizens. She was figuratively symbolized as a whore who was patronized by Satan and earthly kings to engage in her idolatry, trade, and debauchery. On the other hand, New Jerusalem stands in synecdoche of part for whole for the new heaven and earth. It also stands in metonymy for the fullness of the presence of God in the new heaven and earth and for the saints who will live there eternally. She is depicted as the eternal bride of Jesus. As the fullness of the presence of God, she is the source of eternal life whose splendor, eternality, and wholeness are represented by the streets of gold, the river of life, and the tree of life, all emanating from the essence of God. The church will gloriously live (walk on the streets of gold), eternally live (drink from the river of unending life and eat the fruit of the tree of eternal life) in complete wellness (eat its leaves which are for the healing of the nations).

The scene on the mountain top recalls Moses being called by God to the top of Mount Pisgah to behold the promised land (Deut 34:1). This time, however, John is beholding a symbolic ark city which also represents God's eternal presence in the new heaven and new earth coming down from heaven (vv. 10). The wall of sin that separated the impeccable God with peccable world is eternally removed. Here, the ark, the temple and city are merged into a unity that symbolizes the fullness of the presence of God. It's adornment symbolically describe the majesty, holiness, and life-sustaining

---

5. Fee, *Revelation*, 297.
6. Longman, *Revelation*, 290.

nature of God. From it, the dwellers of the new heaven and earth will draw eternal life and wellness as they worship God eternally.

To express and represent the loftiness of the majesty, glory, and holiness of God in the earthly temple, God instructed Moses to overlay the Ark of the Covenant with pure gold. But though precious, gold is common. Here, the majesty, glory, and holiness of God are represented by a very rare jewel—jasper, clear as crystal (vv. 11). The city-ark had a symbolic great high wall (vv. 12a). Usually, a great wall would symbolize the safety of the city's inhabitants. In this scene, it represents the inaccessibility and complete exclusion of sin and sinner. It evoked the need for sanctification to those who wished to dwell in it.

The city had twelve gates and twelve angels standing at the gates. On the gates were written the names of the twelve tribes of Israel—on the east three gates, on the north three gates, on the south three gates, and on the west three gates (vv. 12b-13). The twelve gates and twelve angels guarding each of the twelve gates symbolize discriminatory access to the presence of God. The names of the twelve tribes of Israel could denote the guaranteed entrance of the Old Testament saints into the city. The city had twelve foundations and on each one was the name of the twelve apostles of the Lamb (vv. 14). The names of the twelve apostles could denote the New Testament saints who have been made pillars in the heavenly temple (3:12). The twelve gates having the names of the twelve tribes of Israel and the twelve foundations with the names of the twelve apostles of the Lamb echo the words of Paul that the household of God, the church, is "built on the foundation of the apostles and prophets, Christ Jesus himself being the cornerstone, in whom the whole structure, being joined together, grows into a holy temple of the Lord. In him, you also are built together into a dwelling place for God by the Spirit" (Eph 2:20–22).

[15] The one who spoke with me had a measuring rod of gold to measure the city and its gates and walls. [16] The city lies foursquare, its length the same as its width. And he measured the city with the rod. It was 12,000 stadia in length, width, and height. [17] He also measured its walls, it was 144 cubits by human measurement.

The mighty angel talking to John had a measuring rod of gold to measure the city, its gates, and its walls (vv. 15). A visionary act of measuring the city with a golden measuring rod is symbolically laden with meaning. The gold highlighted the exceeding holiness of God, whose presence the city represented; Gordon D. Fee opines that it represented the holy of holies.[7]

---

7. Fee, *Revelation*, 298.

ETERNAL DWELLING OF THE SAINTS (21:1—22:21)

However, deducing from the symbol of Mount Zion as the new heaven and earth, Jerusalem its capital, and the humongous ark that encompasses the whole city, then the cubed city can be figured out as representing the fullness of God's presence (Ezek 48:35). That is why the city is portrayed as having no need of a temple because they are rendered irrelevant by his presence symbolized by the humongous ark city—the New Jerusalem. The act of measuring the city demonstrated the enormity of this ark city of God's presence in comparison to its type in the earthly tabernacle.

Compared with the ark in the earthly temple, which was a miniature ark, two and a half cubits long, one and a half cubits wide, and one and a half cubits high (Exod 25:10–11), the representation of the presence of God in the new heaven and new earth was a gigantic four-square 12,000 stadia cubed city (vv. 16). This city is just a symbol communicating divine truth to finite humans. God cannot fit or dwell in a specific geographical location in heaven above or earth below. He is *El Shaddai*–almighty (omnipotent, omniscient, and omnipresent). The measurements are meant to contrast the partial relationship between God and man in the extant heaven and earth and the wholesome relationship that will exist in the new heaven and new earth. According to Stephen S. Smalley, the city is 2000 kilometers cubed.[8] Compared with the size of the ark in the earthly tabernacle, one can appreciate God's everlasting and unencumbered presence among the saints in the new heaven and earth. The 144 cubits (approximately 72 feet) thick wall denotes his impeccability. He cannot be permeated by evil.

[18]*The wall was built of jasper, while the city was pure gold, like transparent glass.* [19]*The foundations of the city wall were adorned with every kind of Jewel. The first was jasper, the second sapphire, the third agate, the fourth emerald,* [20]*the fifth onyx, the sixth carnelian, the seventh Chrysolite, the eighth beryl, the ninth topaz, the tenth chrysoprase, the eleventh jacinth, the twelfth amethyst.* [21]*And the twelve gates were twelve pearls, each of the gates made of a single pearl, and the street of the city was pure gold, like transparent glass.*

The ark in the earthly tabernacle was a visible representation of the transcendent God. It could only be approached once a year to plead for the forgiveness of sins committed by God's people in the course of the past year. On the other hand, the visionary ark (New Jerusalem) represented the incoming of the transcendent God whose visible presence would abide eternally in the new heaven and earth. To evoke desire for this future eternal relationship with God and to encourage the audience to persevere in faith to the very end, the city is portrayed as bedecked with very valuable and

---

8. Smalley, *Revelation*, 551.

desirable jewels: jasper, sapphire, agate, emerald, onyx, carnelian, chrysolite, beryl, topaz, chrysoprase, jacinth, and amethyst.

In the preliminary letters to the seven churches, Jesus had promised to make those who will overcome pillars in the house of his God (3:12). Therefore, the foundation and walls could represent the saints in whose hearts God dwells by the Spirit. First Peter 2:5 offers this interim picture: "You also, like living stones, are being built into a spiritual house to be a holy priesthood, offering spiritual sacrifices acceptable to God through Jesus Christ."

[22]And I saw no temple in the city, for its temple is the Lord God the Almighty and the Lamb. [23]And there was no need of the sun nor moon, that they shine in it, for the glory of God gives it light, and its lamp is the Lamb. [24]By its light will the nations walk, and the kings of the earth will bring their glory into it. [25]And its gates will never be shut by day–and there will be no night there. [26]They will bring into it the glory and honour of the nations. [27]But nothing unclean will ever enter it, nor anyone who does what is detestable or false, but only those who are written in the Lamb's book of life.

The earthly community of faith needed a temple for their worship and for storing the relics of their covenant and remembrance of God's salvific deeds. However, the new heaven and new earth does not need a temple. The real and eternal presence of God and the Lamb obviates the need for their typologies. Similarly, there will be no need of the sun and moon which were given to light up the day and night. The glory of God and the Lamb will be sufficient to draw the saints to worship.

In contrast to the merchants of the earth who prostituted with Mystery Babylon, the nations and kings of the earth will bring glory and honor to God (vv. 24). The nations and kings of the earth should be understood as the saintly dwellers of the new heaven and earth, some of whom were kings in the former earth. Saying that "its gates will never be shut by day—and there will be no nights there" (vv. 25), suggests that there will be no evil to warrant any deterrence. The only allowable merchandise is the doxology and honor of the nations who have now become the people of God (vv. 26). This amazingly evocative description is summarized in the audition "nothing impure will ever enter it, nor will anyone who does what is shameful or deceitful, but only those whose names are written in the Lamb's book of life" (vv. 27). This statement speaks very powerfully to the suffering churches that the evil they are suffering at present will not follow them into the new heaven and new earth. The statement is couched with both a warning against falling back into sin and an exhortation to live holy lives.

Strategic and Communicative Acts in Rev 21

The visionary contrast between the new heaven and earth with the old heaven and earth constitutes a strategic act. It evokes contempt for the worldly and high regard and longing for the heavenly. Similarly, the contrast between New Jerusalem, the presence of God in the new heaven and new earth with Rome, the loathsome city that ruled the extant world was meant to elicit a strong loathing of Romish ways and a yearning to live in the heavenly home. It was aimed at strengthening the resolve of those passing through tribulations to persevere and those who were living in sinful slumber to repent.

Description of the city as having been prepared as a bride adorned for her husband compares the longing a husband has for a soon-to-be-married bride and the longing that should subsist in the saints for life with God. The audition "behold, the dwelling place of God is with man. He will dwell with them, and they will be his people, and God himself will be with them as their God" auditions the nature of the existence and relationship that is referenced by the symbolic New Jerusalem.

The audition "he will wipe away every tear from their eyes and death shall be no more, neither shall there be mourning, nor crying, nor pain anymore" (vv. 4), and the voice of God affirming that he is making everything new (vv. 5), are a communicative act. Likewise, the promise of water without cost from the spring of the water of life to the thirsty and that the victorious will inherit all this, and that God will be their God and they will be his sons, are also communicative acts. They are aimed at urging the saints to desire this gorgeous inheritance.

The city's ambiance was compared with the beauty of the most precious jewels. The description showed the city's holiness to elicit a desire for holiness on earth in order to earn a life with God in the new heaven and new earth. The portrayed contrast of the city's holiness with the darkness of sin in the earthly city is a strategic act. The audition "the Kings of the earth will bring their splendour and the doxology and honour of nations will be brought to it" contrasts with the immorality, idolatry, and persecution practiced in the earthly city. The contrast evokes a desire to forsake anything vile and to embrace holiness so as to be counted worthy to partake in the splendor, honor, and glory in the new city.

Finally, the enumeration of those who will not be allowed into the new heaven and earth and saying that they will have their lot in the lake of fire is also a communicative act. Its aim was to highlight the things that should be pursued and the ones that should be shunned in order to inherit the promise of eternal life with God.

Application of Evocations in Rev 21

The scenes recorded in this chapter depict the presence of God in the new heaven and new earth using very lofty symbols, which undoubtedly served to stir the seven churches in seeking the things above (Col 3:1–2). It amplifies Jesus' teaching about the desirability of the kingdom of God in his parable of the costly pearls, for which the one who found them sold everything he had to purchase them (Matt 13:45–46).

Seeing the simulation of the glory of God in the new heaven and earth should make both the primary and secondary readers despise the things that tempt in this world and long for and consequently pursue the things above where Christ is seated with God (Col 3:1). The visionary revelation allows the saints to see the glory awaiting them to cause them to despise trials, temptations, and persecutions that are continually visited on them by the dragon, the beast, and the false prophets of their day.

REV 22

FINAL RAPPROCHEMENT

[1] Then he showed me a river of water of life, clear as crystal, flowing from the throne of God and the Lamb [2] through the middle of the city's street. On either side of the river was the tree of life producing twelve kinds of fruits. It yields its fruit each month, and the leaves of the tree are for the healing of the nations.

John is still on the mountaintop vision stage being shown the bride of the Lamb—standing in metonymy for the New Jerusalem. She is the antithesis of the great prostitute also standing in metonymy for Babylon the Great (Rome). In this scene, he is shown a river of the water of life flowing from the throne of God and the Lamb. On either side of the river was a tree of life. Robert L. Thomas rightly notes, "The best analysis pictures a river flowing down the middle of the city's street with the trees on each side of the river in the middle of the space between the street and each side of the river banks."[9]

This flowing, crystal-clear river of life is a symbolic demonstration of eternal life that will be flowing from God and the Lamb to all the heirs of the new heaven and earth. A street presupposes the saint's eternal walk on it. The word "walk" (Greek: περιπατέω, *peripateō*) is used in the New Testament to denote "to live" (Col 2:6; 3:7). The street, therefore, represents a holy life of unhindered communion with God. Eternal life can be defined as God's perpetual and irrevocable enablement of his new creation to live eternally. The

---

9. Thomas, *Revelation 8—22*, 483.

tree of life on each side of the river that bears twelve crops of fruit, one crop each month, symbolically demonstrates abundant and exceedingly fulfilling life, while the leaves of the tree of life demonstrates the absence of disease and any kind of infirmity in the new heaven and new earth.

³*There will no longer be anything accursed, but the throne of God and of the Lamb will be in it, and his servants will worship him.* ⁴*They will see his face, and his name will be on their foreheads.* ⁵*And night will be no more. They will need no light of lamp or sun, for the Lord God will be their light, and they will reign forever and ever.*

The presence of God and the Lamb is incompatible with anything accursed. Only the throne of God and the Lamb will be in the city. In this scene, thrones are used to represent the ones who sit on them; that is God and the Lamb. The absence of sin ensures unhindered communion between God and his saints. Rebecca Skaggs and Priscilla C. Benham note that "the metaphor of bearing a name on one's forehead is taken from slave imagery. The name indicates ownership and likeness."[10] In view of the then-prevailing slave-master relationships, this supposition is very probable. To see one's face is to be allowed into one's presence (2 Sam 14:24, 32), and to have God's name on the saints' foreheads is to fully reflect the image and likeness of God (Gen 1:26). Sin will be no more, as shown by the light of God and the absence of night—used here as a symbol of calamity.[11] The presence of the throne of God and the Lamb with his servants, the saints, worshiping him perpetually, symbolizes the perpetual reign of the Godhead and the saints. This reign should neither be understood as the heavenly host's subjugation of the human species nor a subjugation of an underprivileged class of people by a favoured class. It is a complete overthrow of Satan, sin, and death that results in a perpetual shalom with God.

⁶*And he said to me, "These words are trustworthy and true. The Lord, the God of the spirits of the prophets, has sent his angel to show his servants what must soon take place."*

The certainty of the events simulated in the entire visionary revelation is avowed by the angel with the words, "These words are trustworthy and true." This statement buttresses the suggestion that this visionary revelation was a prophecy in apocalyptic visionary simulations. It is also meant to urge readers to respond favorably to the evocations generated by the strategic acts embedded in this visionary revelation.

10. Skaggs and Pricilla, *Revelation*, 228.
11. Vine, Unger, and White, *Vine's Dictionary*, 160.

⁷*"And behold, I am coming soon. Blessed is the one who keeps the words of the prophecy of this book."*

This verse starts the epilogue of the entire visionary revelation. Saying "behold I am coming soon" is intended to heighten the urgency and grave importance of watching and living in perpetual preparedness for the soon coming of Jesus Christ. The beatitude "blessed is the one who keeps the words of the prophecy of this book" is intended to further urge the audience to urgently respond to the evocations generated by the entire visionary simulations. It is a fitting conclusion to the visionary revelation. The exhortation to keep the words of the prophecy suggests that John considers the visionary revelation not to be just a message relayed in apocalyptic genre but a genuine prophecy, whose every visionary revelation was to be fulfilled in its due time and circumstance. However, it is meant to meet the now needs of the audience rather than to feed their curiosity of knowing what will happen in the future.

⁸*I, John, am the one who heard and saw these things. And when I heard and saw them, I fell down to worship at the feet of the angel who showed them to me, ⁹but he said to me, "You must not do that! I am a fellow servant with you and your brothers, the prophets, and with those who keep the words of this book. Worship God." ¹⁰And he said to me, "Do not seal up the words of the prophecy of this book, for the time is near. ¹¹Let the evildoer still do evil, the filthy still be filthy, the righteous still do right, and the holy still be holy." ¹²"Behold, I am coming soon, bringing my recompense to repay each one for what he has done. ¹³I am the Alpha and Omega, the first and the last, the beginning and the end." ¹⁴Blessed are those who wash their robes so that they may have the right to the tree of life and that they may enter the city by the gates. ¹⁵Outside are the dogs and sorcerers and the sexually immoral and the murderers and idolaters, and everyone who loves and practices falsehood.*

The phrase "I, John" (vv. 8) shows that John was confident that his audience trusted him to speak truthfully. As in the beginning of the narration, he stamps the authenticity of his vision with his name. Thus, his apostolic credentials were without doubt. Highlighting his reverence at seeing the vision, demonstrated by his falling down, further highlights the importance of the message transmitted through the visionary revelation. Being rebuked by the angel for worshiping him shows that angels, prophets, apostles, and any other person among the saints who would be called in like manner are mere servants of God. They do not deserve to be reverenced and worshiped. Worship is a reserve for God.

The angel told John not to seal up the words of the prophecy of this book, for the time of its fulfilment was near (vv. 10). It calls for an urgent response from the readers. The parallelism in the statements "let the evildoer still do evil, and the filthy still be filthy" and "the righteous still do right, and the holy still be holy" (vv. 11) is expressed in the form of an irony that is both a warning and a plea. It emphasizes that there is little time to persuade people to follow after godliness. Now is the opportune moment to choose to respond to God's rapprochements. This plea and warning are summed up by the words "behold, I am coming soon, bringing my recompense with me, to repay each one for what he has done" (vv. 12). The word "behold" is not an aesthetic nuance; it is a call to attention. It stresses the importance of the statement about to be spoken. The announcement of the imminence of the coming of Jesus aims to prod the saints to urgently respond to the evocations in the strategic acts embedded in the entire visionary revelation. The announcement is framed in the form of a highly evocative strategic act by revealing an attractive reward for those who heed God's grace rapprochements. The parallelism in the phrase "I am the Alpha and the Omega the first and the last, beginning and the end" (vv. 13), emphasizes the finality of God's words. Thus, what he has said cannot be countermanded by any other being; it is true, authoritative, and final.

In the competing choices to either succumb to sin or pursue righteousness, John recommends righteousness in the beatitude "blessed are those who wash their robes so that they may have the right to the tree of life and that they may enter the city by the gates" (vv. 14). Washing their robes is unequivocally shown to be the gate pass to eternal life. The sinners, represented by "dogs, the sorcerers, the sexually immoral, murderers, idolaters, and everyone who loves and practices falsehood" (vv. 14–15) will not be allowed into the city. The metaphor dog signifies backsliders who had once believed but because of either love for the world or pressure from persecutions, forsook the faith and become unfruitful (Mark 4:1–7). The "outside," where they belong, is the lake of fire (20:15), a place of untold torment.

[16]"I, Jesus, have sent my angel to testify to you about these things for the churches. I am the root and the descendant of David, the bright morning star." [17] The Spirit and the Bride say, "Come." And let the one who hears say, "Come." And let the one who is thirsty come; let the one who desires take the water of life without price.

In saying, "I, Jesus, have sent my angel to testify to you about these things for the churches. I am the root of David, the bright morning star," Jesus affirms the authenticity of the visionary revelation, thereby embedding it with greater evocative power. The efficacy of his entreaty to "come!" springs from Jesus' mandate as the Messiah, the root and descendant of David. He is the bright morning star, the one who lit up the night of sin upon the world by his atoning death.

John is still caught up in the Spirit on the symbolic visionary high mountain reminiscent of Moses on Mount Pisgah, beholding the promised land (Deut 34:1). A performance reading should take every reader to this high mountain to behold the promise of God to the victorious saints. The beauty of the city, its golden street, a river of life, and the tree of life that bears fruit every month, complemented by the convicting Spirit who inspired this revelation, are evocatively cajoling the saints in the seven churches, and indeed the saints, in the unfolding history to "come" to Jesus. It is a call to the church to respond to Jesus, who is the way, truth, and life (John 14:9). It entails denying the world, even if it means giving up one's life in martyrdom. The strategic acts in the symbols, visionary simulations, and auditions must have evoked abhorrence for the sinful world and a yearning for the new heaven and new earth. It is time for those whose desire has been kindled to respond to heaven's call, come to Jesus, and receive living water without price. The water of life has already been paid for by the death of the Lamb of God.

[18]I warn everyone who hears the words of the prophecy of this book; if anyone adds to them, God will add to him the plagues described in this book, [19]and if anyone takes away from the words of the book of this prophecy, God will take away his share in the tree of life and in the holy city, which are described in this book. [20]He who testifies to these things says, "Surely I am coming soon." Amen. Come, Lord Jesus! [21]The Grace of God be with you all. Amen.

John issues a warning to everyone who hears the words of the prophecy in this book not to add or take away any word from the prophecy. Each of the visionary simulation, symbol, and audition is complementarily vital. If they do not hearken, they risk receiving the judgments recorded in this book and being disinherited from the pronounced blessings (vv. 18–19).[12] John closes the narration by invoking the words of Jesus, whom he describes as "he who testifies to these things says, 'Surely, I am coming soon'" (vv. 20). With these words, John stresses the message of Jesus' imminent coming and encourages the seven churches to adopt a watchful and prayerful lifestyle. On behalf of himself and the church, John agrees with the appeal of Jesus with the words "Amen, Come, Lord Jesus!" meaning, "may it be so, come Lord Jesus." Finally, John caps the narration of his visionary revelation with

---

12. Ngundu, "Revelation," 1578.

a benediction: "The grace of the Lord Jesus be with all the saints. Amen" (vv. 21). The grace, by which the church is redeemed and prepared for eternal life, is the best wish upon the militant church as she sojourns, in her final exodus through the unfolding history awaiting the soon return of her great God and savior Jesus Christ.

Strategic and Communication Acts in Rev 22

Showing the crystal-clear river of the water of life and the tree of life is a strategic act that generates evocations of deep longing to share in the revealed inheritance in the new heaven and earth. Consequently, it urges the audience to respond by believing in Jesus, resisting sin, patiently enduring tribulations, and performing spiritual disciplines that would bridge the gaps in the visionary situations of the seven churches.

The guiding angel's affirmation that the visionary revelation and auditions were trustworthy and true complemented the simulation's strategic acts. Jesus also affirmed the authenticity of the visionary revelation by saying that he was indeed the one who sent the angel to testify these things. Finally, John complimented the efficacy of the strategic act by authenticating the visionary revelation with the stamp of his name as he did at the beginning of his narration (1:1-9). Thus, John's, Jesus', and the angel's auditions aimed at authenticating the visionary revelation to embed it with enhanced efficacy to bridge the gaps in the seven churches" visionary situations.

Application of Evocations in Rev 22

This visionary revelation gives a preview of life in the new heaven and earth that is the very opposite of the life in the former heaven and earth. The wanting historical situations in the seven churches of Asia Minor (chapters 2-3, 6-20), the outworking of God's retributive and disciplinary judgment decrees (chapters 6-9; 16-20), the tribulation of saints by the evil trinity (chapters 12-13) and even the rapprochements in the preaching of the gospel (6:1-2; 10:1—11-19) will not be part of the new heaven and new earth.

The above evocative contrast is complemented by the final rapprochement, "the Spirit and the Bride say 'Come!' And let the one who hears say, 'Come!' Let the one who hears say 'Come.' And let the thirsty one come; let the one who desires take the water of life without price." It is intended to urge the saints in the seven churches to despise the old heaven and earth and long for the new heaven and earth. It is also meant to prompt endurance in tribulations in the knowledge that their present sufferings are not worthy compared to the glory that will be revealed to us (Rom 8:18).

The churches of God throughout the unfolding history have historical situations with gaps that can be adequately bridged by responding to the evocations generated by the strategic acts embedded in this final visionary revelation. These evocations can be applied in total to the church in every age including ours. The visionary simulation of the beauty, eternal satisfaction, and wholeness in the new heaven and earth can engender comfort to those suffering grief and mourning for deceased loved ones. The present globalized world is being lured into rebellion against the teachings of the Bible through the many media platforms and human rights groups. Sins like abortion, homosexuality, oppression of the poor and vulnerable by the rich and mighty are no longer frowned at by the church. The communicative and strategic acts in this last visionary simulation can indeed bring the change needed to this repugnant historical situation.

RETROSPECTIVE GRAPHIC OVERVIEW OF THE VISIONARY SIMULATIONS

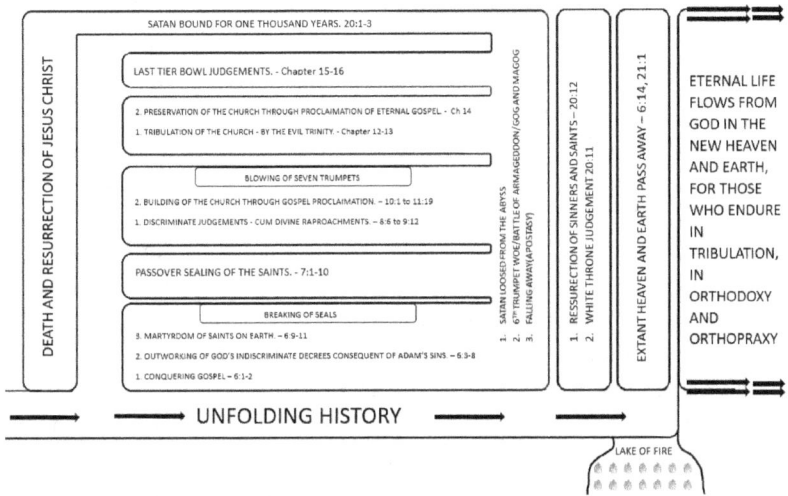

Observations from Graphic Overview

It was suggested in the introduction that because of the symbolic and progressive visionary parallelism employed in structuring the scenes of the visionary revelation, interpretation outcomes of its constituent scenes should be provisionally held until the entire visionary revelation is fully read and interpreted. The above graphic description looks back and summarizes the salient interpretive outcomes.

It concludes that "the things that are and that will take place after this" take place as history unfolds, starting from the death and resurrection of Jesus Christ to his second coming. This period will come to an end when the extant heaven and earth pass away (6:14; 11:15; 16:17–21; and 21:1). It is also observed that the events simulated when the seals are opened, when the trumpets are sounded, and when the bowls are poured on the earth happen concurrently. However, some of the events simulated at the end of these visionary scenes are slated to be outworked at the close of history (6:12–17; 9:1–21; 16:12–16; 19:11–21; 20:7–15). It is also observed that the preaching of the gospel is a constant occurrence in each of these simulated events (6:2, 11:3–7, 14:6–13, and 18:4–5). It is further observed that the church will experience tribulation throughout the unfolding history which will be orchestrated by Satan, civic leaders, and compromised religion (chapters 12–13). This tribulation will escalate towards the end of history to engender the end time obduracy and apostasy (20:7–9). However, notwithstanding these tribulations, Jesus will sustain the church in victory (14:1–5). The gates of hell will never prevail against her.

It is observed that the death of Jesus outworked salvation, power, and sustenance of the church during the unfolding history. This state is simulated in the scene sowing the sealing of the 144,000 (7:4–8), the rest of the throng of the saints (7:8–9), and binding of Satan for the entire history, which is symbolically described as a thousand years (20:1). However, towards the end of history, Satan will instigate a furious tribulation to engender obduracy and apostasy (9:1–21; 16:12–16; 20:7–8). This end-time, short but furious tribulation is compared to the proverbial battle of Gog and Magog (Ezek 38–39). That period is described eerily as a time when Satan is loosed from his erstwhile one-thousand-year incarceration (20:7–9).

The obduracy exhibited by persecutors of the saints and their collaborating world, notwithstanding God's gracious rapprochements, will irk God to the point of outworking the final judgment (white-throne judgment). This event will be preceded by the resurrection of all the dead from the time of Adam (20:13). The sinners will be judged as unworthy of eternal life and consigned to shame and everlasting contempt in to a state compared to a lake of fire burning with sulfur and brimstone (20:15). The righteous will be ushered into eternal bliss in the new heaven and new earth, where the full presence of God will dwell with his people eternally (vv. 14).

Summary

As stated in the introduction to this commentary, the challenge in interpreting John's visionary revelation stems from the unique mode and media in which it is transmitted. The other challenge is the extant lack of a criticism method for interpreting divinely inspired visions and dreams. Though the visionary revelation is majorly a strategic act, interpreters normally use current criticism methods of interpreting communicative acts. Such interpretations result in the inadvertent and not very useful pursuit of identifying the referents to each symbol and the simulated events instead of the very useful endeavor of identifying their embedded strategic acts, the evocations they generate, and applying them to the audiences' varied historical situations.

Interpreters have also been interpreting the visionary revelation as John's inspired message, otherwise transmitted in an apocalyptic genre. They do not view it as a divinely directed vision that reveals the things that are and that were to take place in the course of the unfolding history through visionary simulations. Consequently, they explore John's thoughts and eschatological leanings. This view deflects the reader from an otherwise valuable search for God's intentions in showing visions embedded with less of communicative acts but more of strategic acts.

This commentary's unique and revolutionary contribution is its delineation of the communicative and strategic acts embedded in each scene of the visionary revelation. It has also noted that the communicative acts in the seven personalized covering letters reveal the visionary situations and their gaps. Furthermore, the strategic acts embedded in the visionary revelation have been identified as God's chosen means of generating evocations to engender audience responses that would bridge the gaps in the churches' varied historical situations.

Another unique contribution of this commentary is identification of the letters to the seven churches as personalized covering letters that were to accompany the single narration of the visionary revelation (4:1—22:21).

Their purpose has also been identified as to catalogue the visionary situations and needs that prompted God to show the visionary revelation. The visionary simulations in chapter 4 and chapter 5 have also been identified as a visionary version of the authenticating formula of divine discourse: "thus says the Lord." Here, it can be rephrased as "thus shows/reveals the Lord."

Yet another unique and groundbreaking contribution is identification of synonymity between the function of both the simulation and the event simulated in the sealing of the 144,000 and the throng of worldwide saints and the function of both the simulation and event simulated in binding Satan for a thousand years. This identification opens fresh ground for future research.

The above observations are groundbreaking in interpreting the visionary revelation in three significant ways: first, they have enlarged the interpretation horizons of the visionary revelation by providing a well-argued alternative to the extant methods. They also offer fresh conclusions on the purpose and application of the visionary revelation. Second, they aptly connect the visionary revelation with the needs they are intended to resolve. Third, the commentary observes that since God's rapprochements, the discipline of the wayward, the tribulation of the saints, and the promised rewards of the saints have been a constant throughout history, then the evocations generated by the communicative and strategic acts can be applied in total to the historical situations of the secondary audiences.

The hermeneutical outcomes of using this method agree with Old Testament and New Testament theologies. It shows that the main purpose of this visionary revelation is not to inform but to transform by the readers' responses to the evocations generated by its communicative and strategic acts. It is also observed that there is less use of communicative acts and greater use of strategic acts. Moreover, the primary purpose of showing the visionary revelation is to urgently prepare the church for the soon coming of their great God and savior Jesus Christ.

An issue that has muddled up interpretation of Revelation is a misleading attempt to sketch the events simulated in the visionary revelation to agree with the supposed chronology of the events shown in the vision narrated in Dan 9:24–27. Suffice to say, Revelation is not a road map of future prophetic events. Instead, it is a visionary simulation of God's redemptive deeds that he has accomplished in Christ, the outworking of his indiscriminate decrees, his rapprochements in retributory and disciplinary judgments and the preaching of the gospel in the unfolding history, his eternal rewards to the saints, and wages of sin to the sinner.

The book of Revelation indeed presents a hermeneutical challenge. Even the most astute exegete cannot certainly identify the referent of each symbol. Notwithstanding, the strategic acts embedded in each scene of the visionary revelation can generate evocations that can be applied to any reader's historical situation to arouse greater fidelity to orthodoxy, orthopraxis, and patient endurance when facing issues of theodicy.

In a nutshell, the visionary revelation is a divinely inspired vision aimed at rejuvenating and maintaining the church's spiritual health amid satanic attacks through trials, temptations, and persecutions herein referred to as tribulations. First, the seven churches in Asia Minor were shown the gaps in their fidelity to orthodoxy, orthopraxy, and the spiritual risk posed by Christian suffering in the personalized letters to each of the seven churches (chapters 2–3). Secondly, they were shown a visionary revelation embedded with highly efficacious strategic acts (6:1—22:21) to generate evocations that, if responded to, would eliminate the gaps in their visionary situations.

May this commentary catalyze those who have ears to hear what the Spirit is saying to the churches by guiding them to identify the embedded communicative and strategic acts. May they be engendered by the evocations generated by these communicative and strategic acts to bridge gaps in their varied historical situations as they await their longed-for inheritance in the new heaven and earth. Amen!

Bibliography

Aune, David E. *World Biblical Commentary: Revelation 6–16*. Edited by Bruce Metzger. Nashville: Thomas Nelson, 1998.
Bauckham, Richard. *The Climax of Prophecy*. Edinburgh: T&T Clark, 1993.
Beale G. K. *The Book of Revelation: A Commentary on the Greek Text*. Grand Rapids: Eerdmans, 1999.
———. *Handbook on the New Testament Use of the Old Testament: Exegesis and Interpretation*. Grand Rapids: Baker Academic, 2012.
Beale G. K., and David H. Campbell. *Revelation: A Shorter Commentary*. Grand Rapids: Eerdmans, 2015.
Beale G. K., and Sean M. McDonough. "Revelation." In *Commentary on the New Testament Use of the Old Testament*, edited by G. K. Beale and D. A. Carson, 1081–1161. Grand Rapids: Baker Academic, 2007.
Beasley-Murray, George R. "Revelation." In *Dictionary of the Later New Testament and Its Developments*, edited by Ralph P. Martin and Peter H. Davids, 1025–38. Downers Grove, IL: InterVarsity, 1992.
———. "Premillennialism." In *Revelation: Three Viewpoints*, edited by G. R. Beasley-Murray, Herschel H. Hobbs, and Ray Frank Robbins, 11–72. Nashville: Broadman, 1977.
———. "The Book of Revelation". In *Century Bible Commentary*, edited by Ronald E. Clements and Matthew Black. Grand Rapids: Eerdmans, 1974.
Beckwith, Isbon T. *The Apocalypse of John*. Eugene, OR: Wipf and Stock, 2001.
Beitzel, Barry J. *The New Moody Atlas of the Bible*. Chicago: Moody, 2009.
Bitzer, Lloyd F. "The Rhetorical Situation." *Philosophy and Rhetoric* 1 (1968) 1–14.
Boxall, Ian. *The Revelation of Saint John*. Black's New Testament Commentaries. Peabody, MA: Hendrickson, 2006.
Bullinger, E. W. *Figures of Speech Used in the Bible*. Grand Rapids: Baker, 1968.
Caird, George Bradford. *The Revelation of Saint John*. Black's New Testament Commentaries. Peabody, MA: Hendrickson, 1999.
Charles, R. H. *Studies in Apocalypse*. Eugene, OR: Wipf and Stock, 1996.
———. *The Revelation of St. John*. London: T&T Clark, 2021.
Collins, Adela Yarbro. *Crisis and Catharsis: The Power of the Apocalypse*. Philadelphia: Westminster, 1984.
Cory, Catherine A. *Revelation*. Collegeville, MN: Liturgical, 2006.
DeSilva, David Arthur. *Seeing Things John's Way: The Rhetoric of the Book of Revelation*. Louisville: Westminster John Knox, 2009.

Desrosiers, Gilbert. *An Introduction to Revelation*. London: Continuum, 2000.

Eck, Werner. "Prokonsuln von Asia in der flavisch-traianischen Zeit." *Zeitschrift fur Papyrologie und Epigraphik* 45 (1982) 139–53.

Engen, J. Van. "Anointing Oil." In *Evangelical Dictionary of Theology*, edited by Walter A. Elwell, 21–52. Grand Rapids: Baker, 1984.

Erickson, Millard J. *Christian Theology*. 2nd ed. Grand Rapids: Baker Academic, 1998.

Eusebius, Pamphilus. *The Ecclesiastical History of Eusebius Pamphilus*. Translated by C. F. Cruse. London: Bell & Sons, 1892.

Falwell, Jerry. *Liberty Commentary on the New Testament*. Edited by Edward E. Hindson and Woodrow Michael Kroll. Lynchburg, VA: Liberty, 1978.

Farmer, Ronald L. *Revelation*. Chalice Commentaries for Today. St. Louis: Chalice, 2005.

Fee, Gordon D. *Revelation: A New Covenant Commentary*. 1st ed. Lutterworth, 2011. https://doi.org/10.2307/j.ctt1cg4moq.

Filipiak, Magdalena. "Strategic Actions According to Jürgen Habermas—Some Critical Remarks from the Transcendental-Pragmatic Procedure Viewpoint." *Lingua Posnaniensis* 59.1 (Jun. 2017) 39–52.

Fiorenza, Elizabeth Schussler. *The Book of Revelation: Justice and Judgment*. 2nd ed. Minneapolis: Augsburg Fortress, 1998.

———. *Revelation: Vision of a Just World*. Proclamation Commentaries. Minneapolis: Fortress, 1991.

Gilmour, S. Maclean. "The Revelation to John." In *The Interpreter's One-Volume Commentary on the Bible*, edited by Charles M. Laymon, 945–68. Nashville: Abingdon, 1971.

Goldingay, John. "Isaiah." In *New International Biblical Commentary*, edited by Robert L. Hubbard, Jr., and Robert K. Johnson. Peabody, MA: Hendrickson, 2001.

Goldsworthy, Graeme, *The Gospel in Revelation: Gospel and Apocalypse*. London: Paternoster, 1984.

Grudem, Wayne. *Systematic Theology: An Introduction to Biblical Doctrine*. Leicester, England: InterVarsity, 1994.

Habermas, Jürgen. *The Theory of Communicative Action and Rationalization of Society*, Vol. 1. Boston: Beacon, 1984.

Hanson, C. K. "Right Hand." In *The International Standard Bible Encyclopaedia*, edited by Geoffrey W. Bromiley, et al., 191. Grand Rapids: Eerdmans, 1988.

Hill, Andrew E. "Night." In *The International Standard Bible Encyclopaedia, Vol. 3. K–P*, edited by Geoffrey W. Bromiley, 535–36. Grand Rapids: Eerdmans, 1986.

Huber, Lynn R. *Thinking and Seeing with Women in Revelation*. London: T&T Clark, 2013.

Ingram, David. "Strategic Rationality." In *The Cambridge Habermas Lexicon*, edited by Amy Alken and Eduardo Mendieta, 432–34. Cambridge, UK: Cambridge University Press, 2019.

Jeffers, James S. *Greco-Roman World of the New Testament Era: Exploring the Background of Early Christianity*. Downers Grove, IL: InterVarsity, 1999.

Jenkins, Philip. *New Christendom: The Coming of Global Christianity*. New York: Oxford University Press, 2002.

Johnson, E. Dennis. *Triumph of the Lamb: A Commentary on Revelation*. Phillipsburg, NJ: P&R, 2001.

Josephus, Flavius. *Josephus: The Complete Works.* Translated by William Whiston. Nashville: Thomas Nelson, 1998.

Karura, Mwaniki. *Catalyzing Reader Response to the Oral Gospel: A Rhetorical Analysis of the Convincing and Convicting Devices in the Markan Text.* Carlisle, UK: Langham Monograph, 2020.

———. *Baptism and the Lord's Supper: The Gospel According to Jesus Christ.* Nairobi: Africa Publishing Institute, 2021.

Keener, Craig. *Revelation.* NIV Application Commentary. Grand Rapids: Zondervan, 2000.

———. *New Testament.* IVP Bible Background Commentary. Downers Grove, IL: InterVarsity, 1993.

———. *Miracles: The Credibility of the New Testament Accounts, Vol. 2.* Grand Rapids: Baker Academic, 2011.

Kistemaker, Simon J. *Exposition of the Book of Revelation.* Grand Rapids: Baker, 2001.

Klein, William W., Craig L. Blomberg, and Robert L. Hubbard, Jr., eds. *Introduction to Biblical Interpretation.* 3rd ed. Nashville: Thomas Nelson, 2017.

Koester, Craig R. *Revelation and the End of All Things.* Grand Rapids: Eerdmans, 2001.

———. *Revelation:* A New Translation with Introduction and Commentary. London: Anchor Yale Bible, 2021. eBook.

Ladd, George Eldon. "Revelation." In *The International Standard Bible Encyclopaedia,* edited by Geoffrey W. Bromiley, 171–77. Grand Rapids: Eerdmans, 1988.

Leithart, Peter J. "*Revelation 12–22.*" In T&T Clark International Theological Commentary. New York: T&T Clark, 2018.

Louw, Johannes P., and Eugene A. Nida. *Greek-English Lexicon, Vol. 1.* New York: United Bible Societies, 1988.

Malina, Bruce J., and John J. Pilch. *Social Science Commentary on the Book of Revelation.* Minneapolis: Augsburg Fortress, 2000.

Marshal I. Howard, Stephen Trevis, and Ian Paul. *Exploring the New Testament: A Guide to the Letters and Revelation.* 3rd ed. Downers Grove, IL: InterVarsity, 2021.

Mbiti, John S. *Concepts of God in Africa.* Nairobi: Acton, 2012.

Mburu, Elizabeth. *African Hermeneutics.* Carlisle, UK: Langham, 2019.

Metzger, Bruce M. *A Textual Commentary on the Greek New Testament.* London: United Bible Societies, 1971.

Michaels, I. Ramsey. *Revelation.* Edited by Grant R. Osborne. Downers Grove, IL: InterVarsity, 1997.

———. *Interpreting the Book of Revelation.* Grand Rapids: Baker, 1992.

Morris, Leon. *The Revelation of Saint John.* Grand Rapids: Eerdmans, 1980.

Mounce, Robert H. *What Are We Waiting For?: A Commentary on Revelation.* Grand Rapids: Eerdmans, 1992.

———. "The Book of Revelation." In *The New International Commentary on the New Testament.* Rev. ed. Grand Rapids: Eerdmans, 1997.

Newman, Carey C. *Jesus & the Restoration of Israel: A Critical Assessment of N. T. Wright's Jesus and the Victory of God.* Carlisle, UK: Paternoster, 1999.

Newton, John K. *A Pentecostal Commentary on Revelation.* Eugene, OR: Wipf and Stock, 2021.

Ngundu, Onesimus. "Revelation." In *Africa Bible Commentary.* Edited by Tokunboh Adeyemo. 1543–79. Nairobi: WordAlive, 2006.

Nickelsburg, George W. E. *Jewish Literature Between the Bible and the Mishna: A Literary and Historical Introduction*. 2nd ed. Minneapolis: Augsburg Fortress, 2005.

Osborne, Grant R. *Revelation*. Baker Exegetical Commentary on the New Testament. Edited by Moises Silva. Grand Rapids: Baker Academic, 2002.

Paul, Ian. *Revelation: An Introduction and Commentary*. Downers Grove, IL: InterVarsity, 2018.

———. "Is Revelation a Vision—or an Audition?" Psephizo, Feb. 27, 2018. https://www.psephizo.com/biblical-studies/is-revelation-a-vision-or-an-audition/.

Pentecost, J. Dwight. *Things to Come*. Findlay, OH: Dunham, 1958.

Perlman, Alice L. "Horn." In *The International Standard Bible Encyclopaedia*, edited by G. W. Bromiley, 757. Grand Rapids: Eerdmans, 1982.

Poythress, Vern S. *The Returning King: A Guide to the Book of Revelation*. Phillipsburg, NJ: P&R, 2000.

Ramsey, James B. *Revelation: An Exposition of the First 11 Chapters*. Carlisle, PA: Banner of Truth Trust, 1977.

Rowland, Christopher C. "The Book of Revelation: Introduction, Commentary and Reflections." In *The New Interpreter's Bible, Volume XII*, 503–736. Nashville: Abingdon, 1998.

Ryken, Leland. *How to Read the Bible as Literature and Get More out of It*. Grand Rapids: Zondervan, 1984.

Ryken, Leyland., James C. Wilhoit, Tremper Longman III. *Dictionary of Biblical Imagery*. Downers Grove, IL: InterVarsity, 1998.

Schreiner, Thomas R. *New Testament Theology: Magnifying God in Christ*. Grand Rapids: Baker Academic, 2008.

Skaggs, Rebecca, and Pricilla C. Benham. *Revelation: Pentecostal Commentary*. Dorset, UK: Deo, 2009.

Smalley, Stephen S. *The Revelation of John: A Commentary on the Greek Text of the Apocalypse*. Downers Grove, IL: InterVarsity, 2005.

Spatafora, Andrea. *From the Temple of God to God as a Temple*. Rome: Gregorian University Press, 1997.

Storkey, Allan. "Materialism." In *New Dictionary of Christian Ethics and Pastoral Theology*, edited by David J. Atkinson and David H. Field, 575–76. Downers Grove, IL: InterVarsity, 1995.

Strauss, Lehman. *The Book of the Revelation*. Edinburgh: Loiseaux Brothers, 1964.

Sweet, John. *Revelation*. London: SCM. 1990.

Swete, Henry Barclay. *Commentary on Revelation*. Grand Rapids: Kregel, 1977.

Taylor, John B. "Ezekiel." In *Tyndale Old Testament Commentaries*, edited by D. J. Wiseman. Leicester, England: InterVarsity, 1969.

Thiselton, Anthony C. *Approaching the Study of Theology: An Introduction to Key Thinkers, Concepts, Methods & Debates*. Downers Grove, IL: InterVarsity, 2018.

Thomas. John Christopher, and Frank D. Macchia. "Revelation." In *The Two Horizons New Testament Commentary—Revelation*. Grand Rapids: Eerdmans, 2016.

Tomasino, Anthony J. *Judaism before Jesus*. Grand Rapids: InterVarsity, 2003.

Tremper, Longman III. *Revelation Through Old Testament Eyes: A Background and Application Commentary*. Grand Rapids: Kregel Academic, 2022.

Travis, Stephen H. "Resurrection." In *The IVP Dictionary of the New Testament*, edited by Daniel G. Reid, 896–924. Leicester: InterVarsity, 2004.

Vanhoozer, Kevin J. *First Theology*. Downers Grove, IL: InterVarsity, 2002.

Vine, W. E., Merrill F. Unger, and William White, Jr. *Vine's Complete Expository Dictionary of Old and New Testament Words*. Nashville: Thomas Nelson, 1984.
Wall, Robert W. *Revelation*. Peabody, MA: Hendrickson, 1991.
Walhout, Edwin. *Revelation Down to Earth: Making Sense of the Apocalypse of John*. Grand Rapids: Eerdmans, 2000.
Walvoord, John F. *The Revelation of Jesus Christ*. Chicago: Moody Bible Institute, 1966.
Wilcock, Michael. *The Message of Revelation*. 2nd ed. Nottingham, England: InterVarsity, 1991.
Witherington, Ben. *Revelation*. Cambridge, England: Cambridge University Press, 2003.
Wolterstorff, Nicholas. *Divine Discourse: Philosophical Reflection on the Claim that God Speaks*. Cambridge, England: Cambridge University Press, 1995.
Wright, N. T. *The New Testament and the People of God*. London: SPCK, 1992.

www.ingramcontent.com/pod-product-compliance
Lightning Source LLC
Chambersburg PA
CBHW060601230426
43670CB00011B/1920